ART THERAPY TREATMENT WITH SEX TRAFFICKING SURVIVORS

Facilitating Empowerment, Recovery, and Hope

Edited by
Mary K. Kometiani,
MA, ATR-BC, LPCC

Routledge
Taylor & Francis Group
NEW YORK AND LONDON

First published 2020
by Routledge
52 Vanderbilt Avenue, New York, NY 10017

and by Routledge
2 Park Square, Milton Park, Abingdon, Oxon, OX14 4RN

Routledge is an imprint of the Taylor & Francis Group, an informa business

Library of Congress Cataloging-in-Publication Data
A catalog record for this book has been requested

ISBN: 978-1-138-60227-4 (hbk)
ISBN: 978-1-138-60228-1 (pbk)
ISBN: 978-0-429-46967-1 (ebk)

Typeset in Sabon
by Apex CoVantage, LLC

This book is dedicated to all the survivors I have had the privilege to know. Hearing their stories and witnessing their personal expressions and reflections, and thus becoming part of their journey toward recovery, has been my profound honor. Their strength, courage, and ability to experience vulnerability again following unspeakable trauma is inspiring.

Dear survivors, you are resilient and powerful warriors. Your testimonies are the soul of this book. Thank you for your gift of trust from the bottom of my heart.

Contents

Figures

Contributors

Serena R. Coleman, MA, ATR, AMFT, is a PhD candidate in Notre Dame de Namur University's art therapy program completing her dissertation. She joined the anti-trafficking movement in 2009, which later led to opportunities to work with youth and adults surviving sex trafficking and sexual exploitation in residential facilities as a volunteer, case manager, and art therapist. Serena's areas of interests include social justice, women's issues, youth empowerment, and community relationships.

Chris Drosdick, MA, NCC, CSAC, ATR-BC, ICS, is an art psychotherapist in private practice. Chris is certified in cognitive behavioral therapy for insomnia and yoga nidra. Chris is trained in the Growing Minds mindfulness curriculum, eye movement desensitization reprogramming (EMDR) and schema therapy, a type of cognitive behavioral therapy. Chris enjoys working with children, teens, and adults. Chris presents locally and regionally on art therapy, trauma, and the treatment of sex trafficking survivors.

Kathryn Farmer, MSW, LSW, RA, is the director of Day One at Crime Victim Services. Day One works to prevent violence in West Central Ohio communities and serves survivors of sexual violence and human trafficking. With a deep concern for human rights, Kathryn has extensive experience working alongside oppressed individuals and populations in the areas of poverty alleviation, race relations, and cultural humility.

Tiffany M. Moore, MA, is a project manager funded under the U.S. Office on Violence Against Women and currently sits on the board of directors for Resources and Help Against Marital Abuse within the immigrant and refugee community in Western New York. Tiffany has worked extensively throughout her career with both victims and perpetrators.

Leigha Shoup, MS, RA, is the director of the Child Advocacy Center (CAC) of West Central Ohio and the Special Victims Unit at Crime Victim Services. Leigha provides training locally and nationally to multidisciplinary teams, service providers, and community members regarding diversity and inclusion through the CAC model. Her passion is to help bring awareness and services to all children, adults, and communities to help provide an inclusive, equitable, and holistic healing approach to advocacy.

Smita Singh, MA in Psychology from Calcutta University, Post Graduate diploma in counseling and psychotherapy, Christian Counselling Centre Vellore, is Director of Justice Initiatives of the Mahima Homes project in Kolkata—igniting hope and rebuilding lives. This is an initiative to provide rehabilitation and reintegration services to survivors of sex trafficking and sexual assault and work toward the eradication of sex trafficking in India.

Atira L. Tan, MA, is an art therapist, activist, somatic experiencing practitioner, teacher, and the founder and co-director of the Australian charity Art to Healing (www.arttohealing.org). Born in Singapore and based in Melbourne, Australia, Atira has been an active advocate for the trauma recovery of sex trafficked survivors in South and Southeast Asia, presenting in numerous international conferences, including TEDx.

Cynthia Wilson, PhD, MA, ATR-BC, is registered and board certified as an art therapist in private practice. Dissertation research and individual practicum topics included destigmatization, collaborative care, attunement, communication, trauma, and dissociation. She is a clinical art therapy supervisor and speaks professionally and works clinically with children/adults/groups/families.

Special thanks to Eileen Delaney Kohut, MA, for her editing assistance. Eileen Delaney Kohut, MA (English), MA (Education). After a career teaching English and writing in Cleveland private secondary schools and community colleges, Eileen returned to her Alma Mater, Ursuline College (a women's focused institution and home of the first graduate Art Therapy program in Ohio) as Director of Academic Support for 15 years. In that position, she tutored undergraduate, graduate students, and international students in writing, becoming very familiar with the Art Therapy and Counseling program. She is an ETS grader for AP English exams and has been published in *Inscape*.

Acknowledgments

Since my work started with sex trafficked survivors, I have been surprised by the lack of art therapy research and availability of publications regarding best practices with this population, and it has always been a personal goal to add to this field and publish about this relevant topic. Thank you to Amanda Devine and the editorial board for your enthusiasm and encouragement toward this contribution to the field. I am extremely honored and grateful to be a part of this collaborative and innovative project, and I am especially thankful to the chapter authors who have made this idea into a reality. As the editor, I have learned from each of you, and I appreciate your dedication and commitment to this cause.

I want to thank my husband and our sons George and Liam for allowing this project to become possible. Peter, your unwavering love and support means the world to me. I am also extremely grateful to my mom for her writing expertise and guidance, which consistently grounded me throughout this project and paved the way for this book to be completed. Thank you to the rest of my loved ones, my dear family and friends, I am truly blessed to be surrounded by generous, supportive, and thoughtful individuals. By encouraging my dreams and visions, you have let me believe that anything is possible with heart, purpose, and determination. For this, I am forever grateful.

PART I

FOUNDATION TO SEX TRAFFICKING AND ART THERAPY AS TREATMENT

ONE

Introduction to the Destructive Pandemic of Sex Trafficking

Mary K. Kometiani

Human sex trafficking is a heinous global crime that continues to escalate in the 21st century at an alarming rate with shocking numbers. Formerly an unspeakable and unbelievable crime, trafficking now openly links people from areas and cultures all over the world and victimizes individuals in our own quiet neighborhoods. Young individuals are coerced from villages in third world countries as well as in affluent American suburbs. If the individuals survive (many of those who are sexually exploited are murdered or go missing) the oppressive effects of trafficking and exploitation are overwhelming and devastating to their lives, fracturing their personalities, and damaging all relationships and bonds within their scope.

Once ensnared, the individual's sense of self, personal beliefs, and values are erased by the sex trafficker in a systematic way. Trafficked individuals are silenced, ignored, and treated so inhumanely that their human identity is stripped away; they begin to see and accept themselves as unworthy and low individuals who view the entire world as untrustworthy and unsafe. After undergoing consistent severe sadistic psychological and physical trauma, the trafficked individual is violated and damaged almost beyond comprehension and explanation. Due to the pervasive and powerful consequences of the complex trauma the individual has witnessed, endured, and, perhaps, accepted, many challenges of treating trafficking survivors occur in therapy. However, art therapy treatment has the innate potential to provide a valuable form of expression that is nonthreatening and empowering, letting survivors establish a renewed sense of worth and discover their voices again to regain a healthier and stronger sense of themselves. This book aims to explore art therapy as an effective treatment to survivors all over the world who are recovering from the vicious evils of being trafficked.

This introductory chapter will present relevant statistics regarding the growing issue of human trafficking. A thorough definition and the implications of sex trafficking will be introduced. This chapter establishes the book's focus on three of the foremost areas for sex trafficking: the

United States, Nepal, and India. This diverse trio of sites showcases the different aspects of sexual exploitation and how cultural and societal beliefs affect the occurrence of this crime. Other global troubles, such as poverty, political instability and war, natural disasters, family violence, and devalued status of women, also contribute to sex trafficking (Clawson, Layne, & Small, 2006). Lastly, an overview of the book is provided in this chapter.

For the purposes of this book, "victim" is restricted in use to describe a traumatized individual who has been sexually exploited because "survivor" is the preferred term in this field. Although in true trauma-informed practice, clients choose how to self-refer because they are not identified by their trauma exposure, the meaning of survivor implies a strong and resilient individual who endured the oppressive and horrendous experience of sex trafficking. Lastly, although this crime impacts all people and trafficking criminals can be anyone, women are sex trafficked in epic proportions, so the pronoun "she" may be used to represent survivor and the pronoun "he" may be used to denote the trafficker to simplify the reading in some chapters throughout the book.

Human Trafficking Current Research and Statistics

Human trafficking is modern-day slavery that involves every country in the world. A violation of human rights through exploitation and abuse, sex trafficking concerns all communities because this felonious social injustice endangers all. Regrettably, human trafficking has occurred since the Roman Empire (Litam, 2017), and now slavery prevails in every area of the world (International Labour Office & Walk Free Foundation, 2017). Human trafficking does not transpire from racial and ethnic differences; this exploitation happens as a result of destitution, vulnerability, and profits (Stotts & Ramey, 2009). With low risk and no prerequisite for investment required, sex traffickers regard and use individuals as inexpensive products that can be traded continually (Bales, 2007). The business of sexual exploitation is all about fiscal gains (Snow, 2018). This massive problem is defined simply through supply and demand:

1. Abundant resources of vulnerable youth ensure high profit and fuel an endless cycle of greed;
2. Due to the intense effects of trauma, survivors are hesitant to press criminal charges against traffickers, and some traffickers only suffer mildly with merciful sentences;
3. Unmet sexual desire from perpetrators and pedophiles guarantee high demand.

(Tverdova, 2011)

This modern form of slavery is an epic conundrum that exploits the vulnerable and poor while abundantly rewarding the voracious villains.

Due to the extensive proportions of human trafficking, it is challenging to accurately deliver statistics regarding this furtive crime that affects the unseen and disregarded (Miller-Perrin & Wurtele, 2017). Since many females have disappeared or been murdered, there is no way to deliver an accurate number of how many individuals are affected from this tragic crime (Crawford, 2017). However sexual exploitation is the most recognized form of human trafficking in the world (United Nations Office on Drugs and Crime, 2018). Recent estimates show that over 40 million people were entrapped in global slavery with 4.8 million in forced sexual exploitation and over 70% identified as females (International Labour Office & Walk Free Foundation, 2017). Referred to as the overlooked survivors of trafficking, males account for almost half of the total individuals victimized; however, sex trafficked males are often hidden, underreported, and unsupported by a severe lack of restoration programs (United States Department of State, 2017). The commercial sex industry is financially secure offering exploiters earnings of over US$30,000 per week and generating between almost US$40 million and US$290 million per city (Dank et al., 2014). Globally, commercial sex trafficking generates US$99 billion a year (International Labour Organization, 2014). Currently, sexual exploitation is a massive commercial enterprise that is expanding and prospering without providing necessary supportive services to its devastated survivors.

In contemporary society, the phenomenon of child sex trafficking should be regarded universally as taboo and unfathomable because this crime preys on the human species' most vulnerable and innocent members. Yet sex trafficking is a very prevalent form of exploitation of youth under the age of 18, with 14–16 as the average age of entry into sex exploitation (Shared Hope International, 2017). One in four enslaved individuals are children, with recent calculations of over one million children who are sex trafficked (International Labour Office & Walk Free Foundation, 2017). Even more youth are at risk to be trafficked, and one in seven of reported runaways is likely to become exploited due to lack of protection (National Center for Missing & Exploited Children, 2017). Modern technology adds more danger, and online sexual exploitation is a growing international trend affecting thousands of youth (United States Department of State, 2017). The statistics of children being sold into sexual exploitation are extensive, and even more disturbing is the fact that children are sold into slavery by family members.

Definition and Implications of Human Trafficking

The first international agreement, the Palermo Protocol, defined human trafficking as the employment, transference, and concealing through methods of threatening, forcing, or compelling an individual through intimidation, imprisonment, and deception with the intent to control or exploit an individual through providing or obtaining benefit to attain the authorization of a person having power over another person (United Nations, 2000). An individual's consent is not recognized within these defined means. Although the term trafficking suggests movement, exploited individuals do not have to be moved or transported. Modern-day exploitation occurs through many channels, including forced labor, domestic servitude, organ trafficking, child soldiering, and sex trafficking (United States Department of State, 2017).

Sex trafficking is exploitation, including prostitution and military prostitution (commercial sex for armed forces), stripping, pornography, sex shows, mail-order brides, and traveling for sex, also known as sex tourism (United States Department of Health and Human Services, n.d.). To clarify terminology, prostitution usually meets the definition of trafficking because most prostitutes do not have a choice; they were manipulated, and they do not choose sex work; many prostituted individuals are harassed, raped, tormented, and oppressed, therefore meeting the international definition of trafficking (Contreras & Farley, 2011). The majority of prostitutes have been coerced into prostitution; they have no other feasible alternative, or they are forced due to race/economic/sex inequality (Contreras & Farley, 2011).

When the exploitation of individuals under the age of 18 occurs, with/without force, intimidation, and deception, automatically, the youth are considered to be trafficked (United Nations, 2000). Young persons who are sexually exploited never made a choice; their lack of maturity and experience preclude valid judgment (Smith, 2018b). Commercial sexual exploitation of children (CSEC), the payment of anything valued given for a sex act, includes minor prostitution through sex slavery; sexually explicit photographs and videos; sexual performances, including erotic dancing; and sex tourism (Miller-Perrin & Wurtele, 2017). Domestic minor sex trafficking (DMST), the national term describing the sexual exploitation of youth, includes those who are still living in their homes, the homeless who engage in survival sex (exchanging sex for living necessities), and those who are transported to other areas (Institute of Medicine & National Research Council, 2013). Sex trafficking can occur in escort or massage services, brothels, peep shows, phone sex or live/online sex shows, pornography studios, strip clubs, or street prostitution.

Sex trafficked survivors' situations vary markedly. Survivors are trafficked in a range of experiences, including complex organized crime rings as well as small family village shops (Williamson et al., 2012). While some individuals are lured in by false promises or manipulated through a relationship that leads to exploitation, others are forced into trafficking when sold by family members or a when a false marriage ends in slavery. Human traffickers use force as physical restraint or inflicting bodily harm as a way to acquire and sustain control; fraud through false promises of love, employment, or a better life to vulnerable individuals; and coercion as threats or harm to an individual through manipulation, identification confiscation, and blackmail to expose an individual to families or others (United States Department of Health and Human Services, 2019). These appalling and devious tactics, in addition to the numerous detrimental effects of being sexually exploited, will be further explained in Chapter 2.

Survivors are recruited in countries of origin and may be obscurely transferred to a final destination point where the demand, means, and opportunity for exploitation are higher; some countries are bidirectional, meaning they are both origins and destinations (Farr, 2004). Survivors might be involved in a trafficking situation for a few days to years because of trauma attachment, fear of reprisal for leaving, lack of resources, substance addiction, distrust of authorities, and/or threats of harm for their loved ones. Although human sex trafficking is a worldwide issue, the context and specifics of culture and society are extremely important in understanding the specific concerns of this systematic crime. This chapter presents an international focus on sex trafficking in three areas of the world, including eastern India, midwestern USA, and central Nepal.

Introduction to Global Trafficking Survivors

United States

Brandi came from a dysfunctional home and had a challenging upbringing. She never met her father, and her mother struggled with mental health issues and substance abuse. Brandi was put in foster care at a young age because she was severally sexually abused by a relative during her mother's incarceration. Brandi struggled with feeling unloved and alone until she met an older man while she was in high school. Pretending to be her boyfriend, he provided presents and attention; this was the first time Brandi could remember feeling special and loved. When he asked her to move in with him, it didn't take too long for her to agree. Brandi would have done anything for him, and when he suggested having sex with another man to help pay their bills, she did. Brandi wanted to be faithful to him as "he had been there for her" when she needed help the most. He started to send her to motels and to the streets to provide sexual services. Although she started to despise herself and her situation, after she gave birth to their daughter, she believed she had no escape from this way of life.

The United States is a source, transit, and destination country for the sex trafficking of children, women, men, and transgender individuals (United States Department of State, 2017). Sex trafficking in the United States often occurs in areas with high populations of transient males, including truck stops, military bases, political or business conventions, sporting events, and tourist destinations, as well as street prostitution, brothels that operate out of private homes, motels, massage parlors, spas, and strip clubs (Miller-Perrin & Wurtele, 2017; Polaris, 2019; United States

Department of Health and Human Services, n.d.). The 2010 Super Bowl demonstrated that a major global sporting event increases incidences of human sex trafficking (Finkel & Finkel, 2015). At the Super Bowl of 2015, a huge operation arrested 600 individuals and saved 68 victimized people (Smith, 2018a). It is also reported that some U.S. citizens engage in child sex tourism abroad (United States Department of State, 2017). Reports estimate that 25% of sex tourists are Americans (Mekinc & Music, 2015), and Action Pour les Enfants (2014) reported that Americans account for the majority of foreign sex offenders arrested in Cambodia at 17.1%. Sex trafficking in the United States is linked to the conventional impermanence of males, while culture and media often excuse the gender stereotypical behavior that "boys will be boys." The unwritten action of extreme male bonding is exemplified through fraternity and military gang rapes (Farr, 2004). Glamorizing sex, glorifying violence, and promoting greed at any cost are detrimental influences of the acceptance of sexual exploitation in the United States.

Even though the 13th Amendment abolished slavery over 150 years ago in the United States, modern slavery still continues in sex trafficking. Before 2000, Americans believed that human sex trafficking only occurred in other countries (Smith, 2018b). Due to continued limited awareness and ignorance, people in the United States often rationalize that slavery does not occur close to home, and many are shocked to hear that human trafficking exists locally. However, the crime of human sex trafficking continues to be fast growing and increases every year in the United States; sex trafficking is the most reported type of trafficking from a national hotline with over 7,200 sex trafficking cases in 2017 (Polaris, 2019).

The United States is a highly advanced and prosperous country; albeit, many Americans struggle with poverty and abuse throughout their lives. The opportunity for all people in the United State to achieve success through hard work and ambition is referred to as the *American Dream*. However, deception through employment opportunities and seduction are the two most predominant ways to recruit in U.S. sex trafficking (Kara, 2009), and in some destitute communities, children can be trafficked by their own family members in exchange for money, drugs, or rent payments (National Sexual Violence Resource Center and Pennsylvania Coalition against Rape, 2012). Exploiting the deprived and vulnerable contributes considerably to the sex trafficking industry in the United States and abroad (see Chapters 5 and 6 for case studies about treatment for sex trafficking survivors in the United States).

Nepal

Nina grew up impoverished in a rural and destitute part of Southeast Asia. Domestic violence was common in her village, and she was abused by her father. When Nina was offered an opportunity to move to a larger urban area to receive ample pay to become a housekeeper, she had little doubt about turning down what seemed like the best option for her future. When Nina arrived in a nearby foreign country, she quickly found out that she had been deceived. She was told she owed a large sum of money for her travels, and she needed to pay this off by having sex with others. She was tortured, raped, and drugged to enforce compliance. Nina was alone in a new place where she did not speak the language, she had no resources, and she had no option but to try to survive and do as she was told. She felt very ashamed for what she was doing, and she felt desperate for change, but she was hopeless and believed she had no other options available. Nina had no idea how she had gotten herself into this predicament, and she had no idea how to get out of this situation.

The Global Slavery Index (2018) estimated that two-thirds of sexually enslaved people are identified in Asia and the Pacific. Nepal is a source, transit, and destination country for the sex trafficking of children, women, men, and transgender individuals (United States Department of State, 2017). Nepali women are sexually exploited in Nepal, India, Asia, the Middle East, and Africa (United States Department of State, 2017). In Nepal, sex trafficking usually occurs in private homes, rented rooms, guesthouses, and restaurants (United States Department of State, 2017).

Nepal is known for its exotic diversity in landscape and culture. However, primitive Nepalese beliefs of female inequality and governmental corruption contribute significantly to its issue with sex trafficking. Women in Nepal are considered to be a "commodity" that can be traded, bought, and sold for families and husbands, and violence against women and marital rape are deemed as acceptable actions (Crawford, 2017). Due to substantial political corruption, police solicit bribes from brothels to ignore the illegal businesses; brothel searches may result in only the prostitutes, not the clients or brothel owners, being jailed and paying bail (Kara, 2009). Lack of opportunity, the situation of extreme poverty, cultural beliefs regarding female inequality and family violence, homelessness from environmental calamities, and corruption throughout the government all contribute to sex trafficking in Nepal. Chapter 7 discusses these influences in greater detail and introduces art therapy programming with Nepalese sex trafficked survivors.

India

Arya, aged 13, grew up underprivileged from a lower caste. An older man convinced her family to consent to his marriage to Arya. Since her family was so poor and struggled with enough money for food, they believed that this was the only hope she had in having a better life. Even though she did not want to marry at such a young age, Arya believed she was a burden to her family and would do what they asked. The marriage was quickly revealed to be a deception. Arya's husband sold her to a brothel in a large city, and she was held in debt bondage and forced into sexual exploitation. She was made to watch pornography and learn from other children how to please the customers. Although she was able to eventually escape the brothel, she could not return home because of the debt she had incurred and the stigma from acquiring a sexually transmitted infection while being trafficked. Arya suffered from depression, feelings of hopelessness, and various health issues, but she received counseling, housing, schooling, and medical care through a nonprofit service and was able to survive her traumatic experience.

The Global Slavery Index (2018) estimated that eight million people were enslaved in India. India is a destination, source, and transit country for the sex trafficking of children, women, and men (United States Department of State, 2017). Women from Nepal and Bangladesh, in addition to Europe, Asia, and Africa are trafficked in India (United States Department of State, 2017). The deplorable demand for younger individuals has escalated with auctions for females as young as 8 (Huda, 2006), because they are regarded to be free of STIs (sexually transmitted infections) (Kara, 2009). Sex trafficking in India occurs in brothels, hotels, huts, vehicles, and private homes (United States Department of State, 2017). In India, sexual exploitation is the ultimate motive followed by trafficking for brides and the means to produce offspring (Roy & Chaman, 2017).

India is recognized for its color, cultural richness, and complexity. Most of India's trafficking problem is attributed to its caste system (United States Department of State, 2017). Many Indian females who are trafficked are considered reduced human beings according to their birth status (Smith, 2018b). Corrupted police accept bribes to protect traffickers, thus impeding efforts to save survivors (United States Department of State, 2017). Economic, gender, and caste disadvantage in addition to governmental corruption impact India's issue with trafficking exploitation. These challenges, along with a lack of support in the rehabilitation of survivors, contribute to the re-trafficking of individuals too (Roy & Chaman, 2017). Refer to Chapter 7 for more information about sex trafficking and expressive arts therapy treatment in India.

Invitation to Readers

Reading the content of this book challenges you to confront the ugly reality of international and domestic sex trafficking, to study how best to treat the traumatized survivors, and to seek the prevention of further trafficking progress. I hope to inspire change and encourage readers to become active participants in the current war against human trafficking. You are urged to learn more and become aware of local community organizations involved in this struggle. While facing the reality of this violation against humanity, I hope you will remain optimistic about your opportunity to make a difference, always believing that each individual has worth in society and deserves safety and protection.

As a side note, reading about the trauma of human trafficking can be an emotionally triggering experience. Please remember to read at a pace that allows for some processing and distance, if necessary. Talk to a supportive individual in your life about any effects that this book has on you and take the time for self-care if you find yourself having an adverse reaction to any of the chapters.

Book Overview

This pioneering book introduces the relevant and prominent issue of global human sex trafficking and explores art therapy as a creative and effective treatment. Our text aspires to address the absence of information on prevailing research addressing the mental health needs of survivors (Litam, 2017) and the limited data of art therapy treatment for sex trafficking survivors published in small case studies (Garlock, 2016; Kometiani & Farmer, 2019; Tan, 2012). Consequently, our publication intends to fulfill the need for more literature on the psychological and emotional needs of sex trafficked survivors, and it also demonstrates the beneficial outcomes of art therapy with this population. The book will introduce the personal and professional effects of working with trafficking survivors and the need for advocate staff support in this demanding field. Lastly, the appendix will provide a glossary of human sex trafficking terminology and resources, including references for assessment and further education.

The text aims to

- provide awareness of the epidemic of sex trafficking and introduce the healing benefits of art therapy treatment for survivors;
- define and explain human sex trafficking damage to individuals and the extensive trauma that accompanies this vicious crime;
- present a unique global lens of art therapy treatments for trafficking survivors from the continents of Asia and North America; and
- serve as a handbook for art therapy and mental health professionals and students who encounter and treat this population.

Part 1

Chapter 1, "Introduction to the Destructive Pandemic of Sex Trafficking," provides current research and statistics on human trafficking. This beginning chapter also introduces the definition and cultural implications of sex trafficking through presenting several different examples of trafficked survivors' journeys. A detailed book overview is also provided. Chapter 2, "Deceptive Tactics and Adverse Consequences of Sex Trafficking," details the severe physical, physiological, psychological, emotional, and spiritual effects of sex trafficking. An explanation of the grooming process and trauma bond will clarify why survivors have a difficult time leaving their trafficker and the life of exploitation. A succinct summary of treatment recommendations is provided. Chapter 3, "The Exploration of Vulnerabilities to Sex Trafficking and their Role in Art Therapy Treatment," investigates the benefits of art therapy with at-risk groups of people who are exploited in the sex trafficking industry. Vulnerable populations explored are youth, especially with a history of abuse and substance abuse; the homeless and refugees; and individuals from the lesbian, gay, bisexual, transgender, queer or questioning plus (LGBTQ+) community, foster care, and juvenile detention systems. Chapter 4, "Recommendations for Working With Individuals Affected by Sex Trafficking," summarizes the healing benefits of art therapy and other collaborative modalities with survivors who experience dissociation and complex trauma. Recommended treatment modalities including memory reconsolidation, narrative processing, sensorimotor therapy, eye movement and desensitization reprocessing (EMDR), emotional freedom technique (EFT)/tapping, craniosacral therapy, trauma-focused cognitive behavioral therapy (TF-CBT), trauma-informed mindfulness and yoga, and animal therapy are reviewed. Recommendations for collaborating with other professionals, enforcing boundaries, and working with individuals, groups, adults, and children are also provided.

Part 2

Chapter 5, "Beauty in the Disorder: Art Therapy with Sex Trafficking Survivors in Ohio, United States," provides an introduction to trafficking in North America with a focus on the midwestern state of Ohio. Case examples showcasing art therapy based on trauma recovery stages at a safe house for women survivors of sexual trafficking are provided. This chapter also summarizes recommendations for the best practice when facilitating art therapy with survivors. Chapter 6, "Art Therapy Treatment for Survivors of Sex Trafficking, Boys," presents details from art therapy treatment with two brothers who were survivors of sex trafficking over a three-year period. Resources from many experts in neurobiology, trauma, art therapy, and mindfulness were integrated into treatment interventions. Chapter 7, "Use of the Expressive Art Therapies to Bring Healing From the Trauma of Commercial Sexual Exploitation in Kolkata, India," informs the reader about trafficking in Kolkata and provides case examples from a multimodal expressive arts therapy program. The Mahima Homes of Jatiyo Kristiyo Prochar Samity offer art therapy, music therapy, and dance/movement therapy to recovering survivors of sex trafficking. Chapter 8, "The Women's Transformational Program: An Art Therapy, Life Skills, and Reproductive Health Program in Nepal," introduces minor sex trafficking in Nepal. This chapter describes a creative art therapy and reproductive health program initiated by Art to Healing for adolescent females who experienced sex slavery, exploitation, and abuse.

Part 3

Chapter 9, "Entrusted With Trauma: Advocacy and Human Trafficking," presents the reader with the consequences of working with sex trafficked survivors, the burnout that can ensue, and how to combat distress in the workplace. Research on advocate self-care grounding techniques are provided. Chapter 10, "Challenges and Future Considerations of Treatment for Sex Trafficked Survivors," familiarizes the reader with various challenges in providing treatment for trafficked survivors. Suggestions on how to manage barriers are given. Future considerations for this field and a summation complete the book. Some of the chapters reference the appendices that offer supplementary information and resources to the subject matter presented.

Conclusion

Sex trafficking occurs when females, males, or gender-variant people of all ages are forced or mislead by falsehoods into sexual exploitation for individual or commercial profit. Victimized individuals can be identified around the world and close to home. Typically, the targets of this crime are female and young, which often lessens their status in many undeveloped countries and increases their vulnerability in all countries. Anyone can be trafficked, but those at a higher risk for trafficking are members of vulnerable populations who lack solid support systems and societal resources for personal options and opportunities.

Sex trafficking is an appalling crime that threatens human society on many different levels. The responsible perpetrators and miscreants corrupting our communities break both our modern legal and our ancient moral codes, usually without retribution. Initially, victimized people lose their personal safety; then their identity is physically, emotionally, psychologically, and spiritually compromised and devastated. When innocent children are violated and abused, the consequences are compounded.

Contributing to sex trafficking practices are primitive social and cultural practices, perpetrator greed, political instability, natural disasters, ignorance, poverty, and vulnerability (Bales, 2007). The statistics of human trafficking in today's world are shocking, but human trafficking is a thriving industry due to the unmet worldwide sexual demands and the cunning ability of violent and ruthless evildoers to exploit poor and vulnerable individuals or groups for extensive profits and power. This chapter also introduces the premise for this book by presenting art therapy as an effective and universal form of healing treatment for the brave survivors of trafficking. As the editor, I seek to motivate readers to make a difference in their circles and communities to combat human trafficking. Society regresses when innocent people are knowingly debased in any way, and when we ignore such iniquity, we are part of the problem.

References

Action Pour les Enfants. (2014, February). *Investigating traveling child sex offenders*. Retrieved from https://aplecambodia.org/wpcontent/uploads/2015/03/Analytical-Report-on-Investigating-Traveling-Child-Sex-Offenders-Web-Version.pdf

Bales, K. (2007). What predicts human trafficking? *International Journal of Comparative and Applied Criminal Justice*, *31*(2), 269–279. https://doi.org/10.1080/01924036.2007.9678771

Clawson, H. J., Layne, M., & Small, K. (2006). *Estimating human trafficking into the United States: Development of a methodology*. Fairfax, VA: Caliber an ICF International Company. Retrieved from www.ncjrs.gov/pdffiles1/nij/grants/215475.pdf

Contreras, M., & Farley, M. (2011). Human trafficking: Not an isolated issue. In T. Bryant-Davis (Ed.), *Surviving sexual violence: A guide to recovery and empowerment* (pp. 22–36). Lanham, MD: Rowman & Littlefield Publishers, Inc.

Crawford, M. (2017). International sex trafficking. *Women & Therapy*, *40*(1–2), 101–122. https://doi.org/10.1080/02703149.2016.1206784

Dank, M., Khan, B., Downey, P. M., Kotonias, C., Mayer, D., Owens, C., . . . Yu, L. (2014, March 12). Estimating the size and structure of the underground commercial sex economy in eight major U.S. Cities. *Urban Institute*. Retrieved from www.urban.org/research/publication/estimating-size-and-structure-underground-commercial-sex-economy-eight-major-us-cities

Farr, K. (2004). *Sex trafficking: The global market in women and children*. New York, NY: Worth Publishers.

Finkel, R., & Finkel, M. L. (2015). The 'dirty downside' of global sporting events: Focus on human trafficking for sexual exploitation. *Public Health*, *129*(1), 17–22. https://doi.org/10.1016/j.puhe.2014.11.006

Garlock, L. R. (2016). Stories in the cloth: Art therapy and narrative textiles. *Art Therapy: Journal of the American Art Therapy Association*, *33*(2), 58–66. https://doi.org/10.1080/07421656.2016.1164004

Global Slavery Index. (2018). *Global findings*. Retrieved from www.globalslaveryindex.org/2018/findings/regional-analysis/asia-and-the-pacific/

Huda, S. (2006, July 17). Sex trafficking in South Asia. *International Journal of Gynecology & Obstetrics*, *94*(3). https://doi.org/10.1016/j.ijgo.2006.04.027

Institute of Medicine & National Research Council. (2013). *Confronting commercial sexual exploitation and sex trafficking of minors in the United States*. Retrieved from www.ncjfcj.org/sites/default/files/IOM%20full%20report.pdf

International Labour Office & Walk Free Foundation. (2017). *The global estimates of modern slavery: Forced labor and forced marriage*. Retrieved from www.ilo.org/wcmsp5/groups/public/@dgreports/@dcomm/documents/publication/wcms_575479.pdf

International Labour Organization. (2014). *Profits and poverty: The economics of forced labour*. Retrieved from www.ilo.org/wcmsp5/groups/public/—ed_norm/---declaration/documents/publication/wcms_243391.pdf

Kara, S. (2009). *Sex trafficking: Inside the business of modern slavery*. New York, NY: Columbia University Press.

Kometiani, M. K., & Farmer, K. W. (2019). Exploring resilience through case studies of art therapy with sex trafficked survivors and their advocates. *The Arts*

in Psychotherapy. Advance online publication. https://doi.org/10.1016/j.aip.2019.101582
Litam, S. D. A. (2017). Human sex trafficking in America: What counselors need to know. *The Professional Counselor*, *7*(1), 45–61. https://doi.org/10.15241/sdal.7.1.45
Mekinc, J., & Music, K. (2015, May). Sexual exploitation of children in the tourism-the dark side of tourism. *Innovative Issues and Approaches in Social Sciences*, *8*(2), 64–85. https://doi.org/10.12959/issn.1855-0541.IIASS-2015-no2-art04
Miller-Perrin, C., & Wurtele, S. K. (2017). Sex trafficking and the commercial sexual exploitation of children. *Women & Therapy*, *40*(1–2), 123–151. https://doi.org/10.1080/02703149.2016.1210963
National Center for Missing & Exploited Children. (2017). *Child sex trafficking*. Retrieved from www.missingkids.com/theissues/cse/1in7
National Sexual Violence Resource Center and Pennsylvania Coalition Against Rape. (2012). *Assisting trafficking victims: A guide for victim advocates*. Retrieved from www.nsvrc.org/sites/default/files/publications_nsvrc_guides_human-trafficking-victim-advocates.pdf
Polaris. (2019). *Sex trafficking*. Retrieved from http://polarisproject.org/human-trafficking/sex-trafficking
Roy, S., & Chaman, C. (2017). Human rights and trafficking in women and children in India. *Journal of Historical Archaeology & Anthropological Sciences*, *1*(5), 162–170. https://doi.org/10.15406/jhaas.2017.01.00027
Shared Hope International. (2017). *What is sex trafficking*? Retrieved from http://sharedhope.org/wp-content/uploads/2017/07/What-is-Sex-Trafficking-Printable-Handout.pdf
Smith, L. (2018a). A look at the wins. In L. Smith (Ed.), *Invading the darkness: Inside the historic fight against child sex trafficking in the United States* (pp. 259–266). Vancouver, WA: Shared Hope International.
Smith, L. (2018b). Cries from the shadows. In L. Smith (Ed.), *Invading the darkness: Inside the historic fight against child sex trafficking in the United States* (pp. 1–12). Vancouver, WA: Shared Hope International.
Snow, M. (2018). Identifying victims to change lives. In L. Smith (Ed.), *Invading the darkness: Inside the historic fight against child sex trafficking in the United States* (pp. 135–150). Vancouver, WA: Shared Hope International.
Stotts, E. L., & Ramey, L. (2009). Human trafficking: A call for counselor awareness and action. *Journal of Humanistic Counseling, Education and Development*, *48*, 36–47. https://doi.org/10.1002/j.2161-1939.2009.tb00066.x
Tan, L. A. (2012). Art therapy with trafficked women. *Therapy Today*, *23*(5), 26–31.
Tverdova, Y. V. (2011). Human trafficking in Russia and other post-Soviet states. *Human Rights Review*, *12*(3), 329–344.
United Nations. (2000). *Protocol to prevent, suppress and punish trafficking in persons especially women and children*. Retrieved from ww.ohchr.org/EN/ProfessionalInterest/Pages/ProtocolTrafficking InPersons.aspx
United Nations Office on Drugs and Crime. (2018). *Global report on trafficking in persons 2018*. Retrieved from www.unodc.org/documents/data-and-analysis/glotip/2018/GLOTiP_2018_BOOK_web_small.pdf
United States Department of Health and Human Services. (n.d.). *Sex trafficking fact sheet*. Retrieved from www.acf.hhs.gov/sites/default/files/orr/fact_sheet_sex_trafficking.pdf

United States Department of Health and Human Services. (2019). *What is human trafficking?* Retrieved from www.acf.hhs.gov/otip/about/what-is-human-trafficking

United States Department of State. (2017, June). *Trafficking in persons report.* Retrieved from www.state.gov/documents/organization/271339.pdf

Williamson, C., Karandikar-Chheda, S., Barrows, J., Smouse, T., Kelly, G., Swartz, P., . . . Tame, C. (2012). *Ohio trafficking in persons study commission research and analysis subcommittee report on the prevalence of human trafficking in Ohio to Attorney General Richard Cordray*. Retrieved from www.researchgate.net/publication/260335516_Ohio_Trafficking_in_Persons_Study_Commission_Research_and_Analysis_Sub-Committee_Report_on_the_Prevalence_of_Human_Trafficking_in_Ohio_To_Attorney_General_Richard_Cordray_Research_Committee_Members_At

TWO

Deceptive Tactics and Adverse Consequences of Sex Trafficking

Mary K. Kometiani

Insecure, alone, misunderstood, vulnerable, and chosen;

Empty promises, deception, isolation, fear, intimidation, pain, suffering, degradation, rape, violation, neglect, addiction and danger; and

Criminalized, marginalized, judged, tired, wounded, lost, broken, hopeless, and worthless.

I'm not in control. I am owned. I am for sale.

This narrative could be articulated by any trafficked person. Fraud, force, and coercion as trafficking tactics will be explored. The grooming process and trauma bond are presented as ways to exert control and sexually exploit at-risk people. Individuals are exposed to incommunicable events while being sex trafficked; they are terrorized, violated, dominated, and humiliated. Finally, a myriad of adverse consequences of sex trafficking are thoroughly explained, and a concise overview of holistic treatment recommendations is provided.

Sex Trafficking Tactics

Traffickers entice, recruit, transport, conceal, acquire, manipulate, and patronize to sustain the sex industry. Sexual exploitation transpires from deception for job opportunity, fraudulent romantic relationship, family member selling, kidnapping, or manipulated engagement through another trafficked individual (Kara, 2009). While trafficking may be initiated through purchase or abduction, traffickers often employ a lengthy grooming process that leads to manipulation through a seemingly valid relationship. Usually, traffickers target individuals in need of love, and after establishing a fake relationship of trust and dependence, exploitation is carried out in a systematic manner. Three domineering methods of deception, enforcement, and intimidation complete the exploitation process for at-risk individuals who are sold in the sex trafficking trade.

Fraud

Traffickers use the tactic of fraud to offer false promises of love, employment, or a better life to those who are victimized (United States Department of Health and Human Services, 2019). Traffickers may lure in poor youth by offering them occupational offers of housekeeping, modeling, and dancing, but working conditions and promises of opportunity are entirely fabricated. Children from destitute families are recruited into sex trafficking through promises of financial reimbursement to disadvantaged family members. After deceptive guarantees are made, withholding wages is also a common form of fraudulent behavior in trafficking situations (United States Department of Health and Human Services, 2019). Deceit, the primary way for traffickers to entice the vulnerable, is followed with forceful compliance.

Force

Human traffickers use force through physical restraint or inflicting bodily harm as a way to acquire and sustain control (United States Department of Health and Human Services, 2019). Violent power induces enslavement and resignation. Examples of sex trafficking force tactics include monitoring, intimidation, gang rape/rape, physical abuse, confinement, and controlling personal choices (Polaris, 2014). If individuals do not consent or they disobey the trafficker, increased severity and/or threatening of their loved ones are additional ways to enforce their submittal (Farr, 2004). Traffickers may also use drugs or alcohol as a means to force compliance through addiction or financial reliance (Polaris, 2014). Force, a cruel aspect in the trafficking process, is intended to destroy an individual's opposition and obtain total domination. Coercion follows as the last treacherous maneuver.

Coercion

The United States Department of Health and Human Services (2019) defines coercion as intimidation or harm through manipulation, identification confiscation, bondage, and threats. Using bullying techniques pressures a vulnerable individual into sexual oppression. Sextortion, a form of online exploitation, occurs when perpetrators coerce young individuals through obtaining incriminating photos and threatening exposure if they do not perform sexual acts for audiences via web camera (United States Department of State, 2017). Once individuals have been sold into slavery, further coercive techniques are applied, including inescapable debt bondage with minimal compensation, high interest rates, and charging for other necessary expenses, such as transportation, food, living supplies, and rent (Polaris, 2014; Polaris, 2015; United States Department of Health and Human Services, 2019). Creating and maintaining a high quota of customers and penalizing the trafficked individual for an unmet quantity forces compliance (United States Department of Health and Human Services, 2019). Along with force and fraud, coercion defined as the application of terrorization and devastation, are destructive identification characteristics and provide the foundation for sex trafficking maltreatment.

The Grooming Process

Before and during trafficking, exploited individuals are constantly controlled and victimized (Hom & Woods, 2013). Through the convincing grooming process, traffickers use manipulative tactics to build a dishonest relationship that appears trustworthy and ends in extreme exploitation. This brainwashing process imposes full control over individuals through forced servitude and submission. Even though sex trafficking can occur without grooming, it is a frequently applied con. The United Kingdom's largest charitable organization, Barnardo's (1998), defined the grooming process in these stages:

- developing trust, showing attention, and becoming romantically involved;
- creating dependence through reliance on the trafficker and isolation of other supports;
- control through threats, violence, and demands to prove loyalty; and
- dominance through compliance and cooperation to do whatever the trafficker demands.

First, the trafficking criminal finds potential targets through engaging in charming actions and conversations with the intent of assessing weaknesses. While the perpetrator focuses on these vulnerabilities, he is acting to fulfill a relationship that is lacking in the at-risk individual's life by providing empty promises (Leitch & Snow, 2010). During the second stage, the trafficker secludes the defenseless individual during which he further asserts dependence on him. Following the isolation period, the abuser will start a violent cycle of manipulation, mistreatment, and affection (Leitch & Snow, 2010). The trafficker convinces the innocent individual that she has a choice and that he is not responsible for the abuse. The grooming process exerts psychological control, mental manipulation, emotional abuse, and physical force to control and exploit the vulnerable person.

During the final phase of dominance, the trafficker coerces the individual into prostitution after using violence, gang raping, or exploitation through forced debt, all of which leave the person feeling disgraced, embarrassed, and remorseful (Leitch & Snow, 2010). Total psychological domination, also known as breaking or seasoning, is a method used to establish power over an individual through methodical and consistent infliction of trauma (Herman, 1997). This process involves extreme physical abuse, sexual assault and rape, confinement and torture, and withholding food or water; full control over the individual is exerted by providing a new nickname and regulating all personal details, such as daily arrangements, garments worn, and confiscation of all personal identification. The trafficker's goal is to make the individual willing to agree and to create unquestioned obedience (Herman, 1997). Initiation to sex trafficking can dictate frequent raping or other abusive tactics to ensure passivity and take away an individual's desire to fight back or flee.

The grooming of minors is a process in which traffickers desensitize children to sex through an emerging, devious, authoritarian relationship (Miller-Perrin & Wurtele, 2017). Like these other abusive techniques, using sexually explicit material teaches and exposes the inexperienced individuals to behaviors that are anticipated in a trafficking situation. Watching pornography also numbs the children to the shame, aggression, and mortification of sexual actions that are expected (National Center on Sexual Exploitation, n.d.). Excessive and demoralizing efforts are meant to break the individual and warp the mind by eliminating any sense of control or options for escape.

Trauma Bond

The typical reaction to experiencing significant distress is developing a trauma bond. Through a balance of severe mistreatment and reliance on the trafficker, the trauma bond enmeshes the individual to the abuser. Although the trafficker is feared, he is also the provider of comfort by supplying necessary living supplies, such as food and shelter; the victimized individual becomes dependent on him for survival as well as for emotional connection (Herman, 1997). Exploited persons may not have comprehensive awareness of this sadistic attachment and blindly commit to this toxic relationship. Stockholm Syndrome exemplified the trauma bond after a robbery when hostages who released from captivity defended their perpetrators for being kind while their lives were in mortal danger (Fabrique, Romano, Vecchi, & van Hasselt, 2007). The perpetrator instills fear in addition to gratitude for being able to live in trauma bonding (United States Department of Health and Human Services, n.d.). While the trauma bond is defined through the reaction of prisoner attachment and loyalty to the perpetrator, the grooming process exerts control, manipulation, and force to control and exploit the vulnerable into experiencing a convincing emotional relationship through dependence and obligation. The extensive aftermath that ensues is seemingly unlimited in its comprehensive destruction.

The Adverse Consequences of Trafficking

Sex trafficking involves unrelenting cycles of vicious emotional and psychological abuse and physical violence as individuals are manipulated through intimidating, deceptive, cruel, coercive, and threatening behaviors. The trauma of sex trafficking is considerable enough to have lasting effects (United States Department of State, 2018). There is no limit to the harm of those who are sex trafficked, as they can be murdered if they lack obedience and attempt control in their lives (Kara, 2009). Sex trafficking survivors experience a wide range of physical, physiological, mental, emotional, social, and spiritual consequences from the vast trauma. Devastating long-term outcomes consist of physical effects from abuse, neglect, and infections; physiological disorders and compounded medical issues; psychological trauma, depression, anxiety, and dissociation; emotional disconnection and shame affecting an individual's future and relationships; and spirituality concerns of reducing one's ability to have a meaningful life. Trafficking takes away individuals' rights to feel safe, secure, and protected, and it abandons them into a new life of endangerment without any control.

Physical

The trafficked individual is physically harmed and traumatized in indescribable ways. Destructive consequences include long-term physical trauma from abuse, sexually transmitted infections (STIs), drug addiction, starvation, unwanted pregnancy, and even early death (United States Department of State, 2017). Exploited individuals are beaten, violated, raped, assaulted, and tortured. Research proved most sex trafficked survivors undergo physical and sexual violence while being trafficked that usually starts with being raped and physically battered (Hossain, Zimmerman, Abas, Light, & Watts, 2010; Tsutsumi, Izutsu, Poudyal, Kato, & Marui, 2008; Zimmerman et al., 2008). Considered the most unsafe form of labor, sex industry work is linked to premature mortality from homicide, substance abuse/overdose, accidents, and human immunodeficiency virus (HIV) (Potterat et al., 2004). Throughout the trafficked experience, individuals endure vast amounts of near fatal violence and repeated exposure to deadly infections.

One sex trafficking survivor calculated that by servicing up to 30 men a day for 7 days a week for four years, she was raped 43,200 times (Romo, 2017). The longer an individual is forced to live in exploitation, the greater the health risks that may develop. In a study of sex trafficked survivors, one in four tested positive for HIV; the higher risk for HIV was found to correlate with the earlier age of exploitation and more extended time of trafficking (Silverman et al., 2006). Exposure and high risk of contracting STIs are widespread because perpetrators are reluctant to use protection, and enslaved individuals cannot demand this precaution

(Dandona et al., 2005). Cervical cancer is common for women from the sex industry because of the number of sexual partners and initiation of sexual activity at a young age (Farley, 2004). As a result of unprotected sex beyond their control, trafficked survivors are exposed to diseases that cause additional and often serious medical problems and detriment.

The physical consequences of being trafficked are long term and severe, and chronic health problems can result from a lack of treatment. Severe physical abuse can result in traumatic brain injury (TBI) when an individual suffers with head injuries from being beaten, kicked, strangled, or slammed into an object (Farley, 2004). In addition to numbness, sensory issues, and trouble focusing, many survivors report exhaustion, dizziness, pain, and memory issues as other physical effects from TBI (Crawford, 2017). Other common symptoms reported from a research study of trafficked survivors were headaches, pain, and infections (Zimmerman et al., 2008). Survivors also suffer from additional physical issues, such as burns, wounds, fractures, vaginal and anal tearing, menstrual and fertility issues, pelvic pain, pregnancy and complications resulting from unsafe/forced/illegal abortions, ignored chronic conditions, and dental problems (United States Department of Health and Human Services, n.d.; Williamson et al., 2012). Being exposed to constant, detrimental physical punishment results in many complex physiological ailments.

Physiological

Research demonstrates the extensive and perplexing physiological effects of trauma on the body. Somatic symptoms with unclear sources consisting of migraines, chronic neck and back pain, fibromyalgia, digestion issues, irritable bowel syndrome, asthma, and chronic fatigue are widespread in traumatized individuals (van der Kolk, 2014). The harmful effects of the continued elevation of trauma's stress hormone include attention and memory issues, fatigue, irritability, and other long-term health problems (van der Kolk, 2014). Compounded medical problems, such as skin problems and autoimmune disorders, are also prevalent in those who have survived trauma (Cook, Blaustein, Spinazzola, & van der Kolk, 2003). Survivors of sex trafficking are exposed to the deprivation of necessary living means; they exist in unsanitary and substandard conditions and lack adequate nutrition (Farr, 2004). Survivors who underwent significant trauma are forced to confront the resultant array of its disastrous physiological effects on their bodies.

Undeniably, sex trafficked individuals are exposed to physical and sexual trauma ensuing in widespread health problems. Many adverse consequences develop from the massive abuse that sex trafficked individuals endured. The body remembers trauma, and trauma manifests through a range of physiological symptoms (van der Kolk, 2014). There are many lasting and damaging physiological effects resulting from trafficking trauma, and these are impacted further by the psychological effects.

Psychological

Destructive repercussions from trafficking include persisting psychological trauma, the long-term and extensive effects of complex trauma, and enduring multiple types of abuse and victimization known as *polyvictimization* (United States Department of State, 2017, 2018). Individuals who are sex trafficked are oppressed, dominated, and manipulated by being held captive in confinement. The majority of sex trafficked female survivors reported being threatened and controlled (Hossain et al., 2010). The trafficker lets survivors think they have a choice in being exploited, but this is only a delusion of deciding rather to work as a prostitute or be killed, withstand harm to their loved ones or be blackmailed (Leitch & Snow, 2010; Shared Hope International, 2014). Traffickers also use psychological ruses to maintain continued control and obedience. Violence done in front of other survivors is a warning to defiant behavior persons and a savage demand for loyalty (Leitch & Snow, 2010). Physical harm or the threat of harm of self and/or another is a form of psychological oppression for sex trafficked survivors.

The trafficked survivor experiences a range of interpersonal issues that result in psychological disorders. Some of the initial trauma symptoms to emerge are hyperarousal and affect restriction (Levine, 1997). Early symptoms of trauma include hypervigilance, hyperactivity, and decreased capacity to handle stress. Over time, other symptoms appear, including anxiety, avoidance, sexual interest conflict, and distress over dying or feeling insane (Levine, 1997). If trauma is not resolved, advanced symptoms, such as muteness, depression, and thoughts of self-harm, may settle in an individual (Levine, 1997). Trauma has many intensifying psychological consequences that expand over time.

The results of trauma can include recurrent experienced remembrance and exposure through flashbacks. Trauma flashbacks make individuals feel as if the traumatic event is never ending and continually reoccurring because they are reliving the trauma through memories and a restructured nervous system (van der Kolk, 2014). The same somatic symptoms of increased heart rate and palpitations, sweating, accelerated breathing, and agitation experienced during trauma can be replayed again and again (Rothschild, 2000). Recreating the trauma can be extremely distressing, and the traumatized avoid symptoms and withdraw from others, leading to a deprived existence that is self-protective in nature (Herman, 1997). Flashbacks can be overwhelmingly upsetting for a sex trafficked survivor, causing physical reactions and public evasion through the sudden recollection of harmful events that cannot be forgotten.

Dissociation, explained further in Chapter 4, is a symptom appearing to assist in acclimating an individual to experiencing recurrent trauma (Levine, 1997). Dissociation is a way of disconnecting from reality and what is occurring in order to survive. Dissociation, altered consciousness, amnesia, depersonalization, and derealization are common reactions from complex trauma (Cook et al., 2003). The body changes from experiencing chronic trauma over time to feeling numb as a protective response (van der Kolk, 2014). Being able to separate from the trauma occurrence can be a protective way to endure; however, dissociation has many lasting psychological effects and may perpetually alter the survivor's reality.

Trauma changes an individual. People who are chronically traumatized are constantly anxious, restless, and hypervigilant (Herman, 1997). Research proved that sex trafficked survivors have substantial symptoms of depression, anxiety, and posttraumatic stress disorder (PTSD), and the multiple traumas occurring from trafficking exploitation may lead to comorbid diagnosis of PTSD, anxiety, and severe depression (Abas et al., 2013; Oram, Stockl, Busza, Howard, & Zimmerman, 2012; Tsutsumi et al., 2008). Survivors of sex trafficking may be diagnosed with complex trauma as a result of entrapment, exposure to the abuse of others, and extended physical, psychological, and sexual abuse (Courtois & Ford, 2013).

Further diagnoses include attention deficit hyperactivity disorder, conduct disorder, impulse control issues, and antisocial traits (Williamson, Dutch, & Clawson, 2008). In addition to sexual disorders, sexual trauma ramifications include body image disorder (Cook et al., 2003). Cognitive issues, such as difficulty with processing information, focusing and attention, planning, and learning are typical for complex trauma; aggression, sleep and eating disorders, substance abuse, and oppositional and self-destructive behavior are also widespread in this population (Cook et al., 2003). Lingering substance abuse is common with sex trafficked survivors because drugs and alcohol were either a way of coping with the trauma or a way of being controlled by the trafficker or both (Office for Victims of Crime, n.d.). There is a multitude of mental health issues diagnosed in survivors of sex trafficking that affect their ability to function and lead typical lives.

Trafficking trauma affects the whole person and all aspects of the self, including numerous and vast psychological effects that may remain during lifelong mental health diagnosis. The altering residual results of dissociation and flashbacks are complicated and complex reactions to prolonged, horrific events. Complex trauma leaves a deep self-destructive impact on an individual's psychological and emotional being.

Emotional

Sexual exploitation abuses an individual over and over in humiliating, tortuous, and oppressive ways, and one particularly malicious dilemma is emotional destruction (Farley, 2004). The first traumatic emotional symptom to emerge is powerlessness, leading to amplified feelings and sudden mood changes (Levine, 1997). The trafficked individual is constantly exposed to demeaning language and actions. Emotional abuse occurs through name-calling, threats, and dehumanizing treatment.

The only consistent facet of trafficking is fear (Smith, 2007). Fear alerts an individual to potential a threat or danger, while terror is the maximum fear because it involves a threat to one's life (Rothschild, 2000). Those who are sexually exploited live in terror of their own safety, as well as their loved ones and trafficked companions. Anger is an emotional way for the traumatized to protect the self, a normal response to feeling afraid or harmed, and can intensify into rage when a person feels violated and disrespected (Rothschild, 2000). Rage, uncontrollable and intensified anger, causes dangerous and unhealthy decisions when neglected. Survivors also experience shock, denial, disbelief, and grief as normal responses to suffering through loss and change in their lives. Other common feelings that the trafficked individual deals with are intimidation, hopelessness, despair, distress, lack of control, abandonment, confusion, and sadness. Survivors may think they are to blame for being manipulated into being trafficked, and this belief is frequently reinforced by the trafficker (Shared Hope International, 2014). Because traumatized individuals are isolated and alone, they may feel no one else understands them or can help them, and, because of a lack of support from others, the abusive trafficker is perceived as the only one who cares about them. Sexual trauma survivors feel damaged and worthless from living through intense and incessant abuse.

The trafficked survivor's self-worth is negatively affected by emotional abuse and the accompanying sense of self-blame. Often, women survivors begin to believe their self-worth is related solely to their physical appearance and the value of their bodies. Survivors may experience shame for what they endured while being trafficked, and their self-blame is closely connected to low self-esteem (Polaris, 2014). Trafficking shame is related to feeling foolish for becoming involved with the trafficker, embarrassed for their actions, and regretful of their decisions. Shame is the ultimate expression of self-betrayal because the survivors feel humiliation, remorse, and disgrace regarding a trafficking situation over which they had little control (Herman, 1997). Shame is feeling devalued and worthless at the core of oneself (Marich, 2014). The effects of shame, decreased sense of self-esteem and self-worth, are deeply distressing emotional ramifications of sexual exploitation.

The emotional expense of sexual exploitation is immediate as well as enduring and may lead to lingering social impairment for the survivor. Numerous feelings commonly develop from sexual trauma that lead to poor self-esteem, low self-worth, aggravated self-blame, and tempting self-destruction. The price of survival requires that the individual not expose the pain (Smith, 2007). Those who are sex trafficked may emotionally detach as a coping mechanism to live through the severe mistreatment. After surviving the trauma, individuals may experience ongoing personal struggles because entrenched emotional regulation and detachment affects the ability to establish appropriate boundaries and maintain healthy relationships.

Interpersonal

The trafficked survivor experiences a range of emotional complications that result in interpersonal issues. If trauma does not resolve, isolation may continue (Levine, 1997). Trauma also affects survivors in terms of their future emotional security. Trafficked survivors experience difficulty identifying, expressing, and controlling emotions (Cook et al., 2003). Survivors of exploitation may experience isolation issues during disclosure, revealing their problem with interacting with others.

The outcome for the survivor of sex trafficking is society and community ostracism (United States Department of State, 2017). Sexual trauma, one of the most dangerous and unresolved problems of society, causes trafficking individuals to feel disconnected from themselves, others, and community (Levine, 2008). The manipulative grooming tactics used to build a relationship ending in extreme exploitation makes trust and attachment in future relationships extremely difficult. Trauma makes someone feel constantly out of rhythm with others and unsafe in groups (van der Kolk, 2014). During the trafficking experience, an individual is isolated in an environment that lacks appropriate socialization. Due to trauma, sex trafficked survivors face issues with relationships, boundaries, and attunement (Cook et al., 2003). The United States Department of Health and Human Services (n.d.) documented that survivors may experience hatred toward others, especially males. Feelings become separated from sexual behaviors, initiating intimacy obstacles with future relationships, including friends and possible partners (Farley, 2004). All these effects of trafficking lead to relational problems, including expressing vulnerability, experiencing connection with others, and demonstrating social skills. The interpersonal consequences of sexual exploitation can be worsened from the spiritual effects of trauma.

Spiritual

The survivors of trafficking undergo a process that breaks their innermost being, and the exploitation destroys the individual's spirit. Sex trafficked individuals are denied previous personal identity and are often tattooed to signify ownership (Hom & Woods, 2013). Because trafficking obliterates an individual's identity, privacy, humanity, and dignity, the crime instigates an existential crisis. Spiritual trauma complication is the loss of the sense of oneself (Cook et al., 2003). Sex trafficking takes away the essence of a person, leaving a remnant of the original identity and leaving instead a sense of emptiness and ruin. Some traumatized individuals wish they were dead (Herman, 1997), and they may experience self-hatred (United States Department of Health and Human Services, n.d.). The trafficked survivor feels broken, vacant, discarded, and invisible, as if her existence does not matter. The survivor may not even recognize her former self before the protracted abuse.

Trauma makes an individual feel forsaken, isolated, alienated, and unprotected (Herman, 1997). Faced with incredible hardship over time, the individual is only able to focus on survival one day at a time. Over extended periods of time, individuals may begin to normalize the abuse; enduring severe trauma, abuse, and manipulation impacts their worldview; they believe this is a usual pattern of life (Polaris, 2014). The more destroyed a victimized individual's soul, the more tolerant she became of the trafficking life (Kara, 2009). Those who are exposed to extensive exploitation begin to think of the abuse as a typical and expected way of living, and acceptance of the mistreatment is devastating to a survivor's sense of worth, which is crucial to regain freedom and control.

A wound to the soul is within the deepest part of the self and causes one to feel defective and devoid of meaning (Grassman, 2015). Spiritual ramifications of trauma are loss of identity, demise of hope for the future, and an unclear purpose for living. The survivor who has undergone severe trauma and abuse may feel despair and accept resignation and surrender. Self-harm and suicide stem from depression and hopelessness, and suicidal ideation is common with sex trafficked survivors (Zimmerman et al., 2008). The spiritual effects of sex trafficking are truly life-threatening because the innermost life force of an individual is attacked.

The aftermath of multifaceted trauma is startling. Significant and complex trauma alters a survivor's life in countless ways. Trauma affects an individual physically, physiologically, psychologically, emotionally, socially, and spiritually. The survivor suffers from ongoing physical effects from continuous rape, abuse, neglect of health concerns and infections; physiological pain and body malfunctioning; mental health diagnoses of depression, anxiety, and dissociation; shame and emotional discord affecting an individual's potential; social unacceptance, disconnection, and isolation; and spirituality distress that diminishes a purposeful and predictable life. Sexual exploitation is extremely dangerous for those who suffer through captivity because their lives may end in murder, suicide, overdose, or with complicated and lifelong issues interrupting their ability to recover and live fully after trauma without proper help and support.

Treatment Recommendations

Sexual exploitation impacts individuals differently. Sex trafficked survivors who experience numerous forms of trauma are at increased risk for detriment; however, it is important to explore what individuals consider to be traumatic (Gerassi & Nichols, 2018). Trauma is an individual's reaction to a terrifying event, and every individual responds to trauma differently (United States Department of State, 2018).

Besides establishing safety and basic needs for patients, the United States Department of State (2012) recommends that survivors of human trafficking participate in an environment of empowerment with unconditional support for trust, rage, and shame issues; reestablishing identity; and strengthening self-esteem. Suggested all-encompassing holistic care includes basic necessities and housing, medical care, education, legal services, protection, interpretation/immigration services, living skills, mentorship, educational/vocational training, and job assistance (Miller-Perrin & Wurtele, 2017; National Sexual Violence Resource Center and Pennsylvania Coalition Against Rape, 2012). Mental health care is regarded as the most important treatment for complex trauma for trafficked survivors (Rafferty, 2017). The trafficked survivor experiences a comprehensive range of mental health needs that can be addressed through emotional, psychological, and spiritual support; trauma counseling; expressive arts therapy; both individual counseling and group therapy; psychoeducation regarding trauma, grief and loss, and addictions; mind-body awareness and anxiety management; case management; and client advocacy.

Treatment for sex trafficked survivors needs to be trauma-informed, individualized and survivor-centered, culturally relevant, developmentally appropriate, and gender-responsive (Elkins, Crawford, & Briggs, 2017; Gerassi & Nichols, 2018; Rafferty, 2017; United States Department of State, 2017). Preventing retraumatization focuses on the principles of empowerment, support, and compassion (Rafferty, 2017). Care that is trauma-informed stresses creating physical, emotional, and psychological safety and focuses on an individual's experience and distinct needs (United States Department of State, 2018). Trauma-informed treatment recognizes the impact, signs, and symptoms of trauma on an individual and is active against reexperiencing the event; trauma care also considers how past events impact an individual's behaviors, reactions, and perceptions (United States Department of State, 2017). Furthermore, trauma-informed programs are recommended to be survivor-informed, meaning they receive survivor feedback regarding development, execution, and assessment to ensure effective care (United States Department of State, 2018). Survivor-centered treatment ensures that the individual is essential in the decision-making process and experiences control throughout treatment (Gerassi & Nichols, 2018). Individualized care to promote healing and empowerment, taking into consideration the unique needs of an individual, is required (Rafferty, 2017). Treatment should be respectful, sensitive, and empathetic. Every facet of provided care should be supportive, nonjudgmental, holistic, and empowering (Litam, 2017).

Due to variances in genders, ethnicity, cultures, and any religious or spiritual beliefs, individuals respond differently to trauma and treatment. Men are stigmatized through possible misconceptions and stereotypes regarding sexual orientation; male survivors feel pressured to reassert their masculinity and conflicted between accepting their manhood and the experience of feeling powerless (Elkins et al., 2017). Treatment needs to be consistent with the individual's customs, traditions, and beliefs; cultural variances of emotional expression as well as manifestation of symptoms need to be considered (Rafferty, 2017). Language barriers are also important to address in culturally relevant treatment; interpreters may need to be considered for treatment, and confidentiality needs to be understood and guaranteed (National Sexual Violence Resource Center and Pennsylvania Coalition Against Rape, 2012; United States Department of State, 2017). The individual's background regarding personal, cultural, socioeconomic status, age/development, and traumatic events that occurred while being trafficked will influence all choices regarding treatment. Therapists need to understand how various personal characteristics and cultural expectations can affect the individuality of survivors and their trauma.

Through offering individualized care that meets the needs of diverse survivors of sex trafficking, art therapy provides expression in a universal nonverbal language. Although art therapy can overcome language barriers, therapists need to exert caution with art therapy interventions and their cultural applicability for each individual. Art materials need to represent all cultures, different ethnicities, lifestyles, and values (Malchiodi, 2015). Art therapists are encouraged to use art supplies and media that are representative of the survivor's beliefs, background, gender, and development. Art therapy restores the sense of self that is lost, provides a voice that was silenced and ignored, and gives power back to an individual who had no control. Art therapy plays a vital role in the recovery and reintegration into society of individuals who have experienced the complex trauma of sex trafficking due to the empowering nature of creating art, externalizing emotions, and communicating trauma.

Conclusion

It is fundamental to comprehend the suffering of the trafficked survivors' journey in order to understand the treatment for recovery (Nguyen, Bellehumeur, & Malette, 2014). Trafficked individuals are abused, violated, traumatized, and humiliated in countless ways, experiencing violence and crime that can only be described as worse than a nightmare—the trauma is agonizing, unbearable, and unspeakable. Trafficking objectifies an individual and eliminates human status. A trafficked survivor experiences both visible physical and invisible psychological, emotional, and spiritual wounds. The survivor suffers through betrayal, abuse, and deprivation of basic human rights. Survivors have learned to endure in unsafe and uncertain environments where they had been controlled, their pain was ignored, and their only aim was daily survival. Because their identity is disrupted, their worldview is skewed; they cannot trust others, and future goals have disappeared. Traumatized individuals feel trapped in the past; they struggle to assimilate new experiences. The lives of survivors feel tainted because the trauma continues in the present and is ongoing (van der Kolk, 2014). Given all these burdensome issues, it is clear why some survivors have enormous difficulty in transitioning back to society. Although trauma leaves profound scars, hope in recovery is possible through holistic trauma-informed treatment that includes art therapy.

References

Abas, M., Ostrovschi, N. V., Prince, M., Gorceag, V. I., Trigub, C., & Oram, S. (2013). Risk factors for mental disorder in women survivors of human trafficking: A historical cohort study. *BMC Psychiatry*, *13*(204), 1–11. https://doi.org/10.1186/1471-244X-13-204

Barnardo's (1998). *Whose daughter next? Children abused through prostitution*. Basildon, Essex: Barnados.

Cook, A., Blaustein, M., Spinazzola, J., & van der Kolk, B. (Eds.). (2003). *Complex trauma in children and adolescents*. National Child Traumatic Stress Network. Retrieved from www.nctsn.org/sites/default/files/resources//complex_trauma_in_children_and_adolescents.pdf

Courtois, C. A., & Ford, J. D. (2013). *Treatment of complex trauma: A sequenced, relationship-based approach*. New York, NY: Guildford Press.

Crawford, M. (2017). International sex trafficking. *Women & Therapy*, *40*(1–2), 101–122. https://doi.org/10/1080/02703149.2016.1206784

Dandona, R., Dandona, L., Gutierrez, J. P., Kumar, A. G., McPherson, S., Samuels, F., & Bertozzi, S. M. (2005, August 20). High risk of HIV in non-brothel based female sex workers in India. *BMC Public Health*, *5*(87). https://doi.org/10.1186/1471-2458-5-87

Elkins, J., Crawford, K., & Briggs, H. E. (2017). Male survivors of sexual abuse: Becoming gender-responsive and trauma-informed. *Advances in Social Work*, *18*(1), 116–130. https://doi.org/10.18060/21301

Fabrique, N. D., Romano, S. J., Vecchi, G. M., & van Hasselt, V. B. (2007, July). Understanding Stockholm syndrome. *FBI Law Enforcement Bulletin*, *76*(7), 10–15. Retrieved from www.hsdl.org/?view&did=481801

Farley, M. (2004). "Bad for the body, bad for the heart": Prostitution harms women even if legalized or decriminalized. *Violence Against Women*, *10*(10), 1087–1125. https://doi.org/10.1177/1077801204268607

Farr, K. (2004). *Sex trafficking: The global market in women and children*. New York, NY: Worth Publishers.

Gerassi, L. B., & Nichols, A. J. (2018). *Sex trafficking and commercial sexual exploitation: Prevention, advocacy, and trauma-informed practice*. New York, NY: Springer Publishing Company.

Grassman, D. (2015, June). Help PTSD sufferers heal from "soul injury." *Boston Globe*. Retrieved from www.bostonglobe.com/opinion/2015/06/21/too-many-suffer-too-long-with-soul-injury/KjaS0gXx2vykS4WdtwUf0L/story.html

Herman, J. L. (1997). *Trauma and recovery: The aftermath of violence—From domestic abuse to political terror* (2nd ed.). New York, NY: Basic Books.

Hom, K. A., & Woods, S. J. (2013). Trauma and its aftermath for commercially sexually exploited women as told by front-line service providers. *Issues in Mental Health Nursing*, *34*(2), 75–81. https://doi.org/10.3109/01612840.2012.723300

Hossain, M., Zimmerman, C., Abas, M., Light, M., & Watts, C. (2010). The relationship of trauma to mental disorders among trafficked and sexually exploited girls and women. *American Journal of Public Health*, *100*(12), 2442–2449. https://doi.org/10.2105/AJPH.2009.173229

Kara, S. (2009). *Sex trafficking: Inside the business of modern slavery*. New York, NY: Columbia University Press.

Leitch, L., & Snow, M. (2010). *Intervene: Practitioner guide and intake tool*. Vancouver, WA: Shared Hope International.

Levine, P. A. (1997). *Waking the tiger: Healing trauma*. Berkley, CA: North Atlantic Books.

Levine, P. A. (2008). *Healing trauma*. Boulder, CO: Sounds True.

Litam, S. D. A. (2017). Human sex trafficking in America: What counselors need to know. *The Professional Counselor*, *7*(1), 45–61. https://doi.org/10.15241/sd.al.7.1.45

Malchiodi, C. A. (2015). Ethics, evidence, trauma-informed practice, and cultural sensitivity. In C. A. Malchiodi (Ed.), *Creative interventions with traumatized children* (pp. 24–44). New York, NY: The Guilford Press.

Marich, J. (2014). *Trauma made simple: Competencies in assessment, treatment and working with survivors*. Eau Claire, WI: Pesi Publishing and Media.

Miller-Perrin, C., & Wurtele, S. K. (2017). Sex trafficking and the commercial sexual exploitation of children. *Women & Therapy*, *40*(1–2), 123–151. https://doi.org/10.1080/02703149.2016.1210963

National Center on Sexual Exploitation. (n.d.). *Pornography + sex trafficking: The facts*. Retrieved from http://stoptraffickingdemand.com/facts/

National Sexual Violence Resource Center and Pennsylvania Coalition Against Rape. (2012). *Assisting trafficking victims: A guide for victim advocates*. Retrieved from www.nsvrc.org/sites/default/files/publications_nsvrc_guides_human-trafficking-victim-advocates.pdf

Nguyen, T. T., Bellehumeur, C. R., & Malette, J. (2014). Women survivors of sex trafficking: A trauma and recovery model integrating spirituality. *Counseling and Spirituality*, *33*(1), 111–133. https://doi.org/10.2143/CS.33.1.3044833

Office for Victims of Crime. (n.d.). *Substance abuse needs*. Retrieved from www.ovcttac.gov/taskforceguide/eguide/4-supporting-victims/44-comprehensive-victim-services/mental-health-needs/substance-abuse-needs/

Oram, S., Stockl, H., Busza, J., Howard, L. M., & Zimmerman, C. (2012). Prevalence and risk of violence and physical, mental, and sexual health problems associated with human trafficking: Systematic review. *PLoS Medicine*, *9*(5), 1–13. https://doi.org/10.1371/journal.pmed.1001224

Polaris. (2014). *In their shoes: Understanding victims' mindsets and common barriers to victim identification*. Retrieved from https://humantraffickinghotline.org/resources/understanding-victim-mindsets

Polaris. (2015, May). *Sex trafficking in the US: A closer look at the US citizen victims*. Retrieved from http://polarisproject.org/resources/sex-trafficking-us-closer-look-us-citizen-victims

Potterat, J. J., Brewer, D. D., Muth, S. Q., Rothenberg, R. B., Woodhouse, D. E., Muth, J. B., Stites, H. K., & Brody, S. (2004). Mortality in a long-term open cohort of prostitute women. *American Journal of Epidemiology*, *159*(8), 778–785. https://doi.org/10.1093/aje/kwh110

Rafferty, Y. (2017). Mental health services as a vital component of psychosocial recovery for victims of child trafficking or commercial sexual exploitation. *American Journal of Orthopsychiatry*, *88*(3), 249–260. https://doi.org/10.1037.ort0000268

Romo, R. (2017). *Human trafficking survivor: I was raped 43,200 times*. Retrieved from www.cnn.com/2015/11/10/americas/freedom-project-mexico-trafficking-survivor/index.html

Rothschild, B. (2000). *The body remembers: The psychophysiology of trauma and trauma treatment*. New York, NY: W.W. Norton & Company.

Shared Hope International. (2014). *Domestic minor sex trafficking: Identifying and responding to America's youth*. Vancouver, WA: Shared Hope International.

Silverman, J. G., Decker, M. R., Gupta, J., Maheshwari, A., Patel, V., & Raj, A. (2006). HIV prevalence and predictors among rescued sex-trafficked women and girls in Mumbai, India. *Journal of Acquired Immune Deficiency Syndromes*, *43*(5), 588–593. https://doi.org/10.1097/01.qai.0000243101.57523.7d

Smith, L. (2007). *From Congress to the brothel: A journey of hope, healing, and restoration*. Vancouver, WA: Shared Hope International.

Tsutsumi, A., Izutsu, T., Poudyal, A., Kato, S., & Marui, E. (2008). Mental health of female survivors of human trafficking in Nepal. *Social Science & Medicine*, *66*, 1841–1847. https://doi.org/10.1016/j.socscimed.2007.12.025

United States Department of Health and Human Services. (n.d). *Sex trafficking fact sheet*. Retrieved from www.acf.hhs.gov/sites/default/files/orr/fact_sheet_sex_trafficking.pdf

United States Department of Health and Human Services. (2019). *What is human trafficking*? Retrieved from www.acf.hhs.gov/otip/about/what-is-human-trafficking

United States Department of State. (2017, June). *Trafficking in persons report*. Retrieved from www.state.gov/documents/organization/271339.pdf

United States Department of State. (2018, June 18). *Implementing a trauma-informed approach*. Retrieved from www.state.gov/documents/organization/283795.pdf

United States Department of State Office to Monitor and Combat Trafficking in Persons. (2012, June). *Addressing the internal wounds: The psychological aftermath of human trafficking*. Retrieved from www.state.gov/j/tip/rls/fs/2012/194719.htm

van der Kolk, B. (2014). *The body keeps the score: Brain, mind, and body in the healing of trauma*. New York, NY: Viking.

Williamson, C., Karandikar-Chheda, S., Barrows, J., Smouse, T., Kelly, G., Swartz, P., . . . Tame, C. (2012). *Ohio trafficking in persons study commission research and analysis subcommittee report on the prevalence of human trafficking in Ohio to Attorney General Richard Cordray*. Retrieved from www.researchgate.net/publication/260335516_Ohio_Trafficking_in_Persons_Study_Commission_Research_and_Analysis_Sub-Committee_Report_on_the_Prevalence_of_Human_Trafficking_in_Ohio_To_Attorney_General_Richard_Cordray_Research_Committee_Members_At

Williamson, E., Dutch, N. M., & Clawson, H. J. (2008). *Evidence-based mental health treatment for victims of human trafficking*. Washington, DC: Office of the Assistance Secretary for Planning and Evaluation, U.S. Department of Health and Human Services. Retrieved from https://aspe.hhs.gov/report/evidence-based-mental-health-treatment-victims-human-trafficking

Zimmerman, C., Hossain, M., Yun, K., Gajdadziev, V., Guzun, N., Tchomarova, M., . . . Watts, C. (2008). The health of trafficked women: A survey of women entering posttrafficking services in Europe. *American Journal of Public Health*, *98*(1), 55–59. https://doi.org/10.2105/AJPH.2006.108357

THREE

The Exploration of Vulnerabilities to Sex Trafficking and the Role in Art Therapy Treatment

Serena R. Coleman and Mary K. Kometiani

Introduction

Human trafficking is a global issue that has been increasing at a higher rate without available and reliable data to recognize how many individuals are impacted in cities or across countries (Savona & Stefanizzi, 2007). The vulnerabilities individuals may exhibit prior to trafficking differ from case to case and country to country. Yet the commonalities of labor and sex trafficking are attributed to power and control dynamics and the demand for financial gain. Overall, trafficking is about greed and how to repeatedly use an individual for profit (Bales, 2007). Traffickers exploit the weaknesses and vulnerabilities of individuals.

The purpose of this chapter is to bring awareness to the vulnerabilities that populations face in relation to the sex trade industry. As research continues to grow regarding sex trafficking treatment, a need to understand circumstances that cause an individual to become vulnerable is crucial. This chapter will give a concise overview of common risk factors noted in research, and art therapy with vulnerable populations from available research will be explored. Due to limited literature regarding art therapy and sex trafficking, interviews with art therapists who have worked with survivors or who work with individuals at a greater risk for trafficking have contributed to this chapter and bring awareness to this field.

Vulnerable is defined as "capable of being physically or emotionally wounded" (Merriam-Webster, 2019, para. 1). The terms vulnerable and vulnerability are used within laws to describe the condition of the person and the capability to respond to external factors, yet understanding the full scope of vulnerabilities is a case by case analysis (United Nations Office on Drugs and Crime, 2013). Some people are more susceptible to harm due to environmental factors, which makes them more easily preyed upon or taken advantage of on an individual level. During their lifetime, many individuals are capable of being physically, emotionally, or mentally wounded. Due to the notion that vulnerability can be easily identified in humans, human trafficking can be found anywhere as well (Sadler, 2019). The same vulnerabilities are found globally: poverty, gender discrimination, and marginalization. Becoming more aware of the vulnerabilities our clients face can better equip us to use the most appropriate therapeutic approaches during our encounters with them. This chapter will focus on the vulnerabilities of sex trafficking based from societal, environmental, and individual impacts.

Sex Trafficking Risk Factors

Any individual of any ethnicity, gender, and socioeconomic status can be sex trafficked; however, at-risk populations, including the underprivileged and defenseless minorities are targeted (Contreras & Farley, 2011; Shelley, 2010). Weakness is sought to exploit and manipulate. Traffickers pursue vulnerable individuals because they are easier to control and have decreased self-esteem, indicating their need for attention and protection (Leitch & Snow, 2010). Exploiters are also able to pressure, compel, and manipulate people who are destitute, vulnerable, and want something better (Office for Victims of Crime, n.d.a). Poverty, gender, age, and history of abuse are directly related to sex trafficking risk factors and are considerations for vulnerability (Busch-Armendariz, Nsonwu, & Heffron, 2018); these risk factors are described next.

Gender

Most individuals who are sexually exploited are women. The International Labour Office (2017) reported 40 million people were victims of modern-day slavery on any given day in the year of 2016, wherein women and girls made up 71%; 3.8 million adults and 1 million children were forced into sexual exploitation, of which 99% were women and girls. Trafficking is directly related to society's tolerance of brutality and inequality against females (Crawford, 2017), and gender-based oppression of females increases the risk of sex trafficking (Silverman et al., 2007). Women around the world are at higher risk for poverty than men and are challenged with limited rights to vote, own property, and obtain education (Task Force on Trafficking Women and Girls, 2014). Women who lack accessibility or are denied education and job opportunities are at risk for trafficking because they can be deceived through false promises of employment (Crawford, 2017). Without other choices available, oppressed women who are trying to pursue what they believe is a better opportunity for their future and their families become more vulnerable to exploitation.

Although males are not often thought to be vulnerable to sex trafficking, the risk of gender stereotyping occurs. Male sexual exploitation is undertreated, underreported, and underrecognized due to masculinity myths, cultural norms, and stigma; males are often not recognized as survivors due to the bias, embarrassment, or ignorant views of first responders who believe that sex trafficking is a female problem (United States Department of State, 2017). Particularly during post-trafficking, males are at risk due to misconceptions and misunderstandings. Deplorably, most sexual exploitation of boys is done by adult males who are married men with their own children (Estes & Weiner, 2001). Although females are more likely to be sex trafficked, males are vulnerable in a different regard because they are overlooked for being more apt to suffer silently, and boys are targeted in a disturbing way.

Gender-variant individuals are also at risk. Youth who self-identify as lesbian, gay, bisexual, transgender, queer or questioning plus (LGBTQ+) are more vulnerable to sexual exploitation compared to gender-conforming or heterosexual youth (Xian, Chock, & Dwiggins, 2017). Individuals who identify as transgendered are stigmatized, detached from their peers and families, and they are vulnerable to exploitation (Mitchell, Finkelhor, & Wolak, 2010). Limitations to basic resources and marginalization increase the risks for sex trafficking of the LGBTQ community (Busch-Armendariz et al., 2018). Age can exacerbate gender discrimination, making an individual even more vulnerable to sex trafficking.

Age

Sex trafficking of minors is an unfathomable reality that exploits the vulnerabilities of the developing youth. When individuals under the age of 18 are involved in the sex industry, they are recognized as sex trafficked (Macias-Konstantopoulos & Ma, 2017). Research demonstrates that traffickers usually recruit youth at the average ages of 12–14 (Estes & Weiner, 2001). During the adolescent development stage, young people are maturing and creating identities by exhibiting independence and discovering social connections; hence, traffickers pursue this population, providing a newer, more mature sense of self through manipulative relationships (Herman, 1997; Leitch & Snow, 2010). This phase in teenage brain development also marks an inability to judge safely, problem solve, and experience emotional control (Shared Hope International, 2014). The lack of life experiences and the inability of the developing prefrontal cortex to assess dangerous situations make youth vulnerable to exploitation and manipulative tactics (Greenbaum & Crawford-Jakubiak, 2015). Young individuals are targeted for their innocent minds, developmental milestones, and inability to assess potential risk.

Factors that increase the probability of minor sex trafficking include having friends who are involved in the sex trafficking industry, trouble in school, a record for juvenile detention, parental conflict, and multiracial ethnicity (Chohaney, 2016). Parental involvement in the sex trade normalizes this experience for minors as well as contributes to intergenerational prostitution (Oselin, 2014). Youth exposed to risk factors on a community, individual, and family basis are considered more vulnerable to sex trafficking (Macias-Konstantopoulos & Ma, 2017). The sex trafficking of vulnerable youth, the most defenseless and imperiled population for trafficking, is further explored in Chapters 6, 7, and 8. In addition to age, poverty contributes to the vulnerability of an individual to sex trafficking.

Poverty

Trafficking perpetuates the exploitation of individuals living in poverty (O'Connor & Healy, 2006). With limited prospects, destitute people enter into commercial sex because they feel they do not have any other choice (Gerassi & Nichols, 2018). In areas where all people are threatened by job loss, lack of opportunity, and debt and are desperate to be employed, a person can fall prey to trafficking through deception tactics while searching for a job abroad (Tverdova, 2011). Unemployment as an adult is connected to child labor, poverty, and lack of education; in underdeveloped countries, children start work early because they are used as both primary and secondary earnings for the family (Kelso, 2008). In addition, environmental calamities aggravate poverty and instability in communities, and this increases the extent of vulnerable individuals who can be exploited (Finn, 2016). Human trafficking may be most rampant in areas of the world where poverty is found (Macias-Konstantopoulos & Ma, 2017). Poverty is a significant risk factor in trafficking that can be heightened by the presence of past abuse.

History of Abuse

History of sexual abuse and maltreatment is a common indicator found in literature from those identified as sex trafficked or exploited (Institute of Medicine [IOM] & National Research Council [NRC], 2013). Research has demonstrated sexual abuse was found to be the strongest predictor for trafficking in adolescence; other predictors included neglect, lack of positive relationships with caregivers, exposure to violence for female minors, and sexual and emotional abuse projected trafficking with male youth (Reid, Baglivio, Piquero, Greenwald, & Epps, 2017). Research also suggests that the prior experiences for women and girls of sexual and/or physical abuse before they were trafficked may have contributed to their vulnerability to be recruited (Zimmerman & Borland, 2009). Furthermore, abuse by an authority figure can continue the cycle of victimization (Reid & Jones, 2011; Xian et al., 2017), especially noted with sexual abuse (Oselin, 2014). Age, gender, poverty, and history of abuse lead to increased vulnerability of an individual.

Exploration of Art Therapy as a Treatment for Vulnerable Populations Associated With Sex Trafficking

Human trafficking is attributed to political instability and civil unrest in addition to social and cultural factors, such as female inequality, poverty, and natural disasters (Bales, 2007). Trafficking targets the person who is at-risk individually, domestically, communally, and environmentally. Vulnerability stems from

- risk factors based on the individual, such as homelessness, decreased self-esteem, substance abuse, need to earn money for survival or to support family, truancy, victimized by violence or abuse or trafficking, and lack of citizenship;
- factors related to an individual's family, including low socioeconomic status, little support in the family and community, sexual and/ or domestic violence, family members in the sex trade industry, low level of education, and minority status;
- socioeconomic influences that involve living/working near slums or brothels, high poverty and population, low unemployment, access to international/state border through highways and ports; and
- environmental traits consisting of the presence of child labor, sex tourism, and legal prostitution, or close proximity to migrant camps, military bases, and areas of conflict, and corrupt law enforcement and government.

(International Labour Organization, 2014)

Marginalized and isolated individuals are exploited because they are disregarded, overlooked, and often ignored. Predominantly, at-risk populations include refugees, the homeless, runaways engaging in "survival sex" or gangs; children in foster care or from the juvenile detention system; individuals with substance abuse issues; and those from the LGBTQ+ community (Polaris, 2015; United States Department of State, 2017). Additional deliberations are provided for particular populations.

Substance Abuse

Research demonstrates that substance abuse puts individuals at risk (NRC, 2013). Substance use prior to trafficking can increase vulnerability (Hopper, 2017). The use of substances occurs prior, during, and after one is trafficked. Substance usage and addiction can also contribute to re-trafficking. Substances can be used by the trafficker

- as a way to recruit the individual into an exploited situation;
- exert control to keep an individual in the situation and reduce resistance; or
- as a coping strategy for the trauma experienced.

(Office for Victims of Crime, n.d.b)

Loss is a universal issue for those who use substances; examples of loss include relationships, health, and jobs (Schmanke, 2017). Substances are abused in attempts to forget painful memories and emotions, such as anger, jealousy, fear, anxiety, shame, and guilt (Schmanke, 2017). Childhood trauma, including sexual abuse, attachment issues, and gender-identity issues, are also common for those with addictions (Schmanke, 2017).

Art Therapy and Substance Abuse

For individuals with substance abuse issues, art therapy

- improved negative moods and anxiety (Laurer & van der Vennet, 2015);
- offered valuable insight, explored spirituality concerns, processed trauma and feelings, and aided in recovery through offering group support;
- provided information that can be used in the initial evaluation and subsequent treatment plan (Schmanke, 2017); and
- helped individuals gain awareness of recovery and represented a metaphor for growth, as well as offered information regarding substance use and mental state through the road drawing assessment (Hanes, 2017).

For individuals struggling with substance use issues, art therapy aids in relaxation, mood enhancement, awareness, new identity, and recovery. Substance abuse as a risk factor is worsened by homelessness.

Homeless

Along with addiction and poverty, homelessness is another high-risk condition that often leads to trafficking due to a lack of protection on the street and being more apt to be approached by an exploiter or trafficker (Estes & Weiner, 2001). Sex trafficking due to homelessness extends globally to Cameroon, Hungary, Russia, Tunisia, the United States, and Uruguay (United States Department of State, 2018). Homelessness is attributed to poverty, unemployment, decline in public assistance, lack of affordable housing, domestic violence, mental illness, and addiction (National Coalition for Homeless, 2009b).

Additional factors for youth who lack shelter include familial abuse, neglect, strained relationships, and a history of instable homes or residential placements (National Coalition for Homeless, 2008). Homeless youth are often referred to as runaways and *thrown-aways*, and these terms differ between the choice or being told to leave the home (IOM & NRC, 2013). Survival sex, the exchange of sex for necessary living requirements, is commonly found among homeless youth and young adults (Macias-Konstantopoulos & Ma, 2017). Survival sex also occurs in youth who live within a home without access to basic needs or who are burdened with the responsibility of taking care of family members; homelessness can increase the consideration to trade sex among youth to meet basic needs (Lutnick, 2016). Wolfe's (2017) study across the United States and Canada found one in five homeless youth (out of 1,000 interviews) survived trafficking and 15% reported sex trafficking.

Art Therapy With the Homeless

Art therapy provides a format to tell an individual's story and to connect with others. In art therapy work with the homeless, certain client situations or themes may reoccur. Themes for homeless women who were being trafficked often included a history of molestation with little protection by family members and a need or want to be loved; themes for homeless men who were traffickers often included a loss of a father figure and the want for power (B. Badillo, personal communication, February 28, 2019). Art therapy offered many benefits to homeless individuals that contribute to relationship building and well-being. Examples include the following:

- Art therapy provided a creative healthy lifestyle choice (Prescott, Sekendur, Bailey, & Hoshino, 2008).
- Quilting workshops offered over the years to homeless women were found to contribute to self-efficacy and provided a safe place for social support (Moxley, Feen-Calligan, Washington, & Garriott, 2011).
- Creating a safe environment with clients by becoming the predictable person available week after week instilled therapeutic trust in relationships, and art therapy was used to build rapport with homeless youth.
- Art therapy encouraged the opportunity for creativity, experiencing empowerment, and reclaiming identity (B. Badillo, personal communication, February 28, 2019).

Art therapy with the homeless focuses on building supportive relationships, renewing a sense of self, and offering a healthy option for living.

Refugees

Similar to the homeless, marginalized individuals, such as refugees, are a specific risk for exploitation. Refugee encampment is probably the most successful site for deceiving victims (Farr, 2004; Kara, 2009). Vulnerable, powerless refugees have literally no options (Kara, 2009). Camps are dirty, overcrowded, and disheartening because refugees cannot leave to find work, and due to feeling imprisoned and alienated, desperate emigrants are at particular risk for trafficking (Kara, 2009).

In addition to war, government conflict and instability, environmental calamities, such as hurricanes and tsunamis, heighten the risk for evacuees through homelessness and displacement housing in the refugee camps, making them easy to victimize and abduct for sexual exploitation (Farr, 2004). Natural disasters can leave thousands of individuals homeless and with no resources (National Coalition for Homeless, 2009a), devastating families and leaving orphans in their wreckage (Ebbe, 2008). After a natural disaster, refugees are at high risk for trafficking (United States Department of State, 2018). Examples of natural disasters that contributed to human trafficking include Typhoon Haiyan (Finn, 2016), earthquakes in Nepal (ABC News, 2016), and droughts, floods, and tsunamis in India (Joffres et al., 2008). Isolated, deprived, and displaced individuals who lack opportunities are at particular risk for sex trafficking.

Art Therapy With Refugees

Many refugees have experienced war, political tyranny, and destitution, and art therapy can address the trauma, loss, and distress that accompany their journey to find a new home and adapt to a difference culture (Fitzpatrick, 2002). With refugees, art therapy demonstrated

- the ability to address mental health concerns of anxiety, depression, PTSD, and trauma for youth (Kowitt et al., 2016);
- effective and creative communication regarding memories, grief, and trauma (Fitzpatrick, 2002);
- a way to process mourning, enhance coping and resilience, make meaning, and experience safety (Kalmanowitz & Ho, 2016); and
- a safe environment for children to tell their stories and explore their identities (Akthar & Lovell, 2018).

Art therapists need to be creative to bring cohesiveness and consistency when working with refugees due to recognized attendance issues and language differences (M. Violante, personal communication, January 8, 2019). Communication barriers can be challenging in art therapy with refugees, and therapists may need training on how to work with an interpreter (Yakusho, 2009). All written materials need to be given to survivors in their language (Gerassi & Nichols, 2018). Using an app on a mobile device/tablet can assist with communication in refugee populations (M. Violante, personal communication, January 8, 2019). Although using technology for translations, such as Google Translate (n.d.), can be helpful, it is also challenging because using the website takes time for both parties to learn, and it can be tedious.

Due to weekly changes in attendance, there is a need to provide art interventions or directives that could successfully be completed in one session (M. Violante, personal communication, January 8, 2019). For a group session with female refugees and teenage girls who were identified as vulnerable to human trafficking and commercial exploitation, the following suggestions are recommended:

- check-ins at the start of the session
- breathing exercises
- therapeutic games, such as ice breakers
- success-oriented interventions
- giving options as a positive strategy to gain consistency and safety among the groups
- focusing on positive themes, such as hope.

(M. Violante, personal communication, January 8, 2019)

During the start of a group, a check-in is a way for the therapist to get a sense for what has happened to clients since the last attendance of group. Breathing exercises can be used to experience relaxation and encourage regulation and mindfulness. Success-oriented interventions allow the client to share in a way that is empowering and to experience a sense of mastery. As an example for youth, a success-oriented intervention such as personal collage using strength-based words to portray internal and external strengths, can be used to build empowerment.

Foster Care and Juvenile Detention Systems

Children in the foster care system who leave their placement are at high risk for commercial sexual exploitation and trafficking situations (United States Department of Health and Human Services, Administration for Children, Youth, and Families, 2013). The National Center for Missing and Exploited Children (2017) reported one in seven runaways who were considered to be sex trafficked, and 88% were in the care of either social services or foster care. Many youth who are system involved are both runaways and survivors of childhood abuse and trauma (Gerassi & Nichols, 2018). Many individuals who are in foster care have survived abuse and are from disadvantaged and displaced families, thus increasing their risk for sexual exploitation (NRC, 2013). Often those in foster care have experienced loss, including death or incarceration of a parent, and these individuals struggle with anxiety, depression, and anger, as well as trusting others (Austin, 2007). Moreover, youth who identify as black, Hispanic, Latino, or are of multiple races are disproportionately placed within the foster care system in the United States (Hannan, Martin, Caceres, & Aledort, 2017). Ultimately, many survivors pass through the system's care to end up in the juvenile justice system for juvenile prostitution (National Resource Center on Domestic Violence, 2019) or for other crimes (Gerassi & Nichols, 2018).

Art Therapy With the System Involved

Sometimes, therapy is mandated by the justice system, and this may make the clients feel like they do not have a choice (M. Violante, personal communication, January 8, 2019). As art therapists working on facilitating empowerment, this struggle needs to be acknowledged in therapy. Working with teenagers is often a challenge, especially with teens who are mandated to attend therapy (M. Violante, personal communication, January 8, 2019). Despite this difficulty, there are the following advantages:

- Art therapy with at-risk teenagers addressed relational challenges, feelings, expression, impulsivity, and anger management (Ierarda, Bottos, & O-Brien, 2007).
- Court-mandated clients who attended art therapy connected to their art, accepted themselves, and bonded with the other group members (McKaig, 2003).
- After participating in art therapy, juvenile offenders who had extensive histories of trauma experienced feelings of mastery, self-acceptance, and social connection (Hartz & Thick, 2005).
- Using a trauma-informed approach in art therapy with children in foster care addressed issues of grief, trauma, attachment; creating transitional objects, such as homes and nests, may portray an individual's strength and sense of security, and scrapbooking allowed youth to tell their stories in an empowering way (Malloy, 2017).

Although individuals who are system involved may be mandated to attend art therapy, there are gains, such as improving self-efficacy and self-acceptance in addition to reducing isolation.

Gangs

Trafficking through gangs is a dangerous way for estranged individuals to experience belonging. Gang trafficking offers a sense of family to an isolated person by offering friendship and relationships in the gang community (Leitch & Snow, 2010). Gang members are expected to provide loyalty to the gang by taking care of all members, an assurance which provides faithfulness and devotion to the unit and may appeal to abandoned runaways and homeless persons (Leitch & Snow, 2010). Communities with criminal activity and gang involvement may have acceptable perceptions of commercial sexual exploitation and sex trafficking (IOM & NRC, 2013), and this can pose additional risk.

Art Therapy With Gang Members

Art therapy offers a way to transform individuals who are known for their violence, aggression, and ruthlessness. Examples include the following:

- As a positive form of expression of aggression and vulnerability through a safe and strengths-based approach, art therapy facilitated catharsis from violent urges and a new identity of acceptance (Gussak, 2013).
- An essential service for female gang members or girls at risk for joining a gang, art therapy provided self-expression, emotional outlet, and trauma processing (National Council on Crime and Delinquency, 2012).
- As a form of violence prevention, art therapy offered a sense of community and self-expression (Adler University, 2013).

Art therapy can both aid in prevention and rehabilitation for those involved with gang violence.

LGBTQ+

Individuals from the LGBTQ community are three times more likely to receive a mental health diagnosis and experience substance abuse; they are also at a higher risk for suicide (National Alliance on Mental Illness, 2019). LGBTQ youth are considered to be at high risk for commercial sexual exploitation and sex trafficking based on research evidence (IOM & NRC, 2013). This global issue extends to countries such as Haiti and Equatorial Guinea (United States Department of State, 2018). Sexually exploited young males often experience rejection from loved ones due to their appearance, identity, or sexual preference; they are at particular risk for sex trafficking (Reid, 2012). Individuals who identify as gay who feel isolated from their peers and families are also vulnerable to exploitation (Mitchell et al., 2010). Prostitution can be a form of survival for LGBTQ youth who are homeless or runaways (Raleigh-Duroff, 2004). LGBTQ+ individuals who feel unaccepted and disconnected from their families and communities are at heightened risk for manipulation through sexual exploitation.

Art Therapy With the LGBTQ+ Community

The art therapy community is urged to make sure that clients from the LGBTQ community are not discriminated against (Talwar, 2017). With this population, art therapy focuses on self-reflections:

- Art therapy provided hopeful format for transgendered individuals to represent themselves accurately and with acceptance for their uniqueness while connecting to others (Piccirillo, 1996).

- Using photography as a self-portrait, people who are transgendered were able to portray how they see themselves (Barbee, 2002).
- As a catalyst for discussion and reflection regarding personal identity, art therapy interventions (creating portrait, puppet, mask, or identity collage) for coming out issues assisted individuals in becoming their true selves (Pelton-Sweet & Sherry, 2008).

For the LGBTQ+ community, art therapy explores identity through visual, personal reflections in both an individual and communal format.

Recommendations for Art Therapy With Survivors of Sex Trafficking

Trauma may result from any critical and disturbing event, such as physical, emotional, psychological, and sexual abuse, including sexual exploitation. Art therapy provided to individuals who have experienced trauma facilitates alternative communication, empowerment, and support; art therapy improves symptoms, thus aiding in recovery. The benefits of using art therapy with individuals who have exposure to trauma include the following:

- Children with a history of physical and sexual abuse are less likely to trust someone new, and utilizing art therapy as a form of communication of feelings gives them the opportunity to express unconscious thoughts in a safe approach (Carter, Allan, & Walter, 1992).
- A small pilot study of adults with posttraumatic stress disorder (PTSD) and a history of childhood sexual abuse found that adding art therapy interventions into group treatment decreased symptoms of depression and PTSD (Becker, 2015).
- Art therapy was healing and empowering for adolescent female survivors of rape and incest who also exhibited complex trauma and PTSD (Backos & Pagon, 1999).
- When used in support groups for caregivers of children who have been sexually abused, art therapy provided a way to dialogue and establish support (Pifalo, 2009).
- Klorer (2005) stated the importance of using expressive therapy with severely maltreated children who often exhibit attachment difficulties was helpful because the integration of the arts works with the brain's right hemisphere where early relational trauma is expressed.
- Using art therapy intervention to work with the right brain helped individuals with trauma express emotions before being able to communicate feelings into words (Arrington & Cherry, 2007; Chapman, 2014; Klorer, 2005).

For survivors of sex trafficking, art therapy has many therapeutic advantages, including increased focus, renewed connection to others, reconnection with the self, empowerment, positive self-worth, and new purpose (Clawson, Salomon, & Grace, 2008; Garlock, 2016; Kometiani & Farmer, 2019; Sanar Wellness Institute & Polaris, 2015; Tan, 2012). As there is still much information to uncover regarding art therapy and individuals with a connection to the sex trade industry, the following summaries are recommendations provided from interviews with art therapists who have worked in diverse settings with individuals who have survived sex trafficking.

For survivors of sexual abuse and trauma, safety is of the highest importance. Ways to create safety in the art therapy setting include

- switching to a larger room if the original room size is too crowded;
- sitting near the side of the client as opposed to sitting across from a client, which may appear confrontational;
- creating art alongside the client to increase client comfort and trust in art therapy; and
- not ending the therapy session in a regressed state, instead, provide grounding techniques to achieve mindfulness and attention to the present moment.

(S. Parcell, personal communication, September 24, 2018)

Best practice suggestions for art therapists who work with the trafficked population:

- Your heart needs to be in this work because this is challenging work.
- Become knowledgeable about this population—understand sex trafficking terms, trauma and trauma-informed recommendations, and diagnoses.
- Learn from other professionals about what works in therapy and what approaches are successful.
- Teaching concepts of healthy relationships is needed, especially among youth trafficked or at risk.
- Follow the client's affect to guide the direction of the session and use the client's language and (see Glossary) throughout sessions.
- The importance of safety for the therapist is not to be overlooked—while working with vulnerable youth and young adults in their homes, at parks, and wherever the agency requested. The risks involved may be dangerous due to environments and lack of safety training.

(B. Badillo, personal communication, February 28, 2019)

- Awareness of art materials is crucial because they can
  - cultivate interest (B. Badillo, personal communication, February 28, 2019).
  - prompt regression (S. Parcell, personal communication, September 24, 2018).

    - cause harm to self or others. In residential facilities with survivors who are at risk of suicide and violence, only safe art materials should be used—nontoxic supplies, no glass objects, no sharps, and no long pieces of string.
    - invoke negative reaction—white glue or sticky clay may remind survivors of ejaculation (Hagood, 2000).
    - be triggering. Art therapists are cautioned when using collage to provide precut images/words to avoid inappropriate content (for example, sexual innuendo or alcohol advertising).
- Learn to make the most of each minute of each session through the brief therapy model and provide art directives that can be completed within one or two hours that focus on sparking joy and improving quality of life.
- There can be an additional benefit from personal choice in a creative outlet outside of therapeutic services—applying creativity to engage in flow provides benefits toward well-being (Conner, DeYoung, & Silvia, 2016).
- Lastly, art therapists are encouraged to use trauma-informed, strength-based, and survivor-centered approaches that are culturally appropriate and empowerment oriented (Gerassi & Nichols, 2018).

Conclusion

The crime of human trafficking affects all cultures, ages, and genders (Busch-Armendariz et al., 2018). The invisible, abandoned, disconnected, and suppressed are victimized through the horrendous crime of sex trafficking. When people are considered unequal or treated as lowered status, they are at risk for trafficking. Cultural and societal influences for sex trafficking include destitution, lack of opportunity, governmental corruption, and outdated beliefs; these are further explained in Chapters 7 and 8. Populations that are especially vulnerable to sex trafficking include primarily young, underprivileged women who are searching for a better life; homeless youth and runaways engaging in gang membership; refugees; individuals from foster care and juvenile detention systems; the LGBTQ+ community; and those who have histories of substance abuse or any form of abuse. There are inherent risk factors that predispose individuals to trafficking. However, just as many populations are vulnerable to trafficking, traffickers are not as easily identified. Both biological and foster parents, relatives, neighbors, coaches, gang members, peers, and teachers have been identified as sex traffickers for youth (Leitch & Snow, 2010); both men and women who are business owners, pimps, strangers, and acquaintances have been documented to be traffickers (Office for Victims of Crime, n.d.a).

Art therapists must be aware of marginalization that occurs in communities and promote ways to bring attention to art therapy practices that support individuals with a variety of interventions and frameworks of social justice (Karcher, 2017; Gipson, 2015; Kapitan, 2015; Talwar, 2010). Mental health professionals, including art therapists, need to become more aware of the factors that many youth are challenged to face. Art therapists must also look beyond the individual factors and take into account the impact of violence in both modern society and how art can respond to trauma with cultural humility (Kalmanowitz & Lloyd, 2005). This chapter explores how experiences of abuse and substance usage, as well as age and gender, may increase the chances of an individual being victimized through sex trafficking. Communities with a lower tolerance of sexual violence and a higher level of collective approaches were more likely to help a victim, yet this can only occur if there is an awareness of the problem in the area (IOM & NRC, 2013). Awareness of the risk factors of sex trafficking and commercial sexual exploitation may provide the insight needed to assist clients in connecting them to the right resources and to train clinicians in the use of trauma-informed approaches.

References

The ABC News. (2016, February 14) Nepal earthquake: More than 160 trafficked Nepalis rescued by India in aftermath of quake. *The ABC News*. Retrieved from www.abc.net.au/news/2016-02-15/nepal-earthquakes-cause-spike-in-human-trafficking/7168398

Adler University. (2013, February 18). Art therapy's power to prevent youth violence, improves communities. Retrieved from www.adler.edu/blog/art-therapys-power-to-prevent-youth-violence-improve-communities

Akthar, Z., & Lovell, A. (2018). Art therapy with refugee children: A qualitative study explored through the lens of art therapists and their experiences. *International Journal of Art Therapy*, *24*(3), 139–148. https://doi.org/10.1080/17454832.2018.1533571

Arrington, D., & Cherry, A. R. (2007). Healing trauma using the instinctual trauma response model. In D. Arrington (Ed.), *Art, angst, and trauma: Right brain interventions with developmental issues* (pp. 175–189). Springfield, IL: Charles C. Thomas.

Austin, D. (2007). Lifesongs: Music therapy with adolescents in foster care. In V. A. Camilleri (Ed.), *Healing the inner child* (pp. 92–103). London, UK: Jessica Kingsley Publishers.

Backos, A. K., & Pagon, B. E. (1999). Finding a voice: Art therapy with female adolescent sexual abuse survivors. *Art Therapy: Journal of the American Art Therapy Association*, *16*(3), 126–132.

Bales, K. (2007). What predicts human trafficking? *International Journal of Comparative and Applied Criminal Justice*, *31*(2), 269–279. https://doi.org/10.1080/01924036.2007.9678771

Barbee, M. (2002). A visual-narrative approach to understanding transsexual identity. *Art Therapy: Journal of the American Art Therapy Association*, *19*(2), 53–62. https://doi.org/10.1080/07421656.2002.10129339

Becker, C. L. (2015). Integrating art into group dissociative for adults with post-traumatic stress disorder from childhood sexual abuse: A pilot study. *Art Therapy: Journal of the American Art Therapy Association*, *32*(4), 190–196. https://doi.org/10.1080/07421656.2015.1091643

Busch-Armendariz, N. B., Nsonwu, M., & Heffron, L. C. (2018). *Human trafficking: Applying research, theory, and case studies*. Thousand Oaks, CA: Sage Publications.

Carter, M. A., Allan, J. A. B., & Walter, B. B. (1992). Projective assessment of child sexual abuse: Use of Rosebush Picture Q-sort. *British Journal of Projective Psychology*, *37*(1), 50–59.

Chapman, L. (2014). *Neurobiologically informed trauma therapy with children and adolescents: Understanding mechanisms of change*. New York, NY: W.W. Norton and Company.

Chohaney, M. L. (2016). Minor and adult domestic sex trafficking risk factors in Ohio. *Journal of the Society for Social Work and Research*, *7*(1), 117–141. https://doi.org/10.1086/685108

Clawson, H. J., Salomon, A., & Grace, L. G. (2008, March 15). *Treating the hidden wounds: Trauma treatment and mental health recovery for victims of human trafficking*. Retrieved from https://aspe.hhs.gov/report/treating-hidden-wounds-trauma-treatment-and-mental-health-recovery-victims-human-trafficking

Conner, T. S., DeYoung, G., & Silvia, P. J. (2016). Everyday creative activity as a path to flourishing. *The Journal of Positive Psychology*, *13*(2), 181–189.

Contreras, M., & Farley, M. (2011). Human trafficking: Not an isolated issue. In T. Bryant-Davis (Ed.), *Surviving sexual violence: A guide to recovery and empowerment* (pp. 22–36). Lanham, MD: Rowman & Littlefield Publishers, Inc.

Crawford, M. (2017). International sex trafficking. *Women & Therapy*, *40*(1–2), 101–122. https://doi.org/10.1080/02703149.2016.1206784

Ebbe, O. N. I. (2008a). Causes of trafficking in women and children. In O. N. I. Ebbe & D. K. Das (Eds.), *Global trafficking in women* (pp. 33–38). Boca Raton, FL: CRC Press.

Estes, R. J., & Weiner, N. A. (2001). *The commercial sexual exploitation of children in the US, Canada and Mexico*. Philadelphia, PA: University of Pennsylvania.

Farr, K. (2004). *Sex trafficking: The global market in women and children*. New York, NY: Worth Publishers.

Finn, J. (2016). Human trafficking and natural disasters exploiting misery. *International Affairs Review*. Retrieved from www.iar-gwu.org/content/human-trafficking-and-natural-disasters-exploiting-misery

Fitzpatrick, F. (2002). A search for home: The role of art therapy in understanding the experiences of Bosnian refugees in western Australia. *Art Therapy: Journal of the American Art Therapy Association*, *19*(4), 151–158. https://doi.org/10.1080/07421656.2002.10129680

Garlock, L. R. (2016). Stories in the cloth: Art therapy and narrative textiles. *Art Therapy: Journal of the American Art Therapy Association*, *33*(2), 58–66. https://doi.org/10.1080/07421656.2016.1164004

Gerassi, L. B., & Nichols, A. J. (2018). *Sex trafficking and commercial sexual exploitation: Prevention, advocacy, and trauma-informed practice*. New York, NY: Springer Publishing Company.

Gipson, L. R. (2015). Is cultural competence enough? Deepening social justice pedagogy in art therapy. *Art Therapy: Journal of the American Art Therapy Association*, *32*(3), 142–145.

Google Translate. (n.d.). Retrieved from https://translate.google.com

Greenbaum, J., & Crawford-Jakubiak, J. E. (2015). Child sex trafficking and sexually exploited children: Health care needs of victims. *Committee on Child Abuse and Neglect. Pediatrics*, *135*(3), 566–574.

Gussak, D. (2013). *Drawing out the violence: 5 reasons why art therapy is effective with violent and aggressive people*. Retrieved from www.psychologytoday.com/us/blog/art-trial/201310/drawing-out-the-violence

Hagood, M. M. (2000). *The use of art in counseling child and adult survivors of sexual abuse*. London, UK: Jessica Kingsley Publishers.

Hanes, M. (2017). Road to recovery: Road drawings in a gender-specific residential substance use treatment center. *Art Therapy: Journal of the American Art Therapy Association*, *34*(4), 201–208. https://doi.org/10.1080/07421656.2017.1394124

Hannan, M., Martin, K., Caceres, K., & Aledort, N. (2017). Children at risk: Foster care and human trafficking. In M. Chisolm-Straker & H. Stoklosa (Eds.), *Human trafficking is a public health issue: A paradigm expansion in the United States* (pp. 105–122). Cham, Switzerland: Springer.

Hartz, L., & Thick, L. (2005). Art therapy strategies to raise self-esteem in female juvenile offenders: A comparison of art psychotherapy and art as therapy approaches. *Art Therapy: Journal of the American Art Therapy Association*, *22*(2), 70–80.

Herman, J. L. (1997). *Trauma and recovery: The aftermath of violence—From domestic abuse to political terror* (2nd ed.). New York, NY: Basic Books.

Hopper, E. K. (2017). The multimodal social ecological (MSE) approach: A trauma- informed framework for supporting trafficking survivors' psychosocial health. In M. Chisolm-Straker & H. Stoklosa (Eds.), *Human trafficking is a public health issue: A paradigm expansion in the United States* (pp. 153–184). Cham, Switzerland: Springer.

Ierarda, F., Bottos, M., & O-Brien, M. K. (2007). Safe expression: A community-based creative arts program for at-risk youth. In V. A. Camilleri (Ed.), *Healing the inner child* (pp. 254–267). London, UK: Jessica Kingsley Publishers.

Institute of Medicine [IOM], & National Research Council [NRC]. (2013). *Confronting commercial sexual exploitation and sex trafficking of minors in the United States*. Washington, DC: National Academies Press.

International Labour Office. (2017). *Global estimates of modern slavery: Forced labour and forced marriage executive summary*. Retrieved from www.ilo.org/wcmsp5/groups/public/@dgreports/@dcomm/documents/publication/wcms_575540.pdf

International Labour Organization. (2014). *Commercial sexual exploitation of children and adolescents- The ILO's response*. Geneva, Switzerland: International Programme on the Elimination of Child Labour. Retrieved from www.ilo.org/wcmsp5/groups/public/-africa/-ro-addis_ababa/documents/poster/wcms_237022.pdf

Joffres, C., Mills, E., Joffres, M., Khanna, T., Walia, H., & Grund, D. (2008). Sexual slavery without borders: Trafficking for commercial sexual exploitation in India. *International Journal for Equity in Health*, *7*(22). https://doi.org/10.1186/1475-9276-7-22

Kalmanowitz, D., & Ho, R. T. H. (2016). Out of our mind: Art therapy and mindfulness with refugees, political violence and trauma. *The Arts in Psychotherapy*, *49*, 57–65. https://doi.org/10.1016/j.aip.2016.05.12

Kalmanowitz, D., & Lloyd, B. (2005). Introduction. In D. Kalmanowitz & B. Lloyd (Eds.), *Art therapy and political violence: With art, without illusion* (pp. 4–12). New York, NY: Routledge.

Kapitan, L. (2015). Social action in practice: Shifting the ethnocentric lens in cross-cultural art therapy encounters. *Art Therapy: Journal of the American Art Therapy Association*, *32*(3), 104–111.

Kara, S. (2009). *Sex trafficking: Inside the business of modern slavery*. New York, NY: Columbia University Press.

Karcher, O. P. (2017). Sociopolitical oppression, trauma, and healing: Moving toward a social justice art therapy framework. *Art Therapy: Journal of the American Art Therapy Association*, *32*(3), 123–128.

Kelso, C. M. (2008). Child labor and the trafficking industry in India. In O. N. I. Ebbe & D. K. Das (Eds.), *Global trafficking in women* (pp. 67–78). Boca Raton, FL: CRC Press.

Klorer, P. G. (2005). Expressive therapy with severely maltreated children: Neuroscience contributions. *Art Therapy: Journal of the American Art Therapy Association*, *22*(4), 213–220.

Kometiani, M. K., & Farmer, K. W. (2019). Exploring resilience through case studies of art therapy with sex trafficked survivors and their advocates. *The Arts in Psychotherapy*. Advance online publication. https://doi.org/10.1016/j.aip.2019.101582

Kowitt, S. D., Emmerling, D., Gavarkavich, D., Mershon, C., Linton, K., Rubesin, H., . . . Eng, E. (2016). A pilot evaluation of an art therapy program for refugee youth from Burma. *Art Therapy: Journal of the American Art Therapy Association*, *33*(1), 13–20. https://doi.org/10.1080/07421656.2015.1127739

Laurer, M., & van der Vennet, R. (2015). Effect of art production on negative mood and anxiety for adults in treatment for substance abuse. *Art Therapy: Journal of the American Art Therapy Association*, *32*(4), 177–183. https://doi.org/10.1080/07421656.2015.1092731

Leitch, L., & Snow, M. (2010). *Intervene: Practitioner guide and intake tool*. Vancouver, WA: Shared Hope International.

Lutnick, A. (2016). *Domestic minor sex trafficking: Beyond victims and villains*. New York, NY: Columbia University Press.

Macias-Konstantopoulos, W., & Ma, Z. B. (2017). Physical health of human trafficking survivors: Unmet essentials. In M. Chisolm-Straker & H. Stoklosa (Eds.), *Human trafficking is a public health issue: A paradigm expansion in the United States* (pp. 185–210). Cham, Switzerland: Springer.

Malloy, J. N. (2017). Post-ASFA permanency planning for children in foster care: Clinical and ethical considerations for art therapists. *Art Therapy: Journal of the American Art Therapy Association*, *34*(3), 135–141. https://doi.org/10.1080/07421656.2017.1353334

McKaig, A. M. (2003). Relational contexts and aesthetics: Achieving positive connections with mandated clients. *Art Therapy: Journal of the American Art Therapy Association*, *20*(4), 201–207. https://doi.org/10.1080/07421656.2003.10129604

Merriam-Webster. (2019). *Vulnerable*. Retrieved from www.merriam-webster.com/dictionary/vulnerable

Mitchell, K. J., Finkelhor, D., & Wolak, J. (2010). Conceptualizing juvenile prostitution as child maltreatment: Findings from the national juvenile prostitution study. *Child Maltreatment*, *15*(1), 18–36. https://doi.org/10.1177/1077559509349443

Moxley, D. P., Feen-Calligan, H. R., Washington, O. G. M., & Garriott, L. (2011). Quilting in self-efficacy group work with older African American women leaving homelessness. *Art Therapy: Journal of the American Art Therapy Association*, *28*(3), 113–122.

National Alliance on Mental Illness. (2019). *LGBTQ*. Retrieved from www.nami.org/Find-Support/LGBTQ

National Center for Missing and Exploited Children. (2017). *Children missing from care: Overview*. Retrieved from www.missingkids.com/theissues/cmfc

National Coalition for the Homeless. (2008, June). *Homeless youth*. Retrieved from www.nationalhomeless.org/factsheets/youth.html

National Coalition for the Homeless. (2009a, September). *Natural disasters and homelessness*. Retrieved from https://nationalhomeless.org/wp-content/uploads/2017/09/Natural-Disasters-and-Homelessness-Fact-Sheet-2009.pdf

National Coalition for the Homeless. (2009b, July). *Substance abuse and homelessness*. Retrieved from www.nationalhomeless.org/factsheets/why.html

National Council on Crime and Delinquency. (2012, March). *It's about time: Prevention and intervention services for gang-affiliated girls*. Retrieved from www.nccdglobal.org/sites/default/files/publication_pdf/focus-its-about-time.pdf

National Research Council [NRC]. (2013). Risk factors for and consequences of commercial sexual exploitation and sex trafficking of minors. *Confronting Commercial Sexual Exploitation and Sex Trafficking of Minors in the United States*. Washington, DC: The National Academies Press. https://doi.org/10.17226.18358

National Resource Center on Domestic Violence. (2019). *Domestic child sex trafficking and juvenile justice system*. Retrieved from https://vawnet.org/material/domestic-child-sex-trafficking-and-juvenile-justice-system

O'Connor, M., & Healy, G. (2006). *The links between prostitution and sex trafficking: A briefing handbook*. Retrieved from https://ec.europa.eu/anti-rafficking/sites/antitrafficking/files/the_links_between_prostitution_and_sex_trafficking_a_briefing_handbook_en_1.pdf

Office for Victims of Crime. (n.d.a). *About human trafficking*. Retrieved from https://ovc.ncjrs.gov/humantrafficking/about.html

Office for Victims of Crime. (n.d.b). *Substance abuse needs*. Retrieved from www.ovcttac.gov/taskforceguide/eguide/4-supporting-victims/44-comprehensive-victim-services/mental-health-needs/substance-abuse-needs/

Oselin, S. (2014). *Leaving prostitution: Getting out and staying out of sex work*. New York, NY: New York University Press.

Pelton-Sweet, L., & Sherry, A. (2008). Coming out through art: A review of art therapy with LGBT clients. *Art Therapy: Journal of the American Art Therapy Association*, *25*(4), 170–176.

Piccirillo, E. (1996). In search of an accurate likeness: Art therapy with transgender persons living with AIDS. *Art Therapy: Journal of the American Art Therapy Association*, *13*(1), 37–46.

Pifalo, T. (2009). Mapping the maze: An art therapy intervention following disclosure of sexual abuse. *Art Therapy: Journal of the American Art Therapy Association*, *26*(1), 12–18. https://doi.org/10.1080/07421656.2009.10129313

Polaris. (2015, May). *Sex trafficking in the US: A closer look at the US citizen victims*. Retrieved from http://polarisproject.org/resources/sex-trafficking-us-closer-look-us-citizen-victims

Prescott, M. V., Sekendur, B., Bailey, B., & Hoshino, J. (2008). Art making as a component and facilitator of resiliency with homeless youth. *Art Therapy: Journal of the American Art Therapy Association*, *25*(4), 156–163.

Raleigh-Duroff, C. (2004). Factors that influence homeless adolescents to leave or stay living in the street. *Child and Adolescent Social Work Journal*, *2*(6), 561–572. https://doi.org/10.1007/s10560-004-6404-6

Reid, J. A. (2012). Exploratory review of route-specific, gendered, and age-graded dynamics of exploitation: Applying life course theory to victimization in sex trafficking in North America. *Aggression and Violent Behavior*, *17*(3), 257–271. https://doi.org/10.1016/j.avb.2012.02.005

Reid, J. A., Baglivio, M. T., Piquero, A. R., Greenwald, M. A., & Epps, N. (2017). Human trafficking of minors and childhood adversity in Florida. *American Journal of Public Health*, *107*(2). https://doi.org/10.2105/AJPH.2016.303564

Reid, J. A., & Jones, S. (2011). Exploited vulnerability: Legal and psychological perspectives on child sex trafficking victims. *Victims and Offenders*, *6*, 207–231.

Sadler, R. (2019). *Vulnerable: Rethinking human trafficking*. Nashville, TN: B&H Publishing Group.

Sanar Wellness Institute, & Polaris. (2015, November). *Promising practices: An overview of trauma-informed therapeutic support for survivors of human trafficking*. Retrieved from https://polarisproject.org/sites/default/files/Sanar-Promising-Practices.pdf

Savona, E. U., & Stefanizzi, S. (2007). Introduction. In E. U. Savona & S. Stefanizzi (Eds.), *Measuring human trafficking* (pp. 1–3). New York, NY: Springer.

Schmanke, L. (2017). *Art therapy and substance abuse: Enabling recovery from alcohol and other drug addictions*. London, UK: Jessica Kingsley Publishers.

Shared Hope International. (2014). *Domestic minor sex trafficking: Identifying and responding to America's youth*. Vancouver, WA: Shared Hope International.

Shelley, L. (2010). *Human trafficking: A global perspective*. Cambridge, NY: Cambridge University Press.

Silverman, J. G., Decker, M. R., Gupta, J., Maheshwari, A., Patel, V., Willis, B. M., & Raj, A. (2007). Experiences of sex trafficking victims in Mumbai, India. *International Journal of Gynecology & Obstetrics*, *97*(3), 221–226. https://doi.org/10.1016/j.ijgo.2006.12.003

Talwar, S. (2010). An intersectional framework for race, class, gender, and sexuality in art therapy. *Art Therapy: Journal of the American Art Therapy Association*, *27*(1), 11–17.

Talwar, S. (2017). Ethics, law, and cultural competence in art therapy. *Art Therapy: Journal of the American Art Therapy Association*, *34*(3), 102–105.

Tan, L. A. (2012). Art therapy with trafficked women. *Therapy Today*, *23*(5), 26–31.

Task Force on Trafficking of Women and Girls. (2014). *Report of the task force on trafficking of women and girls*. Washington, DC: American Psychological Association. Retrieved from www.apa.org/pi/women/programs/traffciking/reports.aspx

Tverdova, Y. V. (2011). Human trafficking in Russia and other post-Soviet states. *Human Rights Review*, *12*(3), 329–344.

United Nations Office on Drugs and Crime. (2013, April). *Abuse of a position of vulnerability and other "means" within the definition of trafficking in persons.* New York, NY: United Nations. Retrieved from www.unodc.org/documents/humantrafficking/2012/UNODC_2012_Issue_Paper_-_Abuse_of_a_Position_of_Vulnerability.pdf

United States Department of Health and Human Services, Administration for Children, Youth and Families. (2013). *Guidance to States and services on addressing human trafficking of children and youth in the United States.* Retrieved from www.acf.hhs.gov/sites/default/files/cb/acyf_human_trafficking_guidance.pdf

United States Department of State. (2017, June). *Trafficking in persons report.* Retrieved from www.state.gov/documents/organization/271339.pdf

United States Department of State. (2018). *Office to monitor and combat trafficking in persons.* 2018 Trafficking in Persons Report. Retrieved from www.state.gov/j/tip/rls/tiprpt/countries/2017/271205.htm

Wolfe, D. S. (2017, September 17). 95 percent of homeless youth who experienced sex trafficking say they were maltreated as children. *The Chronicle of Social Change.* Retrieved from https://chronicleofsocialchange.org/research-related/majority-of-homeless-youth-who-experienced-sex-trafficking-say-they-were-maltreated-as-children

Xian, K., Chock, S., & Dwiggins, D. (2017). LGBTQ youth and vulnerability to sex trafficking. In M. Chisolm-Straker & H. Stoklosa (Eds.), *Human trafficking is a public health issue: A paradigm expansion in the United States* (pp. 141–152). Cham, Switzerland: Springer.

Yakusho, O. (2009). Human trafficking: A review for mental health professionals. *Educational Psychology Papers and Publications, 31,* 158–167. https://doi.org/10.1007/s10447-009-9075-3

Zimmerman, C., & Borland, R. (Eds.). (2009). *Caring for trafficked persons: Guidance for health providers.* Geneva, Switzerland: International Organization of Migration.

FOUR

Recommendations for Working With Individuals Affected by Sex Trafficking

Cynthia Wilson and Serena R. Coleman

Introduction

This chapter will focus on recommendations based on trauma-informed practices, research, and expertise to provide support to therapists working with individuals who have survived or are surviving sex trafficking. The use of art therapy is addressed from the perspective of our professional experience and literature. We understand that many therapists are trained in other modalities globally, which may serve the needs of this population and can provide benefits to individuals and groups. It is difficult for us to give definitive recommendations for all persons trafficked due to their unique needs and situations, as the challenges they face can be complex and case by case. Please note that there is extremely scarce literature to be found between the work of art therapists and the trafficked population. It is an honor and privilege for us to coauthor this chapter and bring our knowledge to the field of art therapy. We acknowledge that research is needed in our profession due to the growing problem of trafficking and lack of available resources.

There are complementary treatments to art therapy that may be highly effective when working with individuals who have been sex trafficked. Some trauma-focused treatments consider these alternative practices as best practices when evidence-based approaches are implemented. Some of the modalities may need further training, research, specialized certification, or credentials to ensure competency, and professionals are encouraged to follow national and state requirements. The type of traumas the client has endured, the symptoms the client exhibits, the age and developmental level of the client, the individual or organized criminal group that caused the trauma, the safety of the client, and the current risk(s) of trafficking are all considerations when assessing the complexity for therapy treatment. This chapter aims to provide the therapist with ways to think beyond the typical therapy session to bring more awareness to the client's unique needs. Art therapy is one therapeutic approach that can serve as an effective and meaningful element to the client's healing process while still being open to the use of other modalities.

Preface From the Authors

Cynthia Wilson PhD, ATR-BC

This population inadvertently came to me through my clients in private practice and while previously volunteering as a therapist intern at a nonprofit counseling center. The moment I learned about sex trafficking from that first client, I was passionate about learning more as a means to find ways to help survivors progress, along with an overwhelming desire to find the root cause in order to stop the cycle. From my experience with this client population, all persons were individually motivated adults who came in for therapy for other reasons and revealed that the trauma they were forced to endure as children was a form of sex trafficking. Each client had a unique story and his or her response to the trauma was identified as a core consideration in setting therapeutic goals as well as therapeutic treatment methods. I have learned that flexibility is needed to collaborate with other health professionals and to adapt various treatment modalities with art therapy to produce the most effective client-centered treatment. Over the last decade and half, I have come to realize that stopping the cycle of trafficking may not be a plausible goal for me, but I have not resigned to take it off my "to-do" list. What has risen to the top of my list, however, is education regarding the exposure of the sex trafficking trade and survivors' dissociative symptoms to other health professionals in order to expand the resources of support, care, and hope for all clients in need. Art-based interaction, primarily art therapy, has become my means of finding ways to expand the mind/body connection of the client for increased self-awareness and communication about survivors' needs to health professionals (Wilson, 2019). Art therapy has been specific to the holistic narrative processing of traumas and healing experiences.

Serena R. Coleman, ATR, AMFT

The journey of this work first began with awareness from a statement heard from a friend, "Children and women are being sold for sex . . . in our neighborhoods." Concern, curiosity, and compassion led to my pursuit to learn more about human trafficking (both labor and sex) and eventually to work with the population. The impact of human trafficking in the United States and globally became more evident as I became more educated by grassroots organizations, as did the realization that many of my peers were not talking about this epidemic problem. Volunteering first within nonprofit organizations developed my insight to the challenges adult survivors faced on a daily basis. Working with youth who were commercially sexually exploited proposed different challenges that shifted my focus to the need for quality in health care. Both positions did not originate as art therapist roles, yet they presented opportunities for program development with trauma-informed approaches, collaborations with service providers, and the practice of creating and providing safety (both physically and therapeutically) while learning to apply flexibility and cultural humility. Art has been used as a valuable tool for communication, expression, psychoeducation, and to spark joy or interest. I am continually inspired by the hearts and stories of survivors, leaders, abolitionists, service providers, researchers, and others who confront the issues of human trafficking. I have met amazingly resilient individuals along this journey, and each individual has made an impact on my life. Human trafficking is a challenging issue that cannot be faced alone, yet joining together with genuine hearts and intentional practices can lead to grand and creative solutions.

Complex Trauma

Complex trauma is a form of trauma that results from repeated actions of trauma usually within a period of consecutive time and in connection with relationships, such as domestic violence, prisoner of war, and human trafficking (Courtois, 2004). Research has served to add validity to the diagnosis of complex posttraumatic stress disorder (complex PTSD), otherwise known as type II trauma (Cloitre, Garvert, Brewin, Bryant, & Maercker, 2013; Herman, 1992). The type of severe or complex trauma, often sexual, that results in complex PTSD and/or dissociative states requires a different type of treatment than traditional treatments for the more well-known PTSD (Wilson, 2019). Complex trauma can cause complex PTSD and/or dissociative states in the survivor, requiring additional knowledge and training for the therapist, along with various treatment modalities. Severe sexual abuse was determined to be a marker that causes the various dissociative disorders (DD), such as complex PTSD or dissociative identity disorder (DID), and a marker potentially able to differentiate DDs from other diagnoses because sexual abuse was established to be the most intrusive and complex form of abuse (Dorothy, Middleton, Seager, Williams, & Chambers, 2017). People in the field may recognize the effects of complex trauma with survivors they work with and see the challenges they face firsthand; complex trauma can cause significant effects, such as disempowerment, disability, and dependency when traumas occur during stages of development (Gopal, 2019). The majority of those who have survived sex trafficking have been exposed to chronic traumatic experiences (Hopper, 2017). Being aware of the different effects of complex trauma can assist the therapist in identifying trafficking and in providing effective treatment.

Dissociation

The most severe form of dissociation as defined by the *Diagnostic and Statistical Manual of Mental Disorders, Fifth Edition* (*DSM-5*) (American Psychiatric Association [APA], 2013) is known as DID. DID is common among sexual abuse trauma survivors (Miller, 2012). For example, if a teenager has been sexually assaulted by someone he or she had a trusting relationship with (friend, partner, teacher, family member), the aspects of the experience could develop into several different parts or splits within the mind. There could be parts within the brain that only hold memories of the physical sensations, fragments that hold memories of the sadness or fear, a very angry teenager who hates that he or she didn't fight the attacker off, a younger part that is confused because the teenager loved the attacker so much, and even an abusive side that mirrors the attacker. Sometimes these splits can even be created intentionally by the sex trafficking organization (Miller, 2012). A perpetrating organization/cult intentionally causing trauma to make splits in a human brain seems skeptical, but this practice plays a large role in the survival of the organization/cult's secrecy (Miller, 2012). If the individual who is sex trafficked develops a disconnected/compartmentalized mind in some form of dissociative disorder (DD), then per the sex trafficking organization's hopes, that person will not likely be seriously regarded as a witness, and thus the abusive organization remains secret. Research also suggests that the split aspects of the mind can further be engaged with and developed to the organization's end (Miller, 2012). Unfortunately, this means that the way the brain develops when learning something new can be manipulated and detrimentally used for the purposes of the sex trafficking industry.

Additional Considerations

Therapists and helping professionals working with the trafficked population are encouraged to understand the importance of confidentiality, safety, nonjudgment, collaborative work, and vicarious trauma. Confidentiality is essential in maintaining safety for clients who have been trafficked (International Organization for Migration [IM], 2009). Safety concerns can result from threats and harm from traffickers and exploiters. Similar to domestic violence, individuals surviving, and survivors of, sex trafficking need secure, confidential shelters. Steady housing that provides specialized care of the trafficked population is needed, yet hard to find (Walker, 2013). Beds become more urgent when concerns for the safety of the individual increases, which may be due to a criminal investigation and when the trafficker or exploiter is involved (IM, 2009).

Survivors of sex trafficking also need safety planning. It is important to note that safety planning can be valuable for survivors who have chosen to leave the exploiter or trafficker and those who have chosen to stay (Howard & Sutton, 2018). Creating a safety plan or a plan for care also entails precaution, as many survivors may not identify as victims or survivors, and reporting a crime has the possibility to cause harm to them or their families (Dovydaitis, 2010; Institute of Medicine [IOM] & National Research Council [NRC], 2013). Individuals who have survived trafficking may continue to have strong feelings of connection to their exploiters, which can result in returning to them because of the bond that was created through the suggestion of love, known as trauma bonding. Researchers recognize that traffickers use emotional and psychological abuse that can cause psychological coercion and torture (Task Force on Trafficking of Women and Girls, 2014). There are legal requirements for service providers to contact child protective services for minors who are identified, and when providers need additional assistance in learning or creating specific plans for an individual, the National Human Trafficking Resource Center (1-888-373-7888) can provide resources in the local area and create a plan with the survivor, the clinician, or both (Dovydaitis, 2010, p. 4). (See Sex Trafficking Resources for more information.)

Research Recommendations With Trauma-Informed Approaches

Viewing Sex Trafficking Through the Lens of Trauma

Research indicates that individuals who have endured sexual abuse, such as sex trafficking, can suffer from complex posttraumatic symptoms (Becker, 2015; Pifalo, 2002, 2007, 2009). Sexual abuse, sexual violence, and sexual trauma are all connected to sex trafficking. Survivors of sex trafficking often have to cope with complex trauma (Hopper, 2017). Although empirical research on best practices when working with this population is limited, research on PTSD, complex PTSD, sexual violence, domestic violence, intimate partner violence, sexual abuse, gender-based violence, and other forms of trauma and abuse are more readily available in the literature. Victimized by sexual abuse, individuals can have difficulty communicating their feelings or experiences, which could be perceived as a limitation while working with talk therapists or counselors (Pifalo, 2002; Shenk, Putnam, & Knoll, 2012).

Mental health professionals need to approach working with survivors of sex trafficking through a lens of trauma, specifically relational trauma, which is not often associated with this population. Relational trauma is traditionally viewed as the abuse from a protective caregiver–type individual to a child or that of one loved one to another (Chapman, 2014). This means that relational trauma takes place when someone in a formed trusting relationship causes traumatic harm to the other person in a way that destroys trust and a sense of safety with that other person. It is detrimental to mental and emotional development when a child must protect against an abuser who is also supposed to be the caregiver and upon whom the child must similarly rely on for protection and nurturance (Chapman, 2014). The manipulation of the trafficker enforces a relationship in a way that the individual needs, and then once trust or a bond is established, the trafficker has the opportunity to abuse the individual and create a relational and psychological trauma (Task Force on Trafficking of Women and Girls, 2014).

Trauma-informed approaches are repeatedly recommended in serving the trafficked population. When trauma-informed approaches are implemented, they focus on establishing trust, safety, respect, strengths, and cultural considerations with the individual who has experienced trauma (Hass-Cohen & Findlay, 2015; Lewis-O'Connor & Alpert, 2017). It is recommended that professionals use trauma-informed approaches that apply survivor-centered, strength-based, nonjudgmental, and culturally competent responses to create a safe environment for healing. Based on our observation, many agencies that work closely with the trafficked population, such as nonprofits and advocacy assistance programs, try to educate other professionals who may come in contact with survivors. Further understanding and education about power and control dynamics between the trafficker or exploiter and the vulnerable individual is also needed for professionals. Health-care professionals should consider the complexity of creating thoughtful and realistic treatment plans in collaboration with the individual who has survived any form of sex trafficking. It is recommended that mental health professionals use trauma-informed approaches, including the recognition of strengths and resiliency, awareness of traumatic stress, assistance with self-determination, and addressing the mental health concerns of individuals who have been trafficked with multiple interventions at different system levels (Hopper, 2017).

Collaborative Approach

Growing the treatment team is expected when working with a client who has a vast array of symptomology and complexities associated with the trauma. Collaborative work means the client is finally receiving all the various forms of care that were needed due to the trauma occurrence. It is highly recommended to have a treatment team with various forms of care because that is the natural way of human healing. Perry and Szalavitz (2010) stated that raising an empathetic child takes four adults; likewise, it could then also be said that more than one advocate is needed in recovery for a trafficked survivor due to the variety of aspects of the trauma. Having a treatment team provides clients with all of the multifaceted care that is required for recovery. Research suggests collaborative models of care are beneficial for individuals who have survived trafficking (IOM & NRC, 2013; Hopper, 2017; Gopal, 2019). The Polaris Project (2010) created a Community Model Action Plan, a list of stakeholders who can provide a community-wide response to human trafficking. The list is extensive and ranges from federal- and state-level stakeholders to community-level resources (Polaris Project, 2010). Multidisciplinary approaches are recommended as promising practices for trafficked youth (Greenbaum, 2017; Hannan, Martin, Caceres, & Aledort, 2017).

A suggested trauma-informed approach that appears to support individuals who have been trafficked is the multimodal social ecological (MSE) framework (Hopper, 2017). The MSE framework considers the mental health needs of the population and applies layers of interventions at each level to address and support the individual with a history of complex trauma. The MSE framework focuses on three distinct levels that takes into consideration flexible approaches: the individual level (individual therapy, etc.), the social-environmental level (relationship building, group therapy, family therapy, etc.), and the systems level (education, leadership, etc.) (Hopper, 2017, p. 170). Although research needs to be developed to further assess the suggested approaches with trafficked survivors, the MSE framework offers multiple ways to assist the individual with complex trauma and creatively brings holistic approaches to support resilience and empowerment.

Survivor Knowledge

The knowledge and experiences of survivors of sex trafficking and commercial sexual exploitation can provide another level of care for the trafficked population when used to create policies and support. Survivor-centered approaches with trauma-informed practices are becoming more widely known. More organizations and agencies are incorporating survivor panels and survivor-led organizations to help build better practices for survivors of sex trafficking. Survivor-led programs that include advocacy and housing can build trust among survivors versus other service providers due to shared experiences (Gavin & Thomson, 2017). Survivor-leadership approaches provide opportunities for self-leadership, empowerment, mentorship, and trainings in public speaking and community events (Family and Youth Service Bureau, 2015). Girls Educational and Mentoring Services, GEMS (2018), is an example of an organization whose work is dedicated to empowering young women who have survived commercial sexual exploitation and domestic trafficking. GEMS has encouraged survivor leadership for two decades and created a national Survivor Leadership Institute to continue building a community of survivors and training other organizations on survivor-centered approaches (2018). Providing opportunities for survivors and leaders to share their knowledge with organizations working with the trafficked population is highly encouraged and valuable.

Gender-Responsive

As mentioned earlier, data results find sex trafficking and commercial sexual exploitation of women and girls more common than of men and boys. Due to the high percentages of female survivors of sex trafficking, many service providers have added gender-specific approaches to their treatment programs. It is important to recognize that there are differences between genders; women respond to trauma, such as violence, differently than men, which can be due to their learned coping skills or perception of normalcy (Covington, 2015). Being gender-responsive allows for the opportunity to be intentional and respectful with the services offered in consideration of how one identifies. For example, one report found trauma-informed and gender-responsive yoga significantly supported young girls in the juvenile justice setting with somatic interventions and the promotion of healthy relationships and individual strengths (Epstein & González, 2017). Although this section is using women or females as examples because this information is more widely available, please note that labeling by gender may limit our understandings of individuals who identify as gender variant, transgender, and intersex and have survived or are surviving trafficking (Macias-Konstantopoulos & Ma, 2017), and it is recommended to support and respect the gender identity and sexual orientation of the trafficked population.

Trauma-Focused Cognitive Behavioral Therapy

According to the Child Sexual Abuse Task Force and Research & Practice Core of the National Child Traumatic Stress Network (2004), evidence in research has shown that trauma-focused cognitive behavioral therapy (TF-CBT) has worked in treating trauma in youth and families, has the capability to improve problems that resulted from childhood trauma, and client improvement may be evident after 12–16 sessions of therapy. TF-CBT is an evidence-based practice that has been used for children with symptoms of PTSD (Sigel, Benton, Lynch, & Kramer, 2013). Cohen, Mannarino, and Kinnish (2017) provided strategies for using TF-CBT specifically for commercially exploited youth and discussed the importance of the therapist using adaptive approaches to engage youth in therapy services, work with caregivers, maintain safety, develop trauma narratives, and understand trauma history in addition to making sure youth had accurate diagnoses. Pifalo (2007) emphasized how well trauma-focused art therapy works with the CBT modality to help recall the trauma safely while creating a visual narrative to process and gain awareness for additional issues that might be overlooked due to the strength of the trauma.

Dissociative Effects of Trauma

The symptoms of traumatic experiences in individuals who have been sex trafficked are vast. The sexual abuse is evident, but there is also physiological, relational, and emotional abuse that can all be detrimental. The relational attachment abuse can break the trust of those who were supposed to protect and/or love the individual (Chapman, 2014; Schore, 2009) making it difficult for a child or adult to trust anyone, including him or herself. Dissociation can be a natural human response to protect oneself from all the disturbing aspects of all types of trauma that involve the brain, separating the various aspects of the event from each other and making it difficult to confront the trauma and prevent being overwhelmed (Herman, 1992; van der Kolk, 2014).

The ability to dissociate is a natural effect of human survival (van der Kolk, 2014), and everyone has and does dissociate at times at different levels and in different forms throughout life (Ross, 2015; Ross & Halpern, 2009). Ross and Halpern (2009) report that 3%–11% of Americans have in the past or currently exhibit symptoms for diagnosable dissociation. The act of dissociation provides protection from the overwhelming effects of trauma as well as enables the person to develop coping skills to survive the repeated trauma that comes with sex trafficking. This pattern is a normal reaction to abnormal events for the sake of survival. In working with individuals who have been sex trafficked, it is essential for the therapist to know about DDs of all types and be prepared to collaborate, consult, refer out, and/or learn more about how to treat this aspect of trauma symptoms.

Dissociation is a clear defense mechanism, and its symptoms help to preserve the life of the individual abused when the emotional, relational, sexual, and physical aspects of the trauma are too much to absorb or when there is no other escape from the abuse (Putnam, Harris, & Putnam, 2013; Siegel & Bryson, 2011; van der Kolk, 2014). Various groups and cults who perform satanic ritual abuse (SRA)/ritual abuse (RA) involve sexual torture and the training and selling of children for sexual exploitation. RA occurs when someone has been abused in a ceremonial manner or in a repeated way on a consistent day, season, or time; SRA is orchestrated by satanic religious groups of ceremonial events that take place consistently or routinely due to the seasons, holidays, or other satanic beliefs (Miller, 2012). A child who is trapped in a RA or SRA environment can find that the repeated and extreme cruelty of the abuse demands the body and mind, as well as areas within the mind, disconnect, or a child's growing brain may never fully integrate (Miller, 2012). When a person experiences an event or series of events that are severely traumatic, they may psychologically compartmentalize the memories into separate aspects in order to manage their distress; they may dissociate to protect themselves and survive (Miller, 2012; Spring, 2001).

To be diagnosed with any DD, a person must exhibit different types of dissociation in a way that impedes daily life (APA, 2013). Per the *DSM-5* (APA, 2013), symptoms and signs of DDs can include memory loss of specific times, people, places and events; out-of-body experiences, such as feeling as though you are watching yourself from a different perspective; other mental health problems, such as depression, anxiety, and suicidal thoughts; a sense of disconnection from emotions/emotional numbness; and a lack of a sense of self-identity. Symptoms of DD depend on the type of disorder.

In all, there are three recognized types of dissociation to diagnose, but there are other trauma-related diagnoses that can have a dissociative component per the *DSM-5* (APA, 2013). Nearly half of adults in the United States experience at least one depersonalization/derealization episode at some point in life, but only 2% meet the criteria for a diagnosis with chronic episodes (National Alliance on Mental Illness, 2019). DD can range from having derealization/depersonalization, dissociative amnesia, to the most severe form, DID:

1. Derealization/depersonalization is the disconnected sense from environmental reality and others around you.
2. Dissociative amnesia is a disconnecting lack of remembrance of a traumatic event, but not the complete loss of information from memory.
3. DID occurs when a person has separate areas within the mind that encapsulate the different aspects of the trauma in a way that enable the brain to have fully active personalities that hold those trauma aspects separate.

(APA, 2013)

Therefore, all aspects of DD have a way of keeping the whole person safe from the overwhelming trauma experience whether it was singular or repeated.

In art therapy, there are a few key ways to interact with the dissociative symptoms (Gantt & Tannin, 2007; Lusebrink, 1996) and specific symbols and styles to be aware of in the artwork (Spring, 2001, 2004), each depending on the type of DD and the stage of treatment and healing for the individual. Spring's (2004) 30-year study involving art therapy and trauma found that common elements in the artwork of an individual with a trauma history were disembodied eyes and wedge shapes. In my professional experience (Wilson), a depth of layering and hidden images or messages have been found to be common as well. Key ways to use art therapy with dissociative symptoms include helping each part of the whole persona express the aspect(s) of the trauma they hold for processing and witnessing, to have them use the art to communicate to each other and build internal connections and self-reliance, and/or to have them reground and orient to current time and space through sensory and/or bilateral art directives.

Recommendations for Art Therapy and Complementary Modalities

Art Therapy

Due to the way the brain protectively responds to traumatic experiences (Siegel & Bryson, 2011; van der Kolk, 2014), several art therapists have discussed the importance of understanding the brain and developmental trauma and suggest using art therapy for right-brain interventions for trauma treatment (Arrington & Cherry, 2007; Chapman, 2014; Schore, 2009). Art therapists have the unique ability to assist clients in communication and processing when the trauma of sexual violence has hindered the regions of the brain that enable their ability to express themselves verbally (Siegel & Bryson, 2011; van der Kolk, 2014). Art therapists can draw upon art therapy research and practices working with traumatized populations, such as PTSD, complex PTSD, intimate partner violence, and dissociative spectrum diagnosis. There are many alternatives or additions to traditional talk therapy that are highly effective in the treatment of individuals who have been or are being sex trafficked. Many trauma-focused treatments consider these alternative practices as best practices (Gantt & Vesprini, 2017; Hass-Cohen, Findlay, Carr, & Vanderlan, 2014; Kass & Trantham, 2014; Levine, 1997; Lusebrink & Hinz, 2016; Pifalo, 2002; Tantia, 2014; van der Kolk, 2014).

Specifically pertaining to sexual violence and art therapy, Garlock (2016) provided information regarding using textiles with trauma survivors of gender-based violence, creating narratives with a variety of cloth and sewing to build relationships and to tell stories. Kapitan (2015) informs art therapists about professional ways to apply cultural considerations when working with individuals who have experienced trauma both in the states and abroad and the importance of being aware of one's own bias and shifting our lens to include the cultural norms of the client's heritage. Art therapy continues to build the field with empirical research and publications that can inspire future work with unique populations.

Trauma-Informed Models in Art Therapy

As therapists, we prepare ourselves to work with clients who have trauma backgrounds. Whether the trauma may be connected to relational trauma, generational trauma, or other traumas related to forms of abuse, all traumas can affect our clients. Some art therapists have created specific models to work with clients with trauma backgrounds. As mentioned throughout this chapter, each client is different and has his or her own unique needs to address. To use trauma-informed practices and models, the therapist must rely on intentionality and thoughtful deliverance when incorporating art materials. Chapman (2014) created a trauma-informed neurodevelopmental art therapy model to help children and teens who have been exposed to chronic trauma, violence, and/or abuse. This form of therapy consists of creating a visual narrative of the events, verbalizing, organizing, adding in the missing pieces, and listening to the story with consideration for the right-brain connection and integration of the entire trauma event. Another model that can be used for any age is the instinctual trauma response model, which also involves verbalizations of the traumatic event and a visual trauma narrative that is called the graphic narrative (Gantt & Tinnin, 2007; Arrington & Cherry, 2007). With collaborations between art therapists and other trauma work professionals, best practices in trauma-informed art therapy can safely take place.

Expressive Therapies Continuum

The expressive therapies continuum (ETC) is a model used by art therapists of the different types of expressive art mediums and how they affect the person's ability to connect to the subconscious needs on a multidimensional and multidirectional continuum that includes four creative levels (Lusebrink, 2010). The different types of expressive art mediums, such as watercolor, clay, wood carving, or drawing, can be used to assess the client's mental functioning through the kinesthetic/sensory level, perceptual/affective level, cognitive/symbolic level, and the creative level that flows through and integrates them all (Lusebrink, 2010). For example, if the client is given clay, and he or she focuses on the *sensory* aspects of the media, such as the texture, temperature, or sound of the clay in his or her hand, then the therapist can determine if the client is able to move to the next level of perceptual/affective or over to the kinesthetic aspect of the kinesthetic/sensory level. By viewing a client's art-making process and/or completed artwork using the ETC, art therapists can assess a client's strengths, needs, and disconnect in the four levels of a client's cognitive functioning to allow suggestion or substantiation of a diagnosis or recovery plan from a mental health condition (Lusebrink, 2010). This means that the ETC can be a way to help individuals affected by sex trafficking, with a safe pace that is based on their needs and control while maintaining containment in the artwork and support of the art therapist to help them release their trauma through expression. Figure 4.1 shows an art piece with mixed media because the individual needed to be able to control the flow through the levels of the ETC, going in and out of the perceptual/affective and cognitive/symbolic levels. The image shows how the texture of the mediums helped give depth to the experience and the flow of the

Figure 4.1 Example that used different mediums through the ETC to process trauma

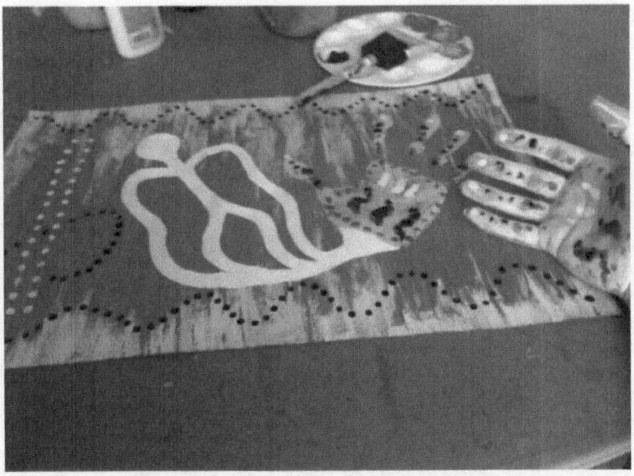

Figure 4.2 Transition through ETC levels of symbolic to affective and ending in sensory

paint was used in a very controlled way to prevent much affect connection. Whereas Figure 4.2 is much more fluid in the use of only paint. It is even incorporating the individual's hand as a paint brush to potentially increase the affective connection and include the kinesthetic/sensory level.

Focusing Oriented Art Therapy®

Mindfulness can be valuable in the healing and treatment of people who have undergone trauma. While focusing on the body is difficult, survivors find it nearly impossible to also focus in the present moment. Rappaport's (2009) Focusing Oriented Art Therapy (FOAT)® is a form of mindfulness used in art therapy. The way the brain is unable to integrate the traumatic event makes activation of the event in the brain overwhelming (van der Kolk, 2014). Rappaport (2009) developed FOAT® as a means of reducing the feeling of being overwhelmed. FOAT® starts with a meditative-type focusing exercise that allows for the much-needed space to respect all the elements of sensory, physical, psychological, and emotional overwhelm of the trauma and handles each piece of the trauma with care. The guided meditation directs setting aside various overwhelming aspects of the trauma to focus on one specific area at a time (Rappaport, 2009), helping to slow down and respect every response and experience. Setting aside gives the client permission to focus on one thing without discounting the other aspects. Then there is creation of an art response to the focusing with a visual expression of internal processing and any visuals that presented in the focusing exercise (Rappaport, 2009). When working with a person who has been sexually abused, a therapist must move very slowly, provide adequate space, and offer the individual control for successful results. FOAT® allows for needed reparative elements for trauma survivors, such as sex trafficked individuals. Figure 4.3 is the result of a guided meditation after setting things aside, to find out what was needed in order to figure out how to better help another's situation. Figure 4.4 is using nature elements in a shadow box display as the mediums to increase focusing inward with containment, for self-care and grounding.

Figure 4.3 Being present in the moment and focusing on increasing awareness of others' needs during FOAT® techniques

Figure 4.4 Being present in the moment and focusing on self-care and self-awareness during FOAT® techniques

Memory Reconsolidation

Hass-Cohen et al. (2014) incorporate memory reconsolidation methods with art therapy to alter a person's perspective of memories and emotional interactions. The Check Protocol (Hass-Cohen et al., 2014) is as an evidence-based model that incorporates five art directives and requires intentional planning of art materials and therapy sessions. This type of reconstructive work can permit not only the mind's emotional memory to be altered also but an overall full body shift and complete relationship change with the self and the way one engages with the world. Currently, there is still no research that a real-life trauma can be defused from the mind (Patihis, Frenda, & Loftus, 2018), and memory reconsolidation does not mean that the memory itself is changed. Neuroscientists have found memory reconsolidation to be helpful for humans (Ecker, Ticic, & Hulley, 2013). The art directives given with memory reconsolidation use the memory of the event to visually process its aspects in a way that can release the effects of the trauma held in the mind and body.

Figure 4.5 is an art piece created with construction paper and tissue paper to show the intense emotional connection to a photograph that holds a memory of a particular person and time. In Figure 4.6 the same materials are used in response to the same photograph, but it shows the change in the emotional presence to the photograph after having done the memory reconsolidation technique.

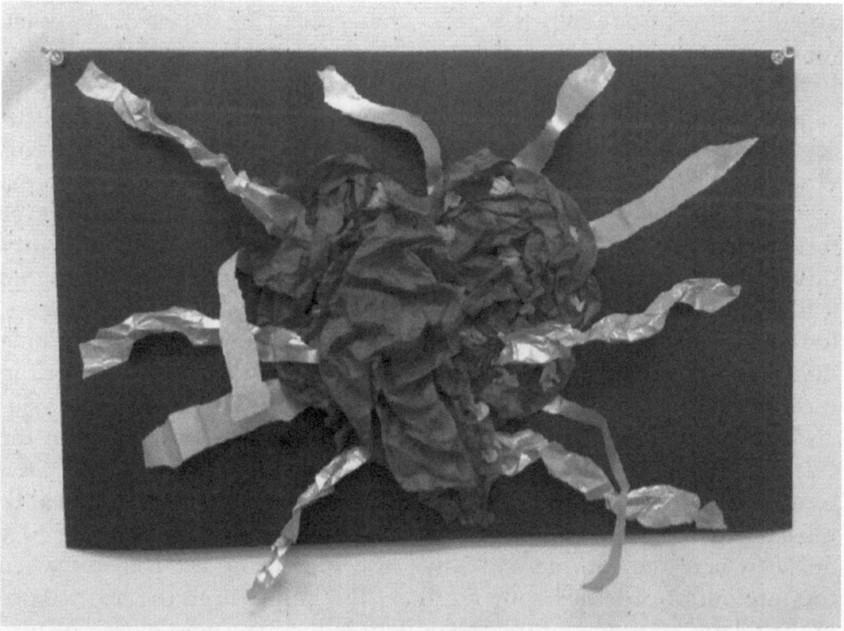

Figure 4.5 Image before the emotional connection to the memory has been processed with the memory reconsolidation technique

Figure 4.6 Change in image after the emotional connection to the memory has been processed with the memory reconsolidation technique

Narrative Processing

Narrative processing done via art therapy can help to organize and structure the traumatic event in a way that gives control back to the individual and gives the perspective of individual aspects of the event that otherwise are not able to be processed (Chapman, 2014; Gantt & Vesprini, 2017). Chapman (2014) explains the narrative directive as a form of focusing attention slowly, one step at a time, while processing the event, allowing for time to see, sense, and think about all that took place in each moment. In other words, by slowing the narrative down in a way that was not possible during the traumatic event, the survivor is able to integrate all the aspects of the event and bring cohesion to both mind and body. The narrative first involves visually recreating the event with one image/trauma scene per one page. One key component that can help alter the view of the trauma and how it is held in the mind and body is to ask the client when or where did someone come along to help (Chapman, 2014). Sometimes it is perceived that no one came to help; however, in doing this process, the client may find that there was someone there at the time of the trauma doing what he or she could to help or even noticing that the therapist in the office now can represent the helpful person. Discussing all of the visuals one image at a time while sharing each part of the event with the therapist and allowing the therapist to restate it for the client to hear is the progression of the process. The therapist listens for something added to the story that doesn't yet have a picture, and the client adds these new images where they are needed while also organizing the pictures when they are out of order. Chapman (2014) also emphasized the importance of the relational model of treatment with individuals who have a history of trauma. Connecting with the client by looking from left eye to left eye during the trauma narrative processing increases the connection from therapist to client on the empathetic emotional level via the right-brain engagement of the left eye (Chapman, 2014; Schore, 2009).

Complementary Modalities

Trauma-Sensitive Mindfulness and Trauma-Informed Yoga

Mindfulness and yoga practices have been increasingly appealing for those searching for holistic ways to heal the mind, body, and spirit. Mindfulness and yoga are being utilized in several settings, including schools, prisons, and companies. In the simplest terms, trauma-informed yoga has been developed to support people with a history of trauma to help them feel safe, comfortable, and less anxious during yoga practice (Castaneda, 2017; Danylchuck, 2015); trauma-sensitive mindfulness understands that mindfulness has the potential to cause harm to survivors of trauma—for example, retraumatization—so in return, trauma-sensitive mindfulness recognizes trauma and responds by trying to minimize threats while still influencing benefits (Trevleaven, 2018). These modalities are recommended to be used by trained instructors, teachers, or clinicians who have received trauma-informed training and certification.

Mindfulness and yoga continue to be researched to bring insight into how they can be applied within clinical psychotherapy. According to Kimbrough, Magyari, Langenberg, Chesney, and Berman (2010), survivors of childhood sexual abuse reported significantly reduced symptoms of depression by 65% at the completion of the eight-week pilot study program. The study included mindfulness practice at home and a mindfulness meditation-based stress reduction program. In other research, women with chronic PTSD completed a 20-week, trauma-sensitive yoga treatment, which resulted in the reduction of PTSD and dissociative symptoms at a quicker rate than other treatments (art therapy not included), and 83% of participants no longer met criteria for PTSD one week after completion (Price et al., 2017). This study had a small sample size and relied on monitored yoga practice at home. However, due to the significant results in decreased symptoms, future research can build support for trauma-informed yoga and mindfulness. Yoga requires little equipment, may be feasible if community training supports therapists, and is predicted to be a valuable tool in adjunct treatment, specifically noted for survivors of partner violence (Clark et al., 2014).

Art, yoga, and mindfulness practices can go hand in hand as collaborative treatments to support people with trauma. Gibbons (2015) stated the importance of professionals being aware that any client may have a trauma background that is not disclosed and can be triggered by yoga or art interventions. Gibbons (2015), an art therapist and yoga therapist, suggested providing choices and being present with the client during sessions. Her book does not focus explicitly on trauma-informed approaches, yet Gibbons (2015) lists examples of art interventions that can be useful to combine with mindfulness and yoga. Sanar Wellness Institute and Polaris Project (2015) recognized therapeutic/restorative yoga, expressive arts therapy, and mindfulness and sensory-based practices as three promising therapeutic supports for survivors of human trafficking "in processing trauma and reconnecting with their bodies" (p. 3). It was noted that further scientific research is needed to support the findings of specific modalities; although the report had some limitations, it was a step toward recognizing which therapeutic interventions can be supportive for human trafficking survivors in trauma-informed care (Sanar Wellness Institute & Polaris Project, 2015). More research is needed nationally and globally on therapeutic supports for survivors of human trafficking. Recommendations for research in art therapy, mindfulness, and yoga are needed to evaluate the successes and challenges of utilizing these modalities with survivors of human trafficking.

Sensorimotor Psychotherapy

Research indicates that the body's memories of a traumatic event stay within the muscles not only as memories of the trauma but also the specific memory when the actions or movements were stopped by the trauma; these actions, such as pushing away, running, or screaming, that the body began could not be completed due to the trauma event. Ogden and Fisher (2015) explained in their sensorimotor psychotherapy that if a client follows through very slowly with movements that were halted during trauma and that are held within the body, then the person can release the body's trauma memory. For example, the sex trafficked survivor moves her/his arms in a way that pushes an attacker away or covers the private areas to prevent harm. Ogden and Fisher (2015) closely observed that the trauma narrative is held in the body not in the mind. Levine (1997) also worked with body memories and has researched the animal kingdom to find ways in which animals respond to trauma that humans have put aside. Through the use of special energy releasing, soothing sounds, and movements produced by the individual with a trauma history, an individual can regain balance, because the person has finally been able to fully respond to the trauma (Levine, 1997). After the release, the body has no need to hold on to this trauma and can go back to homeostasis. For a sex trafficked survivor, this could mean a release of the trauma through allowing the body to do what it couldn't do at the time of the trauma, and then when homeostasis is achieved, it can further allow for the safety of emotional processing.

Conducting art therapy before, during, or after sensorimotor movements can be an active agent of change for therapy (Tantia, 2014), but it does require a location with room for movement and art creation. Artwork can be created before and after the sensorimotor movements or even during the body movements to view aspects of change or to visually represent the body movements. Then the art therapist conducts art therapy dialogue to process and communicate with the images. The artwork created can then be processed by an art therapist to connect to the language of the body and subconscious. The movements may be collaborative, with the therapist recording and replaying the movements the client performed so that the client can witness the movement and create an art response. The opportunity to release the trapped body memory and then connect to the subconscious processing can assist the survivor with fully integrating the body and mind separations during the traumatic event. For individuals who have been sexually exploited, there is a distinct difference in the body work that is needed. Individuals have different experiences and ways of conceptualizing and internalizing their trauma events so that they might survive. With the fight, flight, freeze, faint, and feigned death responses the brain sends out to the rest of the body, there are a variety of combinations of how a person may respond to a sexual trauma (Levine, 1997; Ogden & Fisher, 2015; van der Kolk, 2014). Psychologically, there may be the confusion of the sometimes naturally incongruent desires and reactions of the mind and body. Body betrayal takes place when the body's basic sensory response may indicate pleasure or reproduction needs while the mind is caught in horrified terror and debilitating pain.

Emotional Freedom Technique/Tapping

The emotional freedom technique (EFT) is a form of tapping into the meridian points/acupressure points within the body while directly addressing the negative aspects of things that are held within the bodies while releasing them (Ortner, 2013). Meridian points are the energy points that may also be referred to as acupressure points or the *chakras* that house a person's energy for the different bodily systems. Since EFT works with the body's meridian points, it offers a safe bodily reconnection that can otherwise be uncomfortable for those who have been brutally violated and pairs well with modalities that have proven helpful for the individual who has been sex trafficked.

EFT works well with art therapy directives by providing a platform of mind/body connection and a freedom to nonjudgmentally observe the negative responses that the client is protecting. It is possible to have a client do some tapping to detect the root cause of the distress—the thoughts, feelings, images, or emotions—that arise through the tapping process and provide relevant topics that direct the appropriate art materials and directives needed to process in art therapy. Trust with the body can be developed with the flexibility of EFT use in art therapy because the client can be in control of the speed and direction of focus. There are several ways to do EFT that include having the client watch or listen to the therapist perform the EFT while the client does art regarding the trauma, the client does EFT on him or herself, or the therapist gently taps on the client. For an art therapist, the ways to incorporate EFT into art therapy are a gradual process to help ease the client back into his or her body while providing a sense of control and the expulsion of trauma symptoms into the art container. Figure 4.7 used colored pencils after doing some EFT in order to find a way to express to medical staff what was not able to be expressed in words about the body. Figure 4.8 used acrylic paint also after EFT to connect to the visceral response of another's trauma narrative and find hidden understanding.

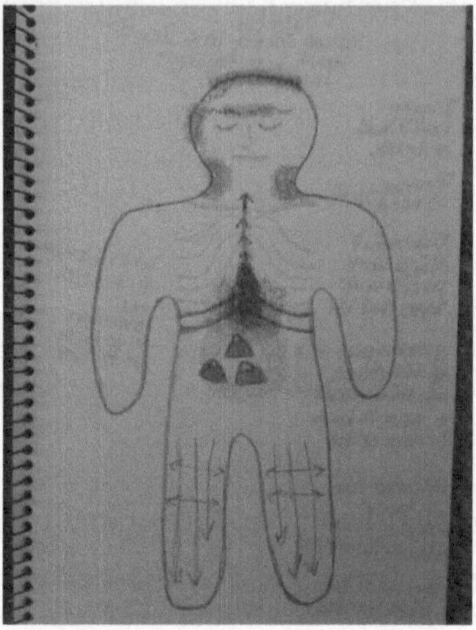

Figure 4.7 Created after EFT to express what the body was trying to express, release, or process

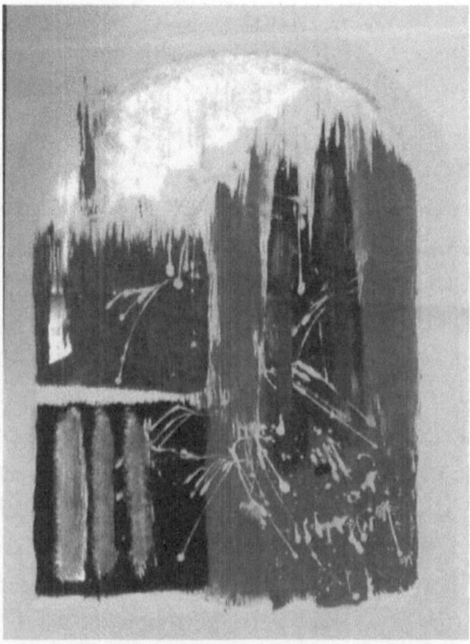

Figure 4.8 Created after EFT to express the visceral body response to another's trauma narrative and give enlightenment on what was being shared verbally

Eye Movement and Desensitization Reprocessing

Eye movement and desensitization reprocessing (EMDR) is still controversial when working with individuals with DID (Miller, 2012; Ross & Halpern, 2009); however, it is a well-researched form of treating individuals with trauma (Parnell, 2008; van der Kolk, 2014). There are modified EMDR options for dissociation that are not yet validated as best practice but have been under study since Shapiro (2001). The International Society for the Study of Trauma and Dissociation (2011) clarifies that EMDR is acceptable to use with dissociation as an adjunctive treatment, but it is not to be conducted as a stand-alone service for the client. It is advised that EMDR for a client with dissociation is performed with caution, and the form of dissociation is determined prior to EMDR treatment. The traditional EMDR specifically works with one single trauma at a time to reprocess the way trauma is held in the body and desensitize its effects while also building strength within (Parnell, 2008; van der Kolk, 2017). Hopper (2017) states that some EMDR protocols have started with creating internal resources before trauma processing and suggests treatments should be paired with the wants and needs of the client.

Doing art therapy with EMDR types of movements can be as simple as involving bilateral/two-handed movements in the creation of the art. The bilateral/two-handed scribble technique can be done for the purposes of regrounding and orienting into current time and space, as well as advancing a client through the developmental stages (Chapman, 2014). Bilateral drawing (Chapman, 2014), clay, and textiles (such as crochet, knitting, and sewing) use bilateral stimulation. The use of the bilateral stimulation with this population can help to ground, soothe, and increase the client's ability to become present or maintain his or her presence in the moment of therapy (Parnell, 2008). These are mindfulness techniques the client can also acquire and practice to feel safe in his or her environment and body. If you are an EMDR practitioner, another way to include art therapy into EMDR is to facilitate the creation of imagery of the resourcing figures that are imagined and do other standard art therapy skills (such as dialogue with the figures or with colors/lines/shapes in the image) to help integrate the resources and process the meaning behind them. Figure 4.9 is a bilateral/two-handed scribble drawing created with oil pastels for a controlled flow of medium within a contained circular space for increased sense of safe containment and grounding in the moment. Figure 4.10 is more of a form of process art using finger paints for fluidity and sensory experience to increase the release of the emotional and visceral body responses to a trauma narrative and explore hidden messages or experiences.

Craniosacral Therapy

Craniosacral therapy (CST) is a noninvasive form of massage therapy or body work that involves light touch (Leonard, 2017). CST is a method of evaluating and improving the functioning of the body's membranes

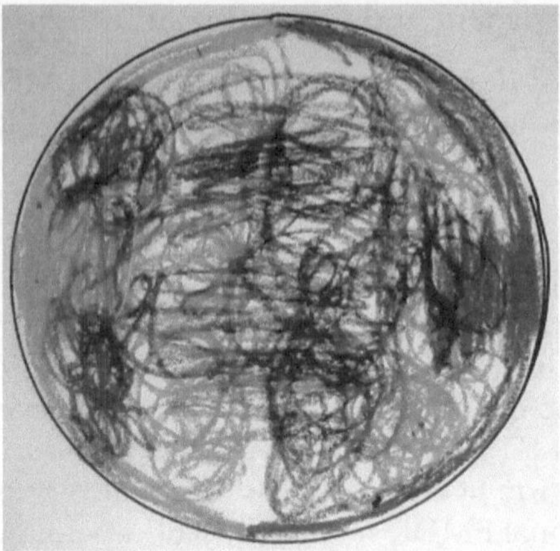

Figure 4.9 Example of art created by bilateral/two-handed art for grounding/orientation into the current space and moment within a contained space

Figure 4.10 Example of bilateral art created with finger paint for releasing of vicarious trauma within the body processing and increasing awareness

and cerebrospinal fluid that flows around the brain and through the spinal cord, called the craniosacral system (Upledger Institute International, 2019). It is important to note that a client with a trauma history may feel unsafe being in a vulnerable position or being touched, but during CST, the client is to leave on all clothing and can choose to sit or lie down while maintaining a greater sense of control and safety. Practitioners of CST believe they can somatically look and physically feel for the tension/blocks in the muscles and/or fascia and flow of the craniosacral fluid that can be caused by trauma.

> A trusting therapeutic relationship enables CST to take clients into altered perceptual states; these in turn facilitate a new level of awareness regarding the interrelatedness of body, mind and spirit, together with an enhanced capacity to care for self and manage health problems.
>
> (Brough, Lindenmeyer, Thistlethwaite, Lewith, & Stewart-Brown, 2015, p. 172)

Through body work, the client can work on releasing the trauma body memories that have been physically blocked (Ogden & Fisher, 2015). With art therapy, the healing flow of the mind can process the memories that coincide with the body blocks while the brain connects the experience and reestablishes the individual in a place of safety.

Practitioners of CST believe it can be used in collaboration with other health-care providers to help with the body's own physical and psychological healing (Leonard, 2017). It can be specifically helpful to combine energy/body work, such as CST, with art therapy for a more holistic and dual approach. With the encouragement of the art therapist, the client drives forward thoughts that arise to verbal expression, and the massage therapist can help reassure the body and ease the flow of craniosacral movement. The incorporation of art therapy usually takes place either before and/or after this type of collaborative session.

During CST, the art therapist can talk with the client about a trauma that has already been discussed in therapy sessions, yet still leave a block in the client's system. The discussion regarding the trauma must be previously discussed and agreed on with the client during CST so that the client continues to feel safe and in control, further allowing for more openness and the release of the trauma from the body. The massage therapist (confidentiality must be insured) may be able to follow the craniosacral fluid, body movements, or body temperature changes and find the blocks associated with the trauma discussed. The artwork created can help the client see the blocks or shifts while processing with the art therapist. This can be as simple as a body scan image using line, shape, and/or color to check on the sensations in the body before and after the collaborative CST session. Having a visual representation of the body sensations allows the art therapist to discuss through visual expression with the client during the CST session to increase any and all release of trauma from the body. The art therapy process also allows for the client's emotional and bodily shift to be visually expressed in the artwork and to integrate a new way of being in the world, potentially decreasing the chances of immediately falling back into the mental state of fear of safety and instability. More research needs to be done in this area to consider it best practices, but in the professional experience of Wilson, this practice has proven highly effective. Figure 4.11 is an image using the controlled medium of writing pen that was created after a craniosacral session showing the increased

Figure 4.11 Portrait of another's needs after craniosacral session showing increased awareness

Figure 4.12 Mask before a collaborative craniosacral session showing a blocked state and inability to connect

awareness of senses and trauma narrative that needed to be looked at. Whereas Figure 4.12 is using a very fluid medium in the increased attempt to amplify the affective awareness, but prior to any craniosacral treatment it left the artist with a stuck inability to connect to the needs of self or other.

Animal Therapy

Having an animal, such as the client's or the therapist's dog, in therapy for therapeutic purposes can be beneficial to the client. Adults and juveniles have benefited from an animal's presence, and research shows that the client becomes more relaxed, open, and has an increased sense of safety when with an animal they have developed an attachment to (Peacock, Chur-Hansen, & Winefield, 2012). The advantages of support animals include giving their companions confidence, affection, and independence while healing from trauma. The use of a support animal can increase trust and connection in the therapeutic relationship. For example, once the individual who has been involved in sex trafficking has a stable residence, letters can be written by the therapist in favor of a support animal for client companionship. Animal-free apartments should accept support dogs under Americans with Disabilities Act (Brennan, Nguyen, & Southwest Americans with Disabilities Act, 2014), and financial help may be available for certified service dogs who are trained in specific tasks in both physical and emotional services. The more a therapist can do to help a client feel safe and in control, the more trust the client will have in the therapist and respond to treatment.

The art therapist can also use an animal in therapy if there is therapeutic resistance or little progress, as a theme or metaphor in the art or even have the animal and the client work on art creations together. Helping the client feel the safety of a relationship, be it with an animal or human, can be the start of the healing processes. Each person has a personal preference in having a service animal present in a session, and the decision should be made with the client.

Professional Experiences With Survivors of Sex Trafficking

Working With Adults in the Sex Trade

Adults who were sex trafficked as children can sometimes find themselves still in the life as sex workers, even when they are no longer trafficked by another. Several of the adults I (Wilson) worked with in California came from criminal organizations that target and traffic children. Some of these organizations/groups solely work with sex trafficking and use people as a form of currency; others use sex trafficking as one way to raise funds for their SRA activities or to pay the larger costs of their organization in other countries. The individuals who are involved in sex work originated from either being manipulated and trained from birth or being lied to as children or young adults; none ever aspired to become a sex worker. Some females of various ages were even used as breeders to have babies who could then be trained from birth to service the organization in various ways.

The ability to make such large quantities of money in a short period of time, the knowledge of how to do sex work, and the ability as an adult to feel in control of when, where, and with whom sex work is conducted can all be driving forces to continue in the life after being trafficked. To remain in a dangerous life, such as sex work as an adult, is familiar

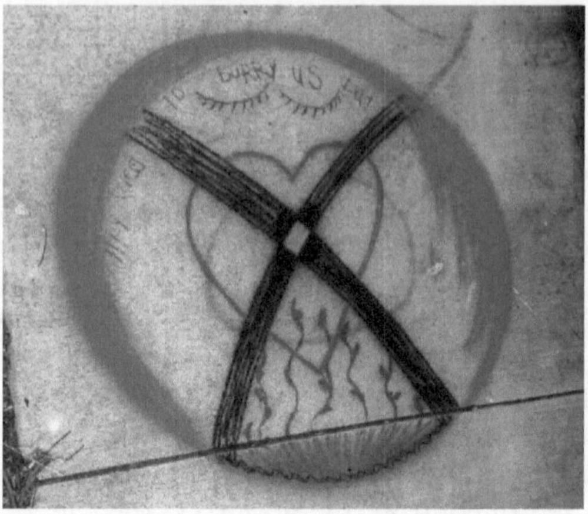

Figure 4.13 Provider response to working with adults who have been or are being sex trafficked

and potentially empowering to the survivor in many ways, no matter how triggering, upsetting, or degrading. To get out of the life, learn a new trade, process the traumas of having been in the life, and learn a new way to exist in the world are all so extremely frightening and challenging to the individual that these choices may even feel dangerous. One important fact in working with adults in the life, even if they are not managed by another, is that they did not choose this life; it was chosen for them, and they don't know other options or know how to obtain and sustain a life in another way (Ross & Farley, 2003). These individuals are not the criminals in the situation, they are human beings striving for survival. Stopping the cycle of sex trafficking ultimately means helping the individuals who have been pulled into the life by providing job skills training, psychoeducation, and therapeutic support to holistically heal. Figure 4.13 is drawn by the provider with soft chalk pastels on the course sidewalk at a university hidden behind a building. It reads "They tried to bury us, but they didn't know we were seeds" and it has a heart that is blocked or protected, closed eyes with red blood dripping around, and then green seedlings pushing up on the restraints just at the point of the break in the sidewalk. This process art helped the provider to explore and express the vicarious trauma being experienced while holding a space for the self and other. It also allowed for much more processing discussion and art to follow.

Working With CSEC

The Victims of Trafficking and Violence Protection Act (TVPA) of 2000 was developed in the United States to combat trafficking and prevent violence against women; section 103 defined sex trafficking as the "recruitment, harboring, transportation, provision, or obtaining a person for the purpose of a commercial sex act," and a commercial sex act is defined as "any sex act on account of which anything of value is given to or received by any person" (U.S. Department of State, 2019b). A commercial sex act with someone under 18 years old is considered a severe form of trafficking under the act (U.S. Department of State, 2019b). CSEC is often exchanged with literature terms such as sex trafficking of minors and domestic minors sex trafficking. Youth who are connected to the sex trade industry are often challenged by the juvenile justice and welfare systems that have not met their needs or have caused further harm (Lutnick, 2016). Commercially, sexually exploited youth face complex trauma and psychological challenges that impact their trust of community supporters (Williams & Frederick, 2009). Through my (Coleman) professional experiences with minors who survived domestic sex trafficking and commercial sexual exploitation, it made sense that building trust would be a challenge, yet frequent running away made it difficult to provide consistent care and build opportunities for trust. By having awareness of the developmental life stages, the emotional effects of trauma, and manipulation of love, in my opinion, trauma bonding seemed to be a main factor for running away with the desire to escape to people they knew versus to stay with those they did not know, such as residential staff. I (Coleman) agree with Smolenski and Ingerman (2017) on the importance of educating not only adults and communities about the possibilities of trafficking and exploitation but also older children about recruitment tactics traffickers use. Chapter 2 describes how exploiters and traffickers prey upon the vulnerable and groom them to believe there is love associated with the want for them, which eventually leads to manipulation and coercion. It is beneficial for the service provider to learn the terms youth are using with each other or when describing situations in therapy, such as daddy (boyfriend, trafficker), bottom (often a female who assists the trafficker or exploiter), and square life (trying to leave the sex trade industry). Please see the glossary for more terminology. I (Coleman) suggest using cultural humility and nonjudgmental approaches to learn more about the experiences they have endured and unknown terms.

Lastly, working with youth who express that they do not want therapy can be challenging. Yet success and opportunity for growth can be a possibility by modeling healthy communication between the service provider and the client. While this can be valuable, it is extremely undervalued in literature. Working with youth who have survived sex trafficking provides the therapist or other service providers with a chance to be genuinely compassionate, nonjudgmental, and honest about ways to work together. In many cases, youth share other needs besides mental health, such as housing and employment (Lutnick, 2016). As providers, this is an opportunity for us to collaborate with the client to explore further goals, recognize resiliency, and begin a process toward building a therapeutic alliance. As art therapists, we are able to use art as a tool to explore

Figure 4.14 Art response by provider working with survivors of sex trafficking

areas of need, to express emotions, and to provide something tangible to visualize goals. It is recommended to use strength-based and survivor-centered approaches. For example, Figure 4.14 is a provider's response to the emotional work of providing and navigating care to those impacted by human trafficking. The heart is heavy; the hands represent both the provider and client interchangeably; and the words reflect themes of suffering, hope, and love.

Working With Groups and Individuals

Any helping professional may find differences between working with individuals versus groups. Working specifically with survivors of sex trafficking, I (Coleman) have found that group dynamics can trigger many responses. Some group members may know each other outside of the group and can have the same exploiter or recognize one another from the same track (an area to buy sex acts in person). This can be problematic, as one group member could be an active recruiter and may know personal information about the others. There can also be triangulation of romantic relationships among individuals or with the trafficker. These relationships can be additionally challenging to manage in the group setting. Depending on what one shares, graphic information and language may trigger others in the group. It is recommended to set clear rules and boundaries (with the group's feedback) prior to starting the group to create safety and to have a coleader or assistant to provide extra support.

I (Wilson) have found that seeing clients individually in the office who have been sex trafficked can have similar responses when healing clients pass each other in the waiting room. There is also the potential for an active recruiter to stage as a client to be able to get other clients back into the trade or to trigger clients to remain quiet about the exploiter.

Screening new clients well before accepting them can help prevent the exploiter from reharming the client, and spreading out the appointment times and days can prevent the client's discomfort or anguish from seeing another client who may have been harmed by the same cult or exploiter in the waiting room. Some therapists may also find it helpful to have separate entrance and exit doors for increased anonymity. The location of the office, lighting, doors, and outside sounds all need to be taken into account when seeing clients individually. There can be triggering sounds, such as a train, ambulance, or lots of people or kids talking or laughing, that may have trained the client to being called back to the exploiter or cult. The sounds and location of the office can also be reminders of the track where the client was sold or had to perform. When working with people who have been sex trafficked, the entire picture of the personal interaction, the physical environment, and the therapeutic process need consideration.

Precautions and Necessities Based on Personal Experiences

The Art Process

Dissanayake (1995) researched how the creation of art must entail an element of making special where nothing special existed before. The importance of making art something special is accomplished by emphasizing the journey of the creation process and the spiritual connection to the final piece. The client can alter the relationship with the art process as well as build rapport with the therapist if the client feels undervalued by the materials offered. As art therapists, we believe providing quality art materials makes a noticeable difference with the trafficked population. For example, brands of glue or markers are often viewed and judged as expensive or cheap. The value of materials may connect to their value of self and importance. Providing quality materials that are not cheap and that will not break may be beneficial to survivors in the art therapy process. Past encounters have increased our appreciation of providing materials and ways we can advocate for materials to be used or purchased, particularly with the trafficked population. We purposely choose materials that survivors may enjoy while keeping the ETC model in mind.

The therapy approach to best fit the client's needs and the therapist's style, theory, and training is to be considered collaboratively between the client and therapist prior to goal setting. Many things must be considered when choosing the treatment modality that works well with one's therapeutic style as an art therapist, as well as with the goals and needs that the client has expressed in discussion with the therapist. All expressive art materials used have a distinct effect on the process (Hinz, 2017; Lusebrink, 2010; Lusebrink & Hinz, 2016. The ETC is the art therapist's guideline to the use of art materials and their functions in relation to the user's emotional and physical responses (Hinz, 2009; Lusebrink, 2010). Art materials have the ability to elicit responses, such as affect or sensory stimulation, even human emotion throughout the body; therefore, when working with a client, a therapist needs knowledge of not only the properties of the art materials and how they work with each other but also how they work in conjunction with the client's needs and therapeutic goals. Knowing the psychological state of the client and where the client can emotionally progress in therapy paired with the ETC will enable the art therapist to create quality sessions and precise clinical and therapeutic notes for treatment that leave no question as to the reason why something was attempted/accomplished in therapy. The ETC provides a way of reasoning which art therapeutic directives or materials can help the client meet goals more effectively and prevent the art therapist from ever feeling lost in the process or undecided about how to help the client move from a stuck place (Hinz, 2017).

Boundaries

Once having had his or her trust broken due to relational trauma as a child or adult, the survivor will have an increased need for genuine empathy and honesty in any therapist. The survivor of trafficking will easily identify deception and accuse falsities in others; imparting trust is not only difficult, but easy to withdraw because a trauma survivor expects the trust to be broken. This does not mean that the therapist should ignore personal boundaries and disclose private information, but it does mean open and honest communication in all client exchanges and ultimately modeling a healthy communicative relationship. Being able to help prepare your client for your own imperfections is important as well as normalizing any anger the survivor may feel toward you; safe expression of anger or disappointment is significant as emotions are discussed, expressed, and repaired in the therapeutic relationship. Mistakes, miscommunications or ruptures in the relationship are bound to happen and giving your client this knowledge helps to prepare him or her for the potential to repair his or her own personal relationships (Siegel & Bryson, 2011).

What a therapist does not want is to cause another situation where the he or she is unwittingly mirroring the perpetrator. Naturally, the therapist/client relationship is bound to be tested time and again to establish safety and trust in the relationship. It is advisable not to attempt some of the listed types of therapy sessions until the rapport is established and/or you are a mature therapist who is highly developed in your empathetic awareness and practice to maintain the containment and boundaries of the therapeutic environment. Supervision is required for those who are still working on credentials to help achieve better awareness of what is happening in session, knowledge of new research/treatment information, and following the best ways to conduct therapy with this sensitive population. Having an extra set of eyes will always help the therapist see alternate perspectives and fresh ideas for treatment as well as provide self-care. It is recommended that a therapist continue consultation groups even after credentialing to remain connected to new ideas, have a support group, reduce burnout, and prevent or process vicarious trauma. Working with the trafficked population has some unique and distinct concerns for professional therapists.

Safety

When working with individuals who have been involved in sex trafficking, you may be going up against an organization, group, or other individuals who do not want you to work with the client and get the client out of the life or potentially implicate the exploiter in the abuse. Depending on the situation, therapists may need to be aware of protecting themselves as well as the client. Although literature discusses vicarious trauma as a mental health concern for professionals (Busch-Armendariz, Nsonwu, & Heffron, 2018), physical safety can also be a concern. The therapist's protection of personal safety means being mindful of dangers in a way that doesn't overwhelm or cause paranoia but that keeps the therapist alert and responsible. Examples of keeping safe (that are useful when working with any client) are having security measures present in the office, not leaving the office alone at night, and providing documentation and following through with any protective services that are required, such as a 24-hour watch on the client to prevent self-harm or going back to the abuser or alerting the police of a stalker. Good documentation and reasoning for therapeutic interactions are important if the client were to ever press charges against the abuser, because the abuser may try to discredit the client through slandering or discrediting the therapist and therapy process. Having a supportive network for therapeutic consultation and education can aid the therapist in maintaining ethical and legal security, as well as peace of mind. Plus, having a sealed record of the client's reported abusers, that another therapist holds on to in the event of any harm to the therapist, can help ensure that the abusers will not attempt any acts against the therapist directly. A note of reassurance for the therapist's and client's protection is that the more they each are out in the world doing things, being seen, being heard, and actively participating, the more visible they are and the less likely the abuser will attempt any harm to them because it will be apparent that the abuser caused the harm (Miller, 2012). Ultimately, the abuser does not want to get caught. Sanders (2015), a writer, advocate, and survivor states, "Safety is not just getting away from the abuser; safety comes from having a sense of security, awareness of self, and efficacy in one's self, too" (p. 126). As clinicians, the main goal is often to cultivate safety in the therapeutic space; yet there is a need to be aware of the dangers clients face outside the office doors and for our own safety as well in different environments.

Assessment Tools

Research recommends using assessment tools to assist professionals in identifying survivors of sex trafficking and commercial sexual exploitation (IOM & NCR, 2014). Assessment tools have been created to be used within different settings. Research recognizes that there is a lack of identifying survivors and training for service providers (IOM & NRC, 2014; Busch-Armendariz et al., 2018). Assessment tools can be used to assist children or adults who have potential of a history of sexual or physical abuse and may need further evaluation via a physician, mental health professional, or human trafficking advocate. If assessment tools cannot be found within the organization or agency, there are government and state websites that can assist in finding more information on ways to recognize signs of trafficking, such as lists posted by setting by the Polaris Project (2019) and the opportunity for online human trafficking awareness training by the U.S. Department of State (2019a).

Collaborating With Other Service Providers

Collaborating with other service providers is recommended (Alpert & Chin, 2017; Busch-Armendariz et al., 2018; Chang & Hayashi, 2017; IOM & NRC, 2013; Hopper, 2017). Examples include trusted resources in the community for advocacy or places to obtain clothes for interviews. Often system-involved youth will have a case manager or social worker whom the therapist will be in contact with. Some confidentiality concerns may be due to the collaborative agency or individual adhering to the Health Insurance Portability and Accountability Act Privacy Rule (Office for Civil Rights, 2013). Therefore, be sure that confidentiality is discussed with the other service providers; in some cases, the therapist may have a nondisclosure/confidentiality statement for them to sign. There will most likely be a need for collaboration and advocacy with other service providers or team members, such as chiropractors, massage therapists, social workers, primary care doctors, pain management clinicians, or psychiatrists.

For practitioners who do not have the same rigorous ethical guidelines as a mental health therapist, a discussion about confidentiality may be needed. Confidentiality needs to be addressed if the art therapy is done in the lobby or waiting room or if the artwork will be viewed by the other service providers. Be sure also that you are only known as the client's therapist by the people the client chooses to inform. Prior to facilitating these types of sessions, there should be a discussion to prepare the client and plan for ways to introduce and label the therapist to various people.

Collaborating in a Therapy Session

Treating people with a history of sexual abuse includes sensitive and flexible approaches to go where the client is able while maintaining safety. A little unorthodox is the idea of collaborating with other health professionals within the office during treatment or going to another health professional's office during treatment with a client. Art therapy can be effectively facilitated in a client's home (Chapman, 2014), hospital room (Malchiodi, 1999a, 1999b), or locations of the trauma for exposure therapy. In switching to any of these locations, there must be clear reasons why this is therapeutic for the client, and the therapist must be able to contain the space and professional boundaries when not in the therapy office. Working with youth may provide opportunities to meet outside the office when needed, such as a library or other safe public areas.

Collaborating with other service providers with the client's input may help the client establish safety/trust while sharing treatment information with the other health professional(s) or receiving the holistic care the client needs. At times, for the survivor to go to a medical doctor, X-ray appointment, or chiropractor can be overwhelming as a result of the trauma because the vulnerable thought of someone touching or examining the body causes the client to avoid/refuse the needed health treatments. Therefore, providing art treatment interventions and/or art therapy while at these appointments can be a way to mentally and physically prepare and engage the client in the process and help to reestablish health care as potentially safe types of physical touching and examination.

Vicarious Trauma

Therapists hearing stories of trauma, essentially the impact of repeated trauma, may cause impactful symptoms that can lead to vicarious trauma. Professionals consistently working with clients who have suffered traumatic experiences or victimization by individuals or systems may be personally affected by the exposures of stories and images that can result in secondary traumatic stress disorder, vicarious trauma, and burnout (Busch-Armendariz et al., 2018). Symptoms of secondary trauma have been identified to almost match the exact same symptoms of PTSD (Jenkins & Baird, 2002). Professionals who have worked with the trafficked population have noted their personal challenges with safety and vicarious trauma (Miller, 2012). In addition, it is important to note the normalcy of professionals to feel emotions when caring for vulnerable populations and to provide and receive support in self-care (Busch-Armendariz et al., 2018).

Conclusion

Due to a lack of clinical research in art therapy with survivors of sex trafficking, there are challenges in providing best practices in psychotherapy, and we encourage the use of evidence-based and trauma-informed approaches. Overall, the main goal with any intervention, therapy approach, or identification is to not cause further harm to any individual

(IOM & NCR, 2013). This chapter used professional experience in combination with research to share practices that we have used effectively with clients who have been sex trafficked and the various settings and collaborations that could be helpful for your clients. More research is needed in the field of art therapy and complementary modalities with the sex trafficked population. Providing care to survivors of sex trafficking includes identifying them and their needs, collaborating with other professionals, responding to meet their needs, and advocacy (Chaffee & English, 2015). This population has complex needs that are unique to each individual. The art therapist must make full use of all referrals to assist survivors. Therapists should take the opportunity to discuss collaboration with other service providers and subsequent benefits and risks with the client. Due to research findings, current literature, and our professional experiences in working with this population, we believe that art therapy can be immensely beneficial to individuals who have been sex trafficked. Art therapists possess the ability to utilize nonverbal communication, to understand the therapeutic art process in trauma recovery, and facilitate the mind/body integration that art encompasses.

References

Alpert, E. J., & Chin, S. E. (2017). Human trafficking: Perspectives on prevention. In M. Chisolm-Straker & H. Stoklosa (Eds.), *Human trafficking is a public issue: A paradigm expansion in the United States* (pp. 363–378). Cham, Switzerland: Springer.

American Psychiatric Association. (2013). *Diagnostic and statistical manual of mental disorders: DSM-5* (5th ed.). Arlington, VA: American Psychiatric Association.

Arrington, D., & Cherry, A. R. (2007). Healing trauma using the instinctual trauma response model. In D. Arrington (Ed.), *Art, angst, and trauma: Right brain interventions with developmental issues* (pp. 175–189). Springfield, IL: Charles C. Thomas.

Becker, C. L. (2015). Integrating art into group dissociative for adults with post-traumatic stress disorder from childhood sexual abuse: A pilot study. *Art Therapy: Journal of the American Art Therapy Association*, *32*(4), 190–196. https://doi.org/10.1080/07421656.2015.1091643

Brennan, J., Nguyen, V., & Southwest Americans with Disabilities Act. (2014). *Service animals and emotional support animals*. ADA National Network. Retrieved from https://adata.org/publication/service-animals-booklet

Brough, N., Lindenmeyer, A., Thistlethwaite, J., Lewith, G., & Stewart-Brown, S. (2015). Perspectives on the effects and mechanisms of craniosacral therapy: A qualitative study of users' views. *European Journal of Integrative Medicine*, *7*(2), 172–183.

Busch-Armendariz, N. B., Nsonwu, M., & Heffron, L. C. (2018). *Human trafficking: Applying research, theory, and case studies*. Thousand Oaks, CA: Sage Publications.

Castaneda, R. (2017, March 29). How yoga helps survivors of trauma: Trauma-informed yoga provides tools for people who deal with emotional scars, experts say. *U.S. News*. Retrieved from https://health.usnews.com/wellness/mind/articles/2017-03-29/how-yoga-helps-survivors-of-trauma

Chaffee, T., & English, A. (2015). Sex trafficking of adolescents and young people in the United States: Healthcare provider's role. *Current Opinion Obstetrics Gynecology*, 27(5), 339–344.

Chapman, L. (2014). *Neurobiologically informed trauma therapy with children and adolescents: Understanding mechanisms of change*. New York, NY: W.W. Norton and Company.

Chang, K. S. G., & Hayashi, A. S. (2017). The role of community health centers in addressing human trafficking. In M. Chisolm-Straker & H. Stoklosa (Eds.), *Human trafficking is a public issue: A paradigm expansion in the United States* (pp. 347–362). Cham, Switzerland: Springer.

Child Sexual Abuse Task Force and Research & Practice Core, National Child Traumatic Stress Network. (2004). *How to implement trauma-focused cognitive behavioral therapy*. Durham, NC and Los Angeles, CA: National Center for Child Traumatic Stress.

Clark, J. C., Lewis-Dmello, A., Anders, D., Parsons, A., Nguyen-Feng, V., Henn, L., & Emerson, D. (2014). Trauma-sensitive yoga as an adjunct mental health treatment in group therapy for survivors of domestic violence: A feasible study. *Complementary Therapies in Clinical Practice*, *20*(3), 152–158.

Cloitre, M., Garvert, D. W., Brewin, C. R., Bryant, R. A., & Maercker, A. (2013). Evidence for proposed ICD-11 PTSD and complex PTSD: A latent profile analysis. *European Journal of Psychotraumatology*, *4*(1). https://doi.org/10.3402/ejpt.v4i0.20706

Cohen, J. A., Mannarino, A. P., & Kinnish, K. (2017). Trauma-focused cognitive behavioral therapy for commercially sexually exploited youth. *Journal of Child & Adolescent Trauma*, *10*, 175–185.

Courtois, C. A. (2004). Complex trauma, complex reactions: Assessment and treatment. *Psychotherapy: Theory, Research, Practice Training*, *41*(4), 412–425.

Covington, S. S. (2015). Becoming trauma-informed: A core element in women's treatment. *Counselor Magazine*, *16*(4), 72–77.

Danylchuck, L. (2015). *Embodied healing: Using yoga to recover from trauma and extreme stress*. McLean, VA: Difference Press.

Dissanayake, E. (1995). *Homo aestheticus: Where art comes from and why*. Seattle, WA: University of Washington Press.

Dorothy, M. J., Middleton, W., Seager, L., Williams, M., & Chambers, R. (2017). Child abuse and neglect in complex dissociative disorder, abuse-related chronic PTSD, and mixed psychiatric samples. *Journal of Trauma and Dissociation*, *17*(2), 223–236.

Dovydaitis, T. (2010). Human Trafficking: The role of the health care provider. *J Midwifery Women's Health*, *55*(5), 462–467.

Ecker, B., Ticic, R., & Hulley, L. (2013). A Primer on memory reconsolidation and its psychotherapeutic use as a core process of profound change. *The Neuropsychotherapist*, *1*, 82–99.

Epstein, R., & González, T. (2017). Gender & trauma-somatic interventions for girls in juvenile justice: Implications for policy and practice. *The Center on Poverty and Inequality, The Art of Yoga Project*. Georgetown Law. Retrieved from www.law.georgetown.edu/poverty-inequality-center/wpcontent/uploads/sites/14/2017/08/gender-and-trauma-1.pdf

Family and Youth Service Bureau. (2015). Using a survivor leadership model to address human trafficking. *Runaway and Homeless Youth Training and Technical Assistance Center*. Retrieved from www.rhyttac.net/index.php?option=com_content&view=article&id=324:htr3-resource--using-a-survivor-leadership-model-to-address-humantrafficking&catid=27:rhy-resources&Itemid=125

Gantt, L., & Tinnin, L. (2007). Intensive trauma therapy of PTSD and dissociation: An outcome study. *The Arts and Psychotherapy*, *34*(1), 69–80.

Gantt, L., & Vesprini, M. E. (2017). Using the instinctual trauma response model in a military setting. In P. Howie (Ed.), *Art therapy with military populations: History, innovation, and applications* (pp. 147–156). New York, NY: Routledge.

Garlock, L. R. (2016). Stories in the cloth: Art therapy and narrative textiles. *Art Therapy: Journal of the American Art Therapy Association*, *33*(2), 58–66. https://doi.org/10.1080/07421656.2016.1164004

Gavin, D., & Thomson, C. (2017). Sex trafficking in one city: Traditional policing and Boston's shift to survivor-centered response. In M. Chisolm-Straker & H. Stoklosa (Eds.), *Human trafficking is a public issue: A paradigm expansion in the United States* (pp. 325–346). Cham, Switzerland: Springer.

Gibbons, K. (2015). *Integrating art therapy and yoga therapy: Yoga, art, and the use of intention*. London, UK: Jessica Kingsley Publishers.

Girls Educational and Mentoring Services. (2018). *Survivor leadership*. Retrieved from www.gems-girls.org/what-is-survivor-leadership

Gopal, A. (2019, February 27). Trauma and mental health consideration in a child sex trafficking response. In webinar National Criminal Justice Training Center *Missing and Exploited Children Training*. Retrieved from https://goto.webcasts.com/starthere.jsp?ei=1224771&tp_key=184764cd15

Greenbaum, J. (2017). Introduction to human trafficking: Who is affected? In M. Chisolm-Straker & H. Stoklosa (Eds.), *Human trafficking is a public health issue: A paradigm expansion in the United States* (pp. 1–14). Cham, Switzerland: Springer.

Hannan, M., Martin, K., Caceres, K., & Aledort, N. (2017). Children at risk: Foster care and human trafficking. In M. Chisolm-Straker & H. Stoklosa (Eds.), *Human trafficking is a public health issue: A paradigm expansion in the United States* (pp. 105–122). Cham, Switzerland: Springer.

Hass-Cohen, N., & Findlay, J. C. (2015). *Art therapy and the neuroscience of relationships, creativity and resilience*. New York, NY: W.W. Norton.

Hass-Cohen, N., Findlay, J. C., Carr, R., & Vanderlan, J. (2014). Check, change what you need to change and/or keep what you want: An art therapy neurobiological-based trauma protocol. *Art Therapy: Journal of the American Art Therapy Association*, *31*(2), 69–78. https://doi.org/10.1080/07421656.2014.903825

Herman, J. (1992). *Trauma and recovery*. New York, NY: Basic Books.

Hinz, L. D. (2009). *Expressive therapies continuum: A framework for using art in therapy*. New York, NY: Routledge.

Hinz, L. D. (2017, November 4). *The ECT at work: Art therapy and possible involved brain networks*. Lecture at Notre Dame de Namur University, Belmont, CA.

Hopper, E. K. (2017). The multimodal social ecological (MSE) approach: A trauma- informed framework for supporting trafficking survivors' psychosocial health. In M. Chisolm-Straker & H. Stoklosa (Eds.), *Human trafficking is a public health issue: A paradigm expansion in the United States* (pp. 153–184). Cham, Switzerland: Springer.

Howard, A., & Sutton, A. (2018). Safety planning with survivors of sex trafficking and commercial sexual exploitation. In A. J. Nichols, T. Edmonds, & E. Heil (Eds.), *Social work practice with survivors of sex trafficking and commercial sexual exploitation*. New York, NY: Columbia University Press.

Institute of Medicine [IOM], & National Research Council [NRC]. (2013). *Confronting commercial sexual exploitation and sex trafficking of minors in the United States*. Washington, DC: National Academies Press.

Institute of Medicine [IOM], & National Research Council [NRC]. (2014). *Confronting commercial sexual exploitation and sex trafficking of minors in the United States: A guide for the health care sector*. Washington, DC: National Academies Press.

International Organization for Migration [IM]. (2009). *Caring for trafficked persons: Guidance for health providers*. Retrieved from https://publications.iom.int/books/caring-traffickedpersons-guidance-health-providers

International Society for the Study of Trauma and Dissociation. (2011). Guidelines for treating dissociative identity disorder in adults, (3rd Rev. ed.). *Journal of Trauma and Dissociation*, *12*(2), 115–187.

Jenkins, S. R., & Baird, S. (2002). Secondary traumatic stress and vicarious trauma. A validation study. *Journal of Traumatic Stress*, *15*(5), 423–432.

Kapitan, L. (2015). Social action in practice: Shifting the ethnocentric lens in cross-cultural art therapy encounters. *Art Therapy: Journal of the American Art Therapy Association*, *32*(3), 104–111.

Kass, J. D., & Trantham, S. M. (2014). Perspectives from clinical neuroscience: Mindfulness and the therapeutic use of the arts. In L. Rappaport (Ed.), *Mindfulness and the arts therapies: Theory and practice* (pp. 288–315). London, UK: Jessica Kingsley Publishers.

Kimbrough, E., Magyari, T., Langenberg, P., Chesney, M., & Berman, B. (2010). Mindfulness intervention for child abuse survivors. *Journal of Clinical Psychology*, *66*(1), 17–33.

Leonard, J. (2017). Craniosacral therapy: Does it work? *Medical News Today*. Retrieved from https://www.medicalnewstoday.com/articles/318490.php

Levine, P. (1997). *Waking the tiger: Healing trauma*. Berkeley, CA: North Atlantic Books.

Lewis-O'Connor, A., & Alpert, E. J. (2017). Caring for survivors using a trauma-informed care framework. In M. Chisolm-Straker & H. Stoklosa (Eds.), *Human trafficking is a public health issue: A paradigm expansion in the United States* (pp. 309–323). Cham, Switzerland: Springer.

Lusebrink, V. B. (1996). Telling without talking: Art as a window into the world of multiple personality. *Art Therapy: Journal of the American Art Therapy Association*, *13*(3), 211–213.

Lusebrink, V. B. (2010). Assessment and therapeutic application of the expressive therapies continuum: Implications for brain structures and functions. *Art Therapy: Journal of the American Art Therapy Association*, *27*(4), 168–177. https://doi.org/10.1080/07421656.2010.10129380

Lusebrink, V. B., & Hinz, L. D. (2016). The expressive therapies continuum as a framework in the treatment of trauma. In J. L. King (Ed.), *Art therapy, trauma, and neuroscience: Theoretical and practical perspectives* (pp. 42–66). New York, NY: Routledge.

Lutnick, A. (2016). *Domestic minor sex trafficking: Beyond victims and villains*. New York, NY: Columbia University Press.

Macias-Konstantopoulos, W., & Ma, Z. B. (2017). Physical health of human trafficking survivors: Unmet essentials. In M. Chisolm-Straker & H. Stoklosa (Eds.), *Human trafficking is a public health issue: A paradigm expansion in the United States* (pp. 185–210). Cham, Switzerland: Springer.

Malchiodi, C. A. (1999a). Introduction art therapy and medicine: Powerful partners in healing. In C. A. Malchiodi (Ed.), *Medical art therapy for adults* [Kindle DX version]. Retrieved from www.amazon.com/Medical-Therapy-Adults-Cathy-Malchiodiebook/dp/B0033WTE04/ref=sr_1_4?keywords=Medical+art+therapy+for+adults&qid=1553038689&s=gateway&sr=8-4

Malchiodi, C. A. (1999b). *Medical art therapy with children*. London, UK: Jessica Kingsley.

Miller, A. (2012). *Healing the unimaginable: Treating ritual abuse and mind control*. London, UK: Karnac Books Ltd.

National Alliance on Mental Illness. (2019). Retrieved from www.nami.org/learn-more/mental-health-conditions/dissociative-disorders

Office for Civil Rights. (2013, July 26). *Summary of the HIPPA privacy rule*. United States Department of Health and Human Services. Retrieved from www.hhs.gov/hipaa/for-professionals/privacy/laws-regulations/index.html

Ogden, P., & Fisher, J. (2015). *Sensorimotor psychotherapy: Interventions for trauma and attachment*. New York, NY: W.W. Norton and Company, Inc.

Ortner, N. (2013). *The tapping solution: A revolutionary system for stress-free living*. USA: Hay House, Inc.

Parnell, L. (2008). *Tapping in: A step by step guide to activating your healing resources through bilateral stimulation*. Boulder, CO: Sounds True.

Patihis, L., Frenda, S., & Loftus, E. (2018). False memory tasks do not reliably predict other false memories. *Psychology of Consciousness: Theory, Research, and Practice*, *5*(2), 140–160. https://doi.org/10.1037/cns0000147

Peacock, J., Chur-Hansen, A., & Winefield, H. (2012). Mental health implications of human attachment to companion animals. *Journal of Clinical Psychology*, *68*(3), 292–303. https://doi.org/10.1002/jclp.20866

Perry, B., & Szalavitz, M. (2010). *Born for love: Why empathy is essential and endangered*. New York, NY: Harper.

Pifalo, T. (2002). Pulling out the thorns: Art therapy with sexually abused children and adolescents. *Art Therapy: Journal of the American Art Therapy Association*, *19*(1), 12–22.

Pifalo, T. (2007). Jogging the cogs: Trauma-focused art therapy and cognitive behavioral therapy with sexually abused children. *Art Therapy: Journal of the American Art therapy Association*, *24*(4), 170–175.

Pifalo, T. (2009). Mapping the maze: An art therapy intervention following disclosure of sexual abuse. *Art Therapy: Journal of the American Art therapy Association*, *26*(1), 12–18. https://doi.org/10.1080/07421656.2009.10129313

Polaris Project. (2010). Community model action plan. *National Human Trafficking Resource Center*. Retrieved from https://polarisproject.org

Polaris Project. (2019). *Recognize the signs*. Retrieved from https://polarisproject.org/human-trafficking/recognize-signs

Price, M., Spinazzola, J., Musicaro, R., Turner, J., Suvak, M., Emerson, D., & van der Kolk, B. (2017). Effectiveness of an extended yoga treatment for women with chronic posttraumatic stress disorder. *The Journal of Alternative and Complementary Medicine*, *23*(4), 300–309.

Putnam, K. T., Harris, W. W., & Putnam, F. W. (2013). Synergistic childhood adversities and complex adult psychopathology. *Journal of Traumatic Stress*, *26*, 435–442. https://doi.org/10.1002/jts.21833

Rappaport, L. (2009). *Focusing-oriented art therapy: Assessing the body's wisdom and creative intelligence*. London, UK: Jessica Kingsley.

Ross, C. A. (2015). Extreme skeptics about DID: Why they're wrong. In *Trauma and dissociation conference*. Seattle, WA: Ivory Gardens Nonprofit Corporation.

Ross, C. A., & Farley, M. (2003). Dissociation among women in prostitution. *Journal of Trauma Practice*, 2, 199–212.

Ross, C. A., & Halpern, N. (2009). *Trauma model therapy: A treatment approach for trauma, dissociation and complex comorbidity*. Richardson, TX: Manitou Communications, Inc.

Sanar Wellness Institute & Polaris Project. (2015, November). *Promising practices: An overview of trauma-informed therapeutic support for survivors of human trafficking*. Retrieved from https://polarisproject.org/sites/default/files/Sanar-Promising-Practices.pdf

Sanders, S. J. (2015). *Sex trafficking prevention: A trauma-informed approach for parents and professionals*. Scottsdale, AZ: Unhooked Books.

Schore, A. N. (2009). Relational trauma and the developing right brain: An interface of psychoanalytic self-psychology and neuroscience. *Self and Systems: Annals of the New York Academy of Sciences*, 189–203. https://doi.org/10.1111/j.1749-6632.2009.04474.x

Shapiro, F. (2001). *Eye movement desensitization and reprocessing: Basic principles, protocols, and procedures* (2nd ed.). New York, NY: The Guildford Press.

Shenk, C. E., Putnam, F. W., & Knoll, G. J. (2012). Experiential avoidance and the relationship between child maltreatment and PTSD symptoms: Preliminary evidence. *Child Abuse and Neglect*, *36*, 118–126.

Siegel, D., & Bryson, T. P. (2011). *The whole brain child: 12 revolutionary strategies to nurture your child's developing mind*. New York, NY: Bantam Books.

Sigel, B., Benton, A. H., Lynch, C. E., & Kramer, T. L. (2013). Characteristics of 17 statewide initiatives to disseminate trauma-focused cognitive-behavioral therapy. *Psychological Trauma: Theory, Research, Practice, and Policy*, *5*(4), 323–333.

Spring, D. (2001). *Image and mirage: Art therapy with dissociative clients*. Springfield, IL: Charles C. Thomas Publisher LTD.

Spring, D. (2004). Thirty-year study links neuroscience, specific trauma, PTSD, image conversion, and language translation. *Art Therapy: Journal of the American Art Therapy Association*, *21*(4), 200–209.

Smolenski, C., & Ingerman, S. (2017). Trafficking of children within the United States. In M. Chisolm-Straker & H. Stoklosa (Eds.), *Human trafficking is a public health issue: A paradigm expansion in the United States* (pp. 93–102). Cham, Switzerland: Springer.

Tantia, J. F. (2014). Mindfulness and dance/movement therapy for treating trauma. In L. Rappaport (Ed.), *Mindfulness and the art therapies: Theory and practice* (pp. 95–106). London, UK: Jessica Kingsley Publishers.

Task Force on Trafficking of Women and Girls. (2014). *Report of the task force on trafficking of women and girls*. Washington, DC: American Psychological Association. Retrieved from www.apa.org/pi/women/programs/traffciking/reports.aspx

Trevleaven, D. A. (2018). *Trauma-sensitive mindfulness: Practices for safe and transformational healing*. New York, NY: W.W. Norton and Company.

Upledger Institute International. (2019, March 13). *Discover craniosacral therapy*. Retrieved from www.upledger.com/therapies/index.php

U.S. Department of State. (2019a). *Human trafficking awareness training: Tip 101*. Retrieved from www.state.gov/j/tip/training/index.htm

U.S. Department of State. (2019b). *Victims of trafficking and violence protection act of 2000*. Retrieved from www.state.gov/j/tip/laws/61124.htm

van der Kolk, B. (2014). *The body keeps the score: Brain, mind, and the healing of trauma*. New York, NY: Penguin Group.

van der Kolk, B. (2017). EMDR vs. fluoxetine vs. placebo. *Evolution of psychotherapy conference*. Lecture at Anaheim Convention Center, Anaheim, CA.

Walker, K. (2013). *Ending the commercial sexual exploitation of children: A call for multi-system collaboration in California*. California Child Welfare Council. Retrieved from https://youthlaw.org/wp-content/uploads/2015/01/Ending-CSEC-A-Call-for-Multi-System_Collaboration-in-CA.pdf

Williams, L. M., & Frederick, M. E. (2009). *Pathways into and out of commercial sexual victimization of children: Understanding and responding to sexually exploited teens*. Lowell, MA: University of Massachusetts Lowell.

Wilson, C. (2019). *Art based communication for individuals with dissociative spectrum disorders*. Unpublished doctoral Dissertation, Notre Dame de Namur University, Belmont, CA.

PART II

POPULATIONS TARGETED BY SEX TRAFFICKING AND THE ROLE OF ART THERAPY IN RECOVERY

FIVE

Beauty in the Disorder

Art Therapy With Sex Trafficking Survivors in Ohio, United States

Mary K. Kometiani

Introduction to Sex Trafficking in Ohio

The United States is one of the top-ten areas for human trafficking (Hepburn & Simon, 2013). In rural, suburban, and urban areas, men, women, and children are trafficked for sex throughout the United States (Polaris, 2015; Shelley, 2010). The midwestern state of Ohio, ranking fourth in the country for human trafficking, is a center in the industry of human exploitation (Bivins, 2018; National Human Trafficking Hotline, 2018b). Ohio's high trafficking numbers are due to the abundance of migrant worker camps within the state and the availability of pornography studios and stores in addition to the accessible state highways, which connect major cities that are significant in domestic sex trafficking networks (Chohaney, 2016). The severe problem in Ohio human trafficking results from these three major causes:

- Ohio has the most truck stops of any state on the broad freeway system;
- the state ranks fifth for strip clubs across the country; and
- there is a staggering high unemployment rate and resultant poverty issues in Ohio.

(Garabrandt, 2016)

Between major cities in other states (Detroit/Pittsburgh/Chicago), an open border with Canada to the north along Lake Erie, and its shipping routes, Ohio offers wide accessibility to vulnerable immigrants and underprivileged people (Williamson et al., 2012). Lastly, Ohio's opioid crisis also contributes to trafficking because addiction is a verified cause for the majority of trafficking cases (Provance, 2018). Ohio's prominent problem with human sex trafficking is escalating due to its location and accessibility, poverty and unemployment issues, substance abuse dilemma, and the extensive number of pornography studios, strip clubs, and truck stops.

Sex trafficking in Ohio continues to expand, although convictions are thought to be highly underreported by the Ohio attorney general (Provance, 2018). In 2017, the number of trafficking investigations increased up to nearly 50% from the previous year (Provance, 2018). The Ohio Trafficking in Persons Study Commission Research and Analysis Sub-Committee Report approximated that over 1,000 minor Ohio girls are trafficked every year (Williamson et al., 2012), and more than 4,000 are at risk for victimization (Anderson, Kulig, Sullivan, & Farrell, 2019). The National Human Trafficking Hotline (2018a) reported 288 sex trafficking cases from Ohio in 2017. These high statistics demonstrate that Ohio has an ineffective response to trafficking; responders to trafficking are uneducated and unprepared; perpetrators receive minimal consequences; and there are many vulnerable youth in Ohio (Williamson et al., 2012). Statistics show that Ohio's issues with sex trafficking are expanding at an alarming rate with even more individuals in jeopardy of exploitation.

This chapter provides an overview of the trauma-informed approach and reasons why this approach is essential when working with survivors of human sex trafficking. Several examples from a safe house for female survivors of sex trafficking illustrate the clear and compelling benefits of art therapy within trauma-informed treatment. Finally, the chapter provides recommendations for best practices when facilitating art therapy with sex trafficked survivors.

Trauma-Informed Approach for Sex Trafficked Survivors

A trauma-informed approach to care is required to adequately support survivors (United States Department of State, 2018). It is crucial to identify sex trafficked survivors as trauma survivors because trauma affects daily life routines and daily existence (Stotts & Ramey, 2009). Trauma from sexual exploitation profoundly alters the mind, produces various physical reactions, and affects a survivor's views of the core of the self, relationships, belief system, and worldview (see Chapter 2 for more details regarding the trauma of sex trafficking). Within trauma-informed care, the therapist

- recognizes trauma as a major experience rather than only a one-time-occurrence;
- holistically views the survivor and understands the individual's behaviors as ways to survive the trauma experience; and
- offers an authentic and sincere partnership that instills the power back to the survivor through a strength-based approach.

(Harris & Fallot, 2001)

In a trauma-informed approach, the survivor's actions are contextualized and understood from a trauma-perspective rather than seen as a separate unconnected issue apart from the individual; behaviors, interactions, and experiences are related to trauma responses (United States Department of State, 2018). Personal control that was taken during the traumatic experience can be regained, returned, and reinstated to the survivor through therapy. Trauma-informed care recognizes the importance of cultural competence, integrated care, and that recovery is possible through healing relationships, experiencing empowerment, and feeling safe (Guarino, Soares, Konnath, Clervil, & Bassuk, 2009). Due to the many complex facets and effects of trauma, sexually exploited individuals require trauma-informed care because, first and foremost, this therapy avoids retraumatization and revictimization, and it prioritizes safety for the survivor.

Safety

Safety is the foundation of trauma-informed therapeutic work with sex trafficked survivors. Providing safety as a therapist is of utmost importance in trauma care, and this is developed over time through an honest, trusting, and authentic partnership (Harris & Fallot, 2001). In order to establish security in the therapeutic relationship, therapists need to demonstrate unconditional positive regard and empathy and thereby build trust with a survivor; providing opportunities for clients to disclose personal details in a safe, nonjudgmental environment can increase the survivor's insight and facilitate growth (Litam, 2017). Survivors require a supportive, success-oriented, and empowering environment that is based on their strengths and their ability to endure (Harris & Fallot, 2001). By establishing a protected and nurturing environment for a trafficking survivor to develop reliance in the therapeutic relationship in addition to providing interventions that are empowering and strength-based, therapists initiate and instill the individual's survivorship.

Trauma-Informed Art Therapy®

Art therapy has many imperative therapeutic gains for sex trafficked survivors, such as increasing focus and positive self-worth, establishing connection to others and reconnection with the self, and experiencing empowerment and new purpose (Clawson, Salomon, & Grace, 2008; Garlock, 2016; Kometiani & Farmer, 2019; Sanar Wellness Institute & Polaris, 2015; Tan, 2012). Trauma-informed art therapy® provides a neurodevelopmental approach to reconnect emotional and sensory (implicit) and factual and declarative (explicit) memory, stabilize an individual's response to stress through self-regulation, and assist with trauma assimilation and healing (Malchiodi, 2015a). Creating art offers a very soothing practice that teaches skills of relaxation and mindfulness through the involvement of a multitude of senses, helping a survivor learn ways to manage their reactions and stabilize responses. Traumatized and exploited individuals process and integrate the broken and confusing trauma recollection through reconnecting trauma memories. Trauma-informed art therapy® emphasizes

- developing safety and consistent expectations,
- empowerment through opportunities to experience a sense of control,
- learning new skills to attain mastery and build self-confidence,
- storytelling to reconnect trauma experiences,
- building support and positive attachment through relationship, and
- enhancing resilience.

(Malchiodi, 2011, 2013, 2015b, 2017)

Most survivors of sex trafficking have survived psychological, emotional, physical, and mental torture; were forced into exploitation against their will; and require the essential aspects of trauma-informed treatment to assist in their recoveries. Malchiodi's method (2011, 2015a, 2015b, 2017) of trauma-informed art therapy® focuses on providing stabilization, self-efficacy, empowerment, attunement, and trauma reintegration while offering the potential to visually narrate the inexpressible and inconceivable. Survivors need to learn they are not to blame and that they are victimized from trauma beyond their control. By providing a success-oriented, predictable, and consistent environment, therapists can help survivors learn to expect a routine, develop safety, and feel a sense of control while achieving mastery (Malchiodi, 2015b). The process of the therapist fostering a healthy relationship with a traumatized individual is the most valuable goal in expressive therapy, because healing happens in relationships (Steele & Malchiodi, 2012). When this basis for therapy is provided, survivors feel protected, empowered, respected, and supported. As a result, trauma recovery through storytelling and memory reintegration is possible.

Case Examples of Art Therapy With Trafficked Survivors

Participants

The following case examples are from a newly established art therapy program that took place in a faith-based ministry safe house in northern Ohio. The goals of the trauma-informed shelter, a 10-bed facility, focused on providing restoration, healing, education, and reintegration skills. The bimonthly support group for survivors of sex trafficking was offered by a registered, board certified art therapist since 2017. The shelter was open to adult females 18 years of age and older, and the participant ages ranged from 19–49 (M = 37). The art therapy participant numbers fluctuated from four to nine participants (M = 6.5) through the program's initial year. Although the women were able to stay for up to two years total in the safe house, the average stay was five months. The group sessions were 1.5 hours long and included art making and discussion.

Setting

The art therapy support group was provided in the communal dining area that offered natural lighting and a large table for art therapy participation. As the attendance of all the women residents was mandated with participation encouraged, this space became closed and confidential during session times. Through facilitation of specific and structured interventions, the art therapist focused on establishing a safe space for the women to make personalized choices and receive individualized, nonjudgmental, and empathetic support.

It was crucial that the participants were involved in other essential individual and group counseling services to effectively cover their psychological and emotional needs. In addition to the bimonthly art therapy group session, the female survivors received extensive psychological, physical, and spiritual care. Support services included weekly trauma counseling, grief counseling, and equine therapy; bimonthly dialectical behavior therapy groups; trauma-informed yoga twice a week; addiction support; dental and medical care; educational and vocational classes; and other activities, such as career assistance, parenting classes, baking and cooking classes, mentoring, and Bible studies.

During the art therapy session, the participants were prompted with various strategic and success-oriented interventions. At the end of group, they were invited to share their artwork and responses with the other participants. They were advised that the emphasis of art therapy is not on the final image but on the thoughtful process of creating. In addition, the processing time following the art making could provide further reflections, understanding, and awareness. The planned interventions were devised by the art therapist and based on Malchiodi's (2011, 2015a, 2015b, 2017) recommendations and Herman's (1997) trauma recovery stages. Goals of the art therapy treatment for the survivors were establishing safety in the group setting; experiencing empowerment, building a community of support, and improving self-worth; and providing opportunity for trauma processing. The art therapy treatment intended to improve social connection, decrease depression and anxiety, increase a sense of control, facilitate coping with life transition, and instill hope for the participants.

Framework

The following art therapy case examples were based on Herman's (1997) three phases of trauma recovery. Herman's (1997) trauma recovery care is recommended through gradual and nonlinear phases (a) survivor safety, (b) trauma memory and loss processing, and (c) adjustment to transition and establishing connection to others. Only possible through healing relationships, recovery focuses on survivor empowerment and creating new connections (Herman, 1997). The following case examples utilized art therapy group sessions because this format provides sex trafficking survivors with the potential to establish restorative relationships, experience a sense of control, and collectively experience healing together. The trauma recovery approach applied through the art therapy group session format proved a solid foundation of support for the traumatized survivors. Within a secure and communal setting, sex trafficked survivors were able to connect to their inner truths, their traumatic pasts, and fellow female survivors, thus instilling the way for recovery.

Therapeutic Process

Trauma Recovery Phases

Survivor Safety

Survivors feel unsafe in their physical bodies and with others, and they feel emotionally and mentally out of control (Herman, 1997). Trauma takes away an individual's sense of control; restoring control and power to the survivor is a primary rule in recovery (Herman, 1997). Trauma recovery can only occur through experiencing an inner sense of safety and self-control. Additionally, ensuring a protected environment and providing opportunities to experience security through relationships is of the utmost importance in art therapy group treatment for sex trafficked survivors. Lastly, providing opportunities to experience empowerment enables the survivor to experience a sense of power that was lost in trauma.

Although appearing unassuming, Teal, a Caucasian in her 30s, had a striking appearance with long blue hair and pretty features. Severely depressed, she often did not meet others' eye contact and presented as downcast. Teal had an extensive history of trafficking and was held captive in a basement for six months. She suffered from suicidal ideation, sleep issues, agitation, significant lack of trust in others, and avoided any physical touch. Throughout her stay, she coped with extensive and time-consuming legal issues from another city's court system, the site of her trafficking.

Due to the effects of her complex trauma, Teal restricted her verbal engagement in the group setting; however, she was able to utilize the art as a safe form of expression to tell her story and experience empowerment. In one memorable session, the group was asked to draw a place that represents safety, and participants were provided with drawing supplies, including markers, pencils, pastels, and drawing paper sized 28 x 44 cm. Using a symmetrical presentation and a few colors, Teal wrote phrases describing her trauma-inflicted viewpoint of her personal safety. Through a reticent processing of her image, Teal said that she only feels safe where she is now living and in her counselor's office at the trauma therapy agency. Teal used the art to illustrate how her trauma had affected her worldview as she inscribed "trust no one" in her image, and she stated that she doesn't feel safe with anyone. She even seemed tearful when other group members attempted to comfort her because of the honest and desolate depiction of her message.

During another group session, Teal was given alcohol inks and ink cardstock (sized 11 x 14 cm) and asked to express her feelings. Teal volunteered, "my brain is a mess;" however, she also specified she wanted to include bright colors to show the "beauty in this disorder" (Figure 5.1). Other than her evocative metaphoric message, she did not engage in any other verbal processing with the group. Often, survivors view themselves as chaotic disorder with erratic behavior because their traumatic pasts do not make sense (Harris & Fallot, 2001). Because many decisions were made by others in their past or while under the influence of alcohol or drugs, a survivor's situation may be difficult to rationalize to others. When given an opportunity to express her feelings using alcohol inks, Teal was able to connect her confusing life experience and the mental effects of trauma while emphasizing her existential hope for the future through using a promising and bright colorful design. Although the trauma of sex trafficking is particularly repulsive and devastating to those it affects, through her image, Teal expressed an ability to recognize some affirmation in her life, and this acknowledgment represented an encouraging step in her journey.

Figure 5.1 Teal's painting expressing beauty in the disorder

Due to Teal's extensive history of trafficking, establishing safety and trust with others remained the main priority in her art therapy treatment. The structured interventions provided throughout her art therapy treatment enabled her to express herself and her feelings through the art materials. Although Teal resisted verbally expressing her vulnerability with the group members, she was provided with a protected environment to allow her to move at her own pace and gradually share through the art interventions with the group and the art therapist. Teal was continually provided with opportunities to experience empowerment, and art therapy provided her with a way to be in control of her story and her disclosure. Although Teal's grave trauma could not be reversed, she was able to gradually advance in art therapy treatment evidenced by sharing an honest expression of her changed worldview and her hopefulness, which displayed a newfound distance between Teal and her trauma.

Trauma and Loss Processing

During the second phase of recovery, the survivor communicates the incommunicable (Herman, 1997). Sharing one's trauma narrative is part of the recovery process, and the expressive arts provide a nonverbal form of communication when verbalization is not possible. When words fail during the narration of the survivor's trauma story, art provides a continual connection through nonverbal expression (Herman, 1997). During this time, the therapist is validating and normalizing responses and sharing the burden of the story (Herman, 1997). During trauma storytelling, the therapist attempts to ease the survivor's troubles by providing emotional and verbal support. Opportunely, art therapy in trauma treatment extends a nonverbal and nonthreatening form of communication for trauma storytelling, and, consequently, the image created is separate from the survivor and signifies an externalization of the burden.

Petite but tough looking, Cathryn was a middle-aged Caucasian. She arrived at the safe house with paranoid thoughts of her being followed and unsure about her safety in the community. As she adjusted to her new living situation, she admitted her frustrations with her memory and not remembering her trafficking past very clearly. During her stay, she dealt with triggering trauma flashbacks and sporadic memory retrieval. Cathryn often felt overwhelmed by her thoughts and her lack of ability to cope, underlined by a constant fear that her traffickers might target her family in retaliation of her departure. She also dealt with physiological issues resulting from her past drug use, including recurrent headaches and a skin disorder. Although she was initially reserved and quiet in art therapy sessions, Cathryn appeared more comfortable with the group setting and established relationships with the participants as time progressed.

After several months of art therapy treatment, Cathryn was provided with an opportunity to express her trauma. The art therapist shared the example poem "I Am From" (Ball & Rosenbluth, 2008), and the group was encouraged to write expressively and create an image about their personal pasts and prompted to write in regard to their life events, family, neighborhood, etc. The group participants were provided with lined paper and writing utensils, drawing supplies to include markers and colored pencils, and collage supplies, including an array of magazines, glue sticks, and scissors. Malchiodi (2015b) advised using drawing and collage supplies with journaling as an art option when choosing materials to accompany an emotional topic because these materials and images provide more power to the client. The survivors, whose voices had been frequently silenced, connected easily with the potential of the art materials available, which served to inspire ideas and suggest words for their journaling.

This structured intervention allowed for trauma processing and grief expressions to be safely communicated and contained through images. The format allowed the survivors to write and create in an honest and nonthreatening format and to exert control by choosing what information from their past to share with the group and with the art therapist. It is crucial that clients are empowered in therapy and reminded that they may talk as much as they want or as little as they want in the session (Malchiodi, 2017). The survivors were given the opportunity to tell their stories and hear others' stories, thus helping to build a community of support through establishing connection and reducing isolation. During this pivotal group, Cathryn recalled her journey:

> Knowing the difference between rite [right] and wrong, choosing to go down the path of self[-]destruction because you don't want to feel or hurt anymore.
> Having dark shadows following you everywhere you go.
> Feeling trapped with no escape no matter what direction you turn.
> Looking for a light, a glimpse of hope on this never ending merry go round of torture[.]
> My fight to escape the darkness, my will to survive the depths of hell, never ending.
> Finally a glimpse of light, my new journey has begun.

A defining moment for Cathryn was as she bravely read aloud her poem that detailed her complex and grim past and expressed her trafficked imprisonment through metaphors and imagery of darkness, shadows, pain, and continuous torment. Her symbols of the "path of self-destruction," "the merry-go-round of torture," and "hell, never ending" express the spiraling process of her journey while her words exemplified feeling "trapped" within a "fight" and persisting with a "will to survive," identifying her enduring perspective. Cathryn communicated her ability to find light over the darkness, discovering hope as she fought and persevered to start anew—"finally a glimpse of light"—a symbol of salvation,

Figure 5.2 Cathryn's drawing illustrating her salvation

redemption for her new and amended independent life. Cathryn's pencil drawing (Figure 5.2) entitled "My Salvation," accompanied her narrative's message of achieving liberation and hope though a large image of a cross, calling to mind her personal crucifixion and resurrection to a new life. Cathryn's illustration portrayed her experience of forgiveness, unconditional love, and grace as her newfound religious beliefs relieved her of the burdensome past.

When a group member makes her trauma story public, the group experiences a universality through offering connection and a symbolic welcome back to the world (Herman, 1997). The group participants listened and supported Cathryn, and they acknowledged her suffering, loss, and strides toward recovery. Healing begins when trauma silence is over (van der Kolk, 2014), and Cathryn demonstrated progress in her trauma healing by sharing the depth of her metaphorical and meaningful narrative with the group, ending her silence and isolation, and establishing trusting relationships with the other participants. Cathryn's poem represented an externalized and concise representation of her troubling and complicated past while being exploited. As a tangible vessel of Cathryn's painful past, her writing might, hopefully, have represented a separation from her trauma and her journey forward away from that past. Cathryn's image visually signified her faith saving her life and redeeming her from the dark, crippling burden of her personal history.

Adjustment to Transition and Establishing Connection to Others

In the third recovery stage, the survivor creates a new sense of self and saves her world, because she is no longer controlled by her trauma (Herman, 1997). During this stage, the survivor experiences success controlling her trauma rather than being controlled by this life-defining event. During this period, the survivor is ready to engage energetically in the world, and the survivor usually feels contentment for her life as she faces her recovery (Herman, 1997). The final phase demonstrates a renewed sense of self and a higher level of progression toward self-control in moving forward from the trauma experience. Examples of this phase are illustrated through subsequent sessions for both Teal and Cathryn.

Later in Teal's art therapy treatment, she was provided with painting supplies, including a 5 x 5 cm mini canvas and easel. In this session, the group members were asked to paint what provides inspiration. Teal chose to share that she is a "survivor" (Figure 5.3). Although she did not participate in verbalizing or processing about her image, she did nonverbally communicate her strength and motivation in enduring trauma through her painting. After using violet, vivid pink, golden yellow, and navy to stipple over the light-blue background, in the middle of her colorful pattern Teal wrote "Survivor" in prominent black paint that encompassed the width of her canvas. She also used the rich pink to paint her easel, ensuring that the colors in her painting radiated. Using bright colors in the appearance of commemoration, the group witnessed her expression of persistence and bravery. Pride in being a survivor is a sign of healthy adaption to trauma, empowerment, and growth (Levine, 1997). Teal's image showed her progress in her acceptance of her new identity as a fighter who endured incomprehensible suffering and unwarranted mistreatment. Survivors need to take control back through engaging with others in the present and by being honest with themselves as survivors (van der Kolk, 2014). Although the effects of Teal's dire trauma could not be undone, she was able to exhibit empowerment and experience a new sense of truth through expressing her acceptance as a survivor through art therapy treatment.

Figure 5.3 Teal's mini canvas representing her identity as a survivor

As she continued to advance in her art therapy sessions, Cathryn was able to experience a renewed sense of worth through the intervention of collaging inner truths that she needs to infuse within herself to heal further. Her collage portrayed two positive self-thoughts: "I am worthy" and "my body is sacred." She also used an image of a cross to demonstrate that her faith is central in her new identity. Her current feelings of peace were conveyed through serene outdoor scenes. A picture of a couple watching the sunset together communicated her hopes to experience a loving relationship one day. Cathryn's religious devotion facilitated new purpose in her life to feel deserving and interested in romantic companionship. She commented that she is working on moving on from her past, and although every day feels like a struggle to her, she attempts to move forward with motivation for her future. Cathryn demonstrated growth through her treatment through discovering a new identity of self-worth, finding reconciliation and acceptance in her past, establishing future relationship goals, and maintaining motivation for personal progression. Through art therapy in the group setting, Cathryn discovered her inner strength, and by modeling openness, she emotionally bonded to others and contributed to their experience. As she became vulnerable with others, Cathryn participated in forming a healing community through giving and receiving support.

These two case examples illustrate the benefits that are achieved when art therapy treatment within a trauma-informed approach is tailored after Herman's (1997) recovery stages. When survivors of sex trafficking are in a protected environment and have the opportunity to experience safety with other group members, an increased sense of self-worth and the acceptance of a new identity as a survivor are possible. Hope for the future and beauty in the chaos becomes conceivable for those who are traumatized, oppressed, and abused in countless ways. An art therapy group setting decreases isolation and increases connection, as the participants are engaging in a common action; provides time for processing about personal emotions, past loss, and trauma; helps the traumatized survivors feel heard and supported through listening to each other's stories; and builds relationships through relating, supporting, and being comforted by one another. Art therapy creates an empowering environment for survivors to retrieve the control that was lost through traumatic experiences. Survivors reclaim their voice and identity, which have been ignored and silenced, through constructing personally meaningful images and creating beauty in a recovering community.

Conclusion

Trauma from being sexually exploited leaves perpetual inner wounds that cannot be healed quickly. These deep injuries affect the survivor's view of the self and of the world. One of trauma's most destructive effects is the loss of purpose in an individual's life due to damage of her inner truth (van der Kolk, 2014). Trauma from trafficking utterly devastates an individual's core identity and strips away the sense of self, whereas recovery is the rebuilding of a new constructive sense of self (Herman, 1997). The trauma of sex trafficking requires a recovering survivor to construct a new identity, purpose, and worldview.

Individuals preserve the innate capability to heal from trauma, and trauma can be healed (Levine, 1997). Trauma healing is possible through connections and rebuilding community (van der Kolk, 2014). In a safe group setting, survivors learn that they are not alone through experiencing a sense of joining, bonding, and affirmation with others. Collective empowerment recognizes each survivor as an equal participant who contributes, nurtures, and bears witness; the group is powerful together and provides a healing force for each member to benefit (Herman, 1997). The group setting offers an effectively supportive environment of shared strength to survivors of sex trafficking.

As it is often not possible to verbalize trauma (van der Kolk, 2014), art provides communication when words fail. The women represented in these cases, through both adaptive and maladaptive ways, have demonstrated strength in surviving. They have lived and survived unbelievable and vicious accounts of trauma. Teal's story exemplified that art therapy provides a sense of choice and control to begin the healing journey, provides an outlet for undisguised emotional processing to resolve emotional trauma, and instills a sense of hope as Teal accepted her identity as a survivor. The progression of Cathryn's art therapy treatment demonstrated that art therapy offers the opportunity to reintegrate trauma, experience a sense of self-worth and self-forgiveness through an acceptance of the past to enable recovery, and enhance resilience through establishing a community of support. Through art therapy, the survivors continued to persevere, revealing their bravery in sharing their heartrending stories: how they are drastically changed, their lives are altered, and how they are also regaining control over themselves and securing their new identities. The survivors reconnected to their chaotic, traumatizing pasts, and found hope, acceptance, and beauty in themselves and each other.

Recommendations for Best Practice

1. Survivors of sex trafficking have experienced traumatic pasts that affect their identities, belief systems, and relationships, and art therapy treatment within trauma-informed care is a fundamental part of a survivor's opportunity to recover.
2. Safety is of greatest importance in art therapy treatment for trafficked survivors. To avoid retraumatization and revictimization, therapy progresses gradually due to the individual's control and extent of traumatization.

3. Trauma takes away one's ability to feel in control, and empowerment in therapy gives the power back to the survivor. This active participation is a crucial aspect of the healing process.
4. Expressive art therapy provides a dynamic, engaging, and structured process that offers the potential to express the inexpressible.
5. Together, the externalized, tangible product created in expressive art therapy that separates the trauma from the future with collective support provided by therapist and group members makes trauma recovery possible in art therapy.

References

Anderson, V. R., Kulig, T. C., Sullivan, C. J., & Farrell, A. (2019, February 1). *Estimating the prevalence of human trafficking in Ohio: Executive summary report*. Retrieved from: https://humantrafficking.ohio.gov/links/Ohio_Human_Trafficking_Prevalence_Study_Executive_Summary.pdf

Ball, B., & Rosenbluth, B. (2008). *Expect respect: A school-based program for preventing teen dating violence and promoting safe and healthy relationships*. Austin, TX: SafePlace.

Bivins, B. (2018, January 17). Ohio ranks fourth in the country for human trafficking cases. *Cleveland 19 News*. Retrieved from www.cleveland19.com/story/37287986/ohio-ranks-fourth-in-the-country-for-human-trafficking-cases

Chohaney, M. L. (2016). Minor and adult domestic sex trafficking risk factors in Ohio. *Journal of the Society for Social Work and Research*, *7*(1), 117–141. https://doi.org/10.1086/685108

Clawson, H. J., Salomon, A., & Grace, L. G. (2008, March 15). *Treating the hidden wounds: Trauma treatment and mental health recovery for victims of human trafficking*. Retrieved from https://aspe.hhs.gov/report/treating-hidden-wounds-trauma-treatment-and-mental-health-recovery-victims-human-trafficking

Garabrandt, K. (2016, April 24). Human trafficking in Ohio? *The News Herald*, pp. A1, A4.

Garlock, L. R. (2016). Stories in the cloth: Art therapy and narrative textiles. *Art Therapy: Journal of the American Art Therapy Association*, *33*(2), 58–66. https://doi.org/10.1080/07421656.2016.1164004

Guarino, K., Soares, P., Konnath, K., Clervil, R., & Bassuk, E. (2009). *Trauma-informed care organizational toolkit*. Rockville, MD: Center for Mental Health, Substance Abuse and Mental Health Services Administration, and the Daniels Fund, the National Traumatic Stress Network, and the W.K. Kellogg Foundation. Retrieved from www.air.org/sites/default/files/downloads/report/Trauma-Informed_Organizational_Toolkit_0.pdf

Harris, M., & Fallot, R. D. (2001). Envisioning a trauma-informed service system: A vital paradigm shift. In M. Harris & R. D. Fallot (Eds.), *Using trauma theory to design service symptoms* (pp. 3–22). San Francisco, CA: Jossey-Bass.

Hepburn, S., & Simon, R. J. (2013). *Human trafficking around the world: Hidden in plain sight*. New York, NY: Columbia University Press.

Herman, J. L. (1997). *Trauma and recovery: The aftermath of violence—From domestic abuse to political terror* (2nd ed.). New York, NY: Basic Books.

Kometiani, M. K., & Farmer, K. W. (2019). Exploring resilience through case studies of art therapy with sex trafficked survivors and their advocates. *The Arts in Psychotherapy*. Advance online publication. https://doi.org/10.1016/j.aip.2019.101582

Levine, P. A. (1997). *Waking the tiger: Healing trauma*. Berkley, CA: North Atlantic Books.

Litam, S. D. A. (2017). Human sex trafficking in America: What counselors need to know. *The Professional Counselor*, 7(1), 45–61. https://doi.org/10.15241/sd.al.7.1.45

Malchiodi, C. A. (2011). Trauma informed art therapy with sexually abused children. In P. Goodyear-Brown (Ed.), *Handbook of child sexual abuse: Prevention, assessment, and treatment* (pp. 341–354). New York, NY: Wiley.

Malchiodi, C. A. (2013). Introduction to art therapy in health care settings. In C. A. Malchiodi (Ed.), *Art therapy in health care* (pp. 1–12). New York, NY: Guilford Press.

Malchiodi, C. A. (2015a). Ethics, evidence, trauma-informed practice, and cultural sensitivity. In C. A. Malchiodi (Ed.), *Creative Interventions with traumatized children* (pp. 24–44). New York, NY: The Guilford Press.

Malchiodi, C. A. (2015b). Trauma-informed art therapy and group intervention with children from violent homes. In C. A. Malchiodi (Ed.), *Creative Interventions with traumatized children* (pp. 258–278). New York, NY: The Guilford Press.

Malchiodi, C. A. (2017). Art therapy approaches to facilitate verbal expression; Getting past the impasse. In C. A. Malchiodi and D. A. Crenshaw (Eds.), *What to do when children clam up in psychotherapy* (pp. 3–17). New York, NY: The Guilford Press.

National Human Trafficking Hotline. (2018a). *Ohio*. Retrieved from ttps://humantraffickinghotline.org/state/ohio

National Human Trafficking Hotline. (2018b). *States*. Retrieved from https://humantraffickinghotline.org/states

Polaris. (2015, May). *Sex trafficking in the US: A closer look at the US citizen victims*. Retrieved from http://polarisproject.org/resources/sex-trafficking-us-closer-look-us-citizen-victims

Provance, J. (2018, January). Ohio trafficking investigations soared in 2017. *The Blade*. Retrieved from www.toledoblade.com/State/2018/01/29/Ohio-human-trafficking-investigations-spiked-last-year.html

Sanar Wellness Institute, & Polaris. (2015, November). *Promising practices: An overview of trauma-informed therapeutic support for survivors of human trafficking*. Retrieved from https://polarisproject.org/sites/default/files/Sanar-Promising-Practices.pdf

Shelley, L. (2010). *Human trafficking: A global perspective*. Cambridge, NY: Cambridge University Press.

Steele, W., & Malchiodi, C. A. (2012). *Trauma-informed practices with children and adolescents*. New York, NY: Routledge Taylor and Francis Group.

Stotts, E. L., & Ramey, L. (2009). Human trafficking: A call for counselor awareness and action. *Journal of Humanistic Counseling, Education and Development*, *48*, 36–47. https://doi.org/10.1002/j.2161-1939.2009.tb00066.x

Tan, L. A. (2012). Art therapy with trafficked women. *Therapy Today*, *23*(5), 26–31.

United States Department of State. (2018, June 18). *Implementing a trauma-informed approach*. Retrieved from www.state.gov/documents/organization/283795.pdf

van der Kolk, B. (2014). *The body keeps the score: Brain, mind, and body in the healing of trauma*. New York, NY: Viking.

Williamson, C., Karandikar-Chheda, S., Barrows, J., Smouse, T., Kelly, G., Swartz, P., . . . Tame, C. (2012). *Ohio trafficking in persons study commission research and analysis subcommittee report on the prevalence of human trafficking in Ohio to Attorney General Richard Cordray*. Retrieved from www.researchgate.net/publication/260335516_Ohio_Trafficking_in_Persons_Study_Commission_Research_and_Analysis_Sub-Committee_Report_on_the_Prevalence_of_Human_Trafficking_in_Ohio_To_Attorney_General_Richard_Cordray_Research_Committee_Members_At

SIX

Art Therapy Treatment for Survivors of Sex Trafficking, Boys

Chris Drosdick

Introduction

Trauma-informed care is challenging due to the personal taxing effects; complex and complicated cases requiring multifaceted coordination of care among physicians, law enforcement, child protective service (CPS), and therapists; maintenance of records for details of disclosure; and difficulty reconciling with the shocking and horrific reality of sex trafficking. Child Sexual Abuse Statistics (2018) demonstrate this vileness:

- The incidence of boys experiencing sexual abuse is one in 20.
- Ninety-three percent of children who have been sexually abused knew their attacker well.
- Over a third of abusers are part of a child's family.
- Over 73% of child targets do not disclose the abuse for a year or more, and another 45% of child targets do not disclose for five or more years.

More specific statistics of sex trafficking report 122 calls in 2018 relating to sex trafficking in Wisconsin and 13% of the victims were boys (National Human Trafficking Hotline, 2019).

Working with children who have been sexually abused and involved with sex trafficking is difficult for many reasons but especially because youth are vulnerable and helpless against manipulative traffickers. Trauma-informed art therapy® was a major part in working with this family because of its effectiveness in addressing self-esteem, anxiety, safety and boundary issues, family communication, shame, gender role and healthy sexuality, and resiliency. This chapter will cover my work with two boys who are survivors of sex trafficking. The chapter will close with final recommendations for working with this population, including the importance of self-care for trauma therapists.

Population and Programming

Through a referral to my private practice, over the course of 24 months, I have had the privilege of working with two brothers who were victims of sex trafficking. The boys have made tremendous progress, and art therapy played a major role in their treatment.

Background

The brothers (all names are pseudonyms), Henry (12) and Matt (8), come from a two-parent household in an upper-middle-class neighborhood in the Midwest. Mom, Angela, works as a stay-at-home-mom and has not worked outside of the home. Dad, Edward, is a professional in the financial industry. Dad is entirely from Greek descent, and mom is entirely Peruvian. The family owns their own home, and the children attend a high-ranked public school in their community. The family practices the Greek Orthodox religion. The mother was a practicing Catholic prior to marriage. The boys participate in sports activities and have friend playdates. Both the mother and the father have relatives in the area. The family has two dogs. From an outsider's perspective, their lives are very comfortable and enviable. The tragedy is well hidden.

When the boys were 6 and 10, they revealed that they were being sexually abused by a male family member. The younger brother, Matt, was the first to make the disclosure. The disclosures that followed over the next two years revealed a sex trafficking web with many facets of abuse. Voyeuristic actions, animal sacrifices, drugs, pornography, and sex parties/orgies were all part of what seemed too awful to be true in this family's case. Furthermore, the abuse went on for three years before the boys reported it to their parents.

Acute Stages of Treatment

Henry and Matt began treatment with another therapist several months before I became involved. She helped them begin to process the abuse with eye movement desensitization reprogramming (EMDR), cognitive behavioral therapy (CBT), and art therapy. After approximately nine months, the therapist felt she was getting burned out in the treatment process. The therapist contacted me and inquired if I was willing to take the family on for the next phase of treatment, the trauma reintegration phase, and I agreed. I considered the therapist a skilled clinician and had no concerns about the transfer. The therapist and I spent an hour on the telephone reviewing the case and preparing me for the transfer. Given the complexity of the case, this was not enough time, and we had additional conversations during the first 60 days of treatment. What I found most helpful were copies of all the reports the original therapist made to CPS.

Reviewing the dozens of reports gave me great insight into what had transpired to date. Then the really hard work began.

The mom, as well as Matt and Henry, struggled with anxiety and panic symptoms as effects of abuse. They were also nervous about changing therapists. We agreed I would see the brothers twice a week for six to eight weeks and then reevaluate their treatment needs. The boys were seen individually for therapy sessions. The mother was seen with the boys for a portion of each session. The mother was also seen individually on a weekly basis to discuss the boys' progress in treatment and for help with parenting. When working with families, I typically find monthly sessions generally are enough for transferring skills and coaching parents. Since there were two children involved in treatment and complex trauma, I increased the family sessions to weekly for a year. The father joined when he was able, but his work schedule often made attending sessions difficult.

During the intake, I learned that mom had been a victim of sexual abuse during her childhood from age 4, which occurred in her home country of Peru. During Angela's childhood, she did not receive treatment for the abuse, as her mother did not believe the abuse occurred. Angela revealed the abuse to her mother a few years after the abuse started. This made the situation with her sons especially painful. Angela understood their pain all too well and never imagined her boys would be sexually abused. Angela also felt immense guilt related to her stay-at-home mother status and her inability to protect the boys from harm. Angela never thought this situation would happen in her family again. She had never left her children with a nonfamily babysitter.

The original therapist's *Diagnostic and Statistical Manual, Fifth Edition (DSM-5)* diagnosis for each boy was posttraumatic stress disorder (PTSD), depression, and generalized anxiety disorder (GAD). Their symptoms of PTSD included

> spontaneous or cued recurrent, involuntary, and intrusive distressing memories of the traumatic events, recurrent distressing dreams in which the content or affect (i.e. feeling) of the dream is related to the events, flashbacks or other dissociative reactions in which the individual feels or acts as if the traumatic events are recurring, intense or prolonged psychological distress at exposure to internal or external cues that symbolize or resemble an aspect of the traumatic events, physiological reactions to reminders of the traumatic events.
>
> (APA, 2013)

The type of trauma the boys experienced is classified as a Type 2 trauma, as it was repeated and prolonged. Judith Herman's work in Type 2 trauma treatment was helpful: "Given the nature and frequency, and duration of Type II trauma, an individual's basic functioning and fundamental capacities for coping are more significantly disrupted" (2015, p. 121). Matt, for example, experienced dissociation and somatic preoccupation. Henry, on the other hand, experienced dissociation paranoia and different somatic preoccupations. Herman's approach is three phased, beginning with creating safety, building stabilization, and improving functioning in day-to-day life.

Theoretical Framework and Therapeutic Process

My initial treatment goals were to continue to process the trauma of the abuse, rule out any additional diagnoses, and reduce the overall stress level in the family. At the beginning of treatment, I often felt the family was like a group of spinning tops, each one going in a different direction. I would work to get them spinning in the same direction and then slow down a bit to get their brains out of the fight-flight-freeze response. For instance, Henry would arrive for a session with Angela, and Henry would talk very fast (racing thoughts evident) and report being in great distress. Angela would interject frequently in the conversation and appeared distressed and panicked. Angela was often panicked over something that occurred at home, as well as over the boys' behavior in the session.

Trauma-informed art therapy® approach takes into consideration these four points:

- how the mind/body/spirit respond to the trauma,
- awareness of symptoms as coping mechanisms,
- cultural sensitivity, and
- teaching resilience and building a thrive mentality.

(Malchiodi, 2011)

Matt and Henry responded differently to the trauma. Matt's mind often went to avoidance: "I don't want to talk about it." Even though Matt was the younger brother and revealed the abuse to his parents first, he still did not like to talk about the painful memories. Matt would often hide behind my couch when we discussed traumatic memories too long. At times, Matt would wrap himself up in a blanket, so I could not see his face. Matt would frequently sit with the heels of his feet placed on his rectum, putting pressure on that area, when feelings came up in session. The anal area is rich in nerve endings, and the parents believed the pressure caused by the heels of the feet pressing on the rectum was self-stimulating behavior. Peter Levine has done extensive research on experiencing the body in trauma treatment (Levine, 2015). Henry struggled with anxiety, obsessive thoughts, and compulsions. Henry showed more physical signs of distress. For example, his legs became straight and increased in movement during session. He would pat his thighs repetitively with his hands and ask for positive affirmation, asking "I am not a bad person, am I?"

Henry was often fatigued at the end of a session; he would exhale loudly and lie back on the couch in relief. Being older, Henry was able to say, "this session helped me" or "this intervention will be useful."

As for theoretical framework, I was focused on trauma-informed art therapy®, EMDR, CBT, and dialectical behavioral therapy (DBT), and mindfulness. The boy's mother had her own psychologist to continue to work with on her personal anxiety, attention deficit hyperactivity disorder inattention type (ADHD), PTSD, and depression. For a time, the couple saw a marriage counselor to work on the strain the revelation of the abuse had put on their relationship. My role with the parents was as an education and parenting coach. For example, the parents attributed most of the boy's behavior to the sexual abuse. Some of our sessions dealt with teasing out normal developmental behavior with trauma responses. I also provided psychoeducation on the various diagnoses the brothers would come to have. Matt was diagnosed with PTSD, major depression, and ADHD combined type. Henry was diagnosed with PTSD, major depression, obsessive-compulsive disorder, and ADHD inattention type. Angela also felt the need to continue therapy at home, which meant the boys were talking about the abuse 24/7. Together, we worked to make home the safe place and to limit talk about the abuse to my office. CBT is an evidence-based practice for reducing serious trauma reactions, such as PTSD, anxiety, and depression symptoms (APA, 2008). CBT helped to restructure some of the boys' negative thought patterns. DBT continued to restructure thought patterns and added mindfulness skills. EMDR assisted in identifying the emotions and body sensations that accompanied the disturbing memories. Through the process of EMDR, the distress of the memories was reduced or eliminated. CBT, DBT, and EMDR all integrated easily with art therapy. For example, responses in EMDR were often visual images versus verbal responses.

There are several theorists that support art therapy in the use of trauma treatment:

> The Freudian view sees formation of creativity in personal conflict where man responds to symptoms through unconscious defense mechanisms. Freud recognized the role of art in psychotherapy as a process of spontaneous imagery, released from the unconscious (Bonier, 2016). For example, Matt repressed his memories of the sexual abuse; he did not deny that the abuse occurred but often stated that he didn't "need" to talk about it. Henry, on the other hand, struggled with projection in his peer relationships. He projected his feelings of not fitting in, mean statements, and cruel behavior onto his peers. Initially, he believed he was never at fault and could not understand why conflict with peers kept happening to him.

> The Jungian's view emphasizes art making or creative expression as assisting in restoring the psychological balance within (Ferrell, 2015). Initially, the boy's artwork with very messy and chaotic. Over time, as the psychological balance began to be restored, their artwork became more orderly and less chaotic.
>
> Ulman (1975), one of the pioneers in art therapy, believed the process of putting feelings into images can be less threatening than speaking the words. For instance, Matt would often respond to the EMDR rounds in a visual format instead of words.

The Journey Begins

So, they begin their healing journey. My office has two distinct treatment areas. I have a comfortable living room space, which is the talking space. I also have a spacious art therapy studio, which is the creating space. The brothers happened to love art, so we were able to utilize art as a mean of communication frequently. I tried to balance between art making and talk therapy, sometimes integrating both in the sessions. For instance, during EMDR sessions, the boys would sometimes draw their responses between bilateral stimulation. Bilateral stimulation is visual, auditory, or tactile stimuli that occurs in a rhythmic left to right pattern. Bilateral stimulation is one of the core elements of EMDR; bilateral stimulation produces four main effects, including a relaxation effect, decreased physiological arousal, increased attentional flexibility, and distancing effect and decreased worry (Shapiro, 2017).

Initially, the boys' art had notable themes. The pictures were often chaotic images made from lots of mess and often included both red and black in the colors (Figure 6.1). Both boys attributed red to blood, as

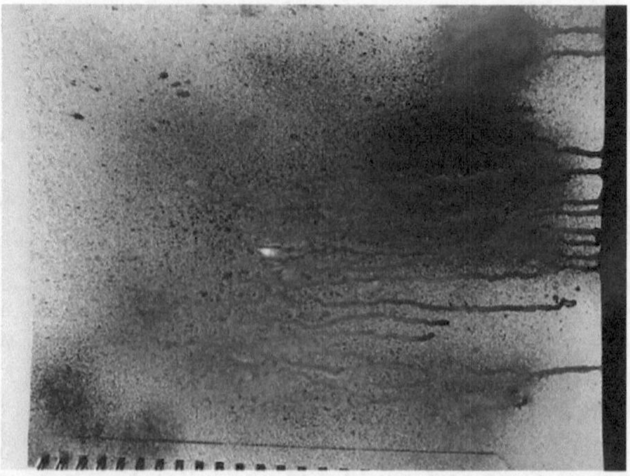

Figure 6.1 Matt—art journal

many of their traumatic memories included blood. For instance, blood coming from their rectums after the sexual abuse. The shapes were angular and often phallic. At times, they would only use charcoal pencils to draw. Both boys struggled with perfectionism, and they would become very frustrated if their art did not evolve as they wanted. Matt would often throw out his artwork. We worked together to reduce frustration by taking a break and briefly shifting to another activity. I always saved the boys' paintings, and we learned to enhance or love them in the future or repurpose the canvases for future projects. I repeatedly taught the boys that their art was a process and not "garbage," a concept that was important for their emotional development. Due to the extent of their trauma, it was valuable for them to realize their messy art was an expression of themselves as survivors. Learning to improve and reclaim their images, and for me to bear witness to their work and find value in their art, addressed and enhanced their self-esteem during the initial sessions. Jung and Freud both theorized that the process of symbol formation creates order and connectedness within the self and may also provide a bridge from one's inner experiences to the outer world (Bonier, 2016; Ferrell, 2015).

How the Mind/Body/Spirit Responds to Trauma: Mindfulness

In an effort to reduce the overall stress in the family and build the heart/head connection, mindfulness was integrated into the treatment plan (Davidson, 2012). The heart/head connection premise is that the head is where logic, analysis, and strategy live. The heart is where empathy, connection, and emotion reside. Trauma victims often report feeling a disconnect between the heart and the head. The head reins in decisions from the heart or from our impulses. The boys' brains were on constant alert, often in the fight-flight-freeze response.

I encouraged mom and the brothers to participate in *yoga nidra* sessions. Yoga nidra, or yogic sleep as it is commonly known, is an immensely powerful meditation technique, and one of the easiest yoga practices to develop and maintain. In 2015, I was trained to facilitate yoga nidra sessions. Yoga nidra was successfully used in treating combat veterans with a diagnosis of PTSD (Nassif et al., 2015).

While the participant rests comfortably in savasana (corpse pose), this systematic meditation takes the individual through the pancha *maya* kosha (five layers of self), leaving a sense of wholeness. Yoga nidra promotes deep rest and relaxation that is not found in the average meditation practice. The stages of body scan and breath awareness alone can be practiced to calm the nervous system, leading to decreasing stress, and better health. Yoga nidra offers a space to explore what one needs in the moment, as well as an opportunity to work on releasing long-held emotions (Saraswati, 1984). Henry and Matt's entire family found peace in the practice of yoga nidra. Henry found yoga nidra was helpful in the evening when he was having difficulty settling down before bed, and Angela would play a yoga nidra YouTube video that they had previously bookmarked. In the office, Henry would ask for a yoga nidra session when he was feeling panicky.

Bessel van der Kolk (2014), a psychiatrist who has spent decades researching trauma and the effects on the body states, "Neuroscience research shows that the only way we can change the way we feel is by becoming aware of our inner experience and learning to befriend what is going on inside ourselves" (p. 206). Yoga nidra helped the family reduce the feeling of being "on-edge" and unable to relax, which can be attributed to anxiety, depression, and PTSD.

I am trained in the Growing Minds curriculum, which is a nonprofit in the Midwest focused on building mindfulness in schools (Growing Minds, 2018). Their mission is to bring mindful focus to every student in every school. Many of the Growing Minds interventions were utilized over the course of treatment with this family. For instance, *wringing out* worked well when the boys had a lot of energy and anxiety. Wringing out was simple to do in my office setting. During several sessions, to take breaks or allow time for them to focus, the boys would simply stand straight with their arms outstretched. Then they would twist at the waist and wring their arms like an agitator in a washing machine. As they picked up speed, they would slowly lower their arms and continue wringing. Once their arms had been lowered to the thighs, they would twist back up. As the facilitator, I would continue to ask them to move up and down for approximately three minutes. This intervention is beneficial for several reasons. The left to right rhythmic movement is a form of bilateral stimulation, which calms the body. The activity also created some physical activity for the boys, which burned off some anxiety and pent-up energy.

In addition to their regularly scheduled sessions, the boys also participated in a community-based art therapy class I teach called Mindful Masterpieces. Each week, the participants created a 16" x 20" acrylic painting based on a famous artist. The five artists focused on during the series were Picasso, Matisse, Monet, Kahlo, and Kandinsky. During each class, the participants were also taught three mindfulness activities. For instance, one activity was based on mindful listening. The students listened to Brazilian coffeehouse music (Urena, 1997) for three minutes and shared the feelings generated by the piece of music. The boys found the music was energizing and made them want to move. The music also created feelings of peace and happiness. Another mindfulness activity they experienced was the slow breathing of a four-three-seven count breath. Participants were taught to inhale to a count of four, hold for a count of three, and then exhale to a count of seven. This forces the stale air out of the lungs, encourages deeper breathing, and the increased oxygen triggers the relaxation response. This intervention also helped with reducing anxiety and physical distress.

How the Mind Responds to Trauma: Boundary Issues

Trauma, almost by its occurrence, sets clients up for boundary issues. The family members struggled with their sense of protection, feelings of safety, and sense of self as a unit. The family lived in emergency mode. "Not knowing where 'I' ends and the 'Other' begins creates chaos and confusion in the client's inner world, which echoes strongly in the therapeutic relationship" (Heitzler, 2013, p. 28). During the first few weeks of treatment, I noticed boundary pushing with the family. I became aware that the prior therapist had spoken to the brothers every night before they went to bed to ease them into sleep. Bedtime routines had been a big problem, as both the brothers struggled with nightmares and flashbacks in the evening and before bedtime. Because this practice did not fit into my schedule, and due to ethics and boundaries standards, I started a new practice. The brothers were provided with journals to write in and capture their thoughts. The content of the journals could then be reviewed in session. I also coached mom and dad on how to encourage the brothers to go to bed without outside assistance. Bedtime continued to be a challenge for Matt more so than Henry. Sleeping in his own bed was a challenge. We used CBT to reshape his negative thoughts about bedtime. Matt made positive artwork to hang above his bed and place on his nightstand to encourage positive and pleasant thoughts at bedtime. Together, we created prayer flags to provide a sense of safety for both boys. The family was educated on the use of essential oil, and Matt placed a diffuser on his nightstand. Frankincense, lavender, and ylang was a blend found helpful in creating a sense of calm. Matt and I set goals regarding sleeping in his own bed, and he was held accountable for making progress toward those goals.

The prior therapist had also made a few house calls or in-person visits to the home, the purpose being to analyze the home from a trauma-informed lens. Since this had already been done, I did not feel the need to replicate the practice. I also wanted to maintain the boundaries between my office and the family's home. The mother also telephoned frequently with updates on disclosures the brothers were making. I had to let the family know that while I would listen to the messages, I would not reply every time they called me. We would discuss the messages at our next scheduled session. I explained that frequently when they called, I was with other clients and was unable to take their call. This initial boundary setting was important for my own self-care, as well as starting our therapeutic relationship off on the right foot.

Over time, I realized the importance of teaching the boys grounding techniques. At bedtime, they were often ungrounded and dissociating.

> Often when we feel ungrounded, dissociated, shocked or over-tired we turn—without even thinking—to our bodies to regain a sense of reality and grounding: a sense of ourselves. We pinch ourselves, rub our eyes or arms, jump up and down or unconsciously stroke and hold ourselves. It is this felt sense of our physical existence that brings us back to reality and into direct contact with ourselves. Many people who have been traumatized have lost access to their body and with that have lost a sense of their physical container. Dissociating and fragmenting daily, they live in exile, dis-embodied, not able to find their way back home, to themselves.
>
> (Heitzler, 2013, p. 39)

Grounding techniques included utilizing the five senses to come back to the present moment, citrus blend essential oils, the body scan, and breathing exercises.

How the Mind Responds to Trauma: Parenting Coaching

In addition to the brothers' sessions, therapy began with the parents on a weekly basis to discuss ongoing legal issues, parenting struggles, and stress reduction. Initially, the parents were pursuing legal action against the perpetrator. The legal process can be long and frustrating; expectations of time needed to be managed. Likewise, there were some language barriers with mom, so often I would do my best to interpret responses from CPS and the police to the parents. Mom tended to take things personally, due to her own history of abuse and unresolved issues. I had to be direct at times and tell her she was personalizing. Many reports were filed with CPS by the prior therapist and me. In addition, I met with the various detectives on the case. Counselors are mandated reporters; however, I learned from the police the details of the abuse are not as necessary in a complex case. The images created during sessions and narratives of specific events were utilized as evidence.

While the parents had two children who were victims of repeated sexual abuse over the course of three years, their sons also had some normal developmental issues. For instance, Matt and Henry fought at times. This is completely normal sibling behavior and is not attributed to the trauma. Typical children also have peer conflicts, and those conflicts cannot be attributed entirely to the trauma. Assisting the parents in determining "normal" behavior from triggers and trauma-related behavior was important. The parents lumped all behavior as trauma-related behavior initially. I also found the parents excused a great deal of the boys' behavior based on their guilt. Together, we worked to implement structure and consequences for inappropriate behavior. Mom and dad awarded positive behavior with experiences or items the boys were interested in, for instance, tickets to a basketball game with dad or new art supplies.

How the Mind Responds to Trauma: Guilt and Shame

The parents shared very little with friends or neighbors in the community and felt very isolated in trying to cope with this tragedy alone. They were ashamed of what people might think of them. The parents were concerned people would judge them and label them as bad parents. "How could you let this happen to your children?" and "How could you not have known?" were common worries for Angela and Edward. Signs of abuse were not obvious or clear during the three years the abuse was going on. For example, torn or stained underwear is often a sign for parents to observe. In this case, there never was a single incident when underwear was torn or stained. The boys reported that they were often stripped of their clothes at the beginning of a session of abuse. Afterward, they were thoroughly cleaned and showered and their clean clothes put back on before they went home. Nor did the boys have urinary infections, while they did struggle with constipation at times. The mother took them to the pediatrician during those times and followed the doctors' instructions to treat, which was a fiber supplement and more fruits and vegetables in the diet. The brothers also exhibited anger outbursts, tantrums, depression, and withdrawn mood during the three years of abuse. Survivors of sexual abuse often struggle with depression, anxiety, PTSD, personality disruptions, attachment issues, and, later in life, addiction or eating disorders (van der Kolk, 2005).

You may be asking those same questions as you read this. The parents were not neglectful. This was a horrifying revelation as well as a dire violation of family trust (Figure 6.2). The mother was very close

Figure 6.2 Angela, hurt, pain, sick, fear—art journal

to her sister and the sister's family, who lived in a neighboring town. They planned get-togethers often. The sister had a son a few years older than the brothers. In family counseling sessions, we discussed the guilt both parents felt around the abuse and in not being able to protect the children from their own family. Matt and Henry had been abused by their maternal uncle and forced to participate in sexual activities with their cousin.

It appears the boys were groomed for participation in the abuse. The abuser, a maternal uncle, gradually drew the boys into a sexual relationship. At first, there were fun outings, like meals out, sleepovers, the circus, and special events together. The boys had gained special attention and were ashamed to admit they enjoyed the attention at first. Gradually, physical boundaries were crossed, and the sexual abuse began. For instance, the boys were taught to share a bed at night or for "naps" with the uncle. During those times, the uncle would touch the boys inappropriately while they were awake and asleep. Later, the uncle progressed to having the boys disrobe and each touch his genitals. Eventually, the boys experienced anal plugs which enlarged their rectums in preparation for penile penetration. Those activities culminated in a sex trafficking ring where the boys were brought to perform various sexual activities for a fee. The children showed no signs of abuse upon returning home. The abuse was well hidden, and the boys were manipulated through a seemingly trusting relationship that followed with both manipulation and threats. Both boys disclosed that the abuser threatened to kill their parents if the boys told about their "club."

How the Mind Responds to Trauma: Negative Thoughts and the Brain

During the first few months of sessions, Henry continually asked, "Am I a bad person?" Sometimes he would ask this repeatedly and work himself into a state of panic. Later, I determined Henry struggled with obsessive thoughts and compulsions. His mother also has a diagnosis of obsessive-compulsive disorder. We worked on cognitive distortions, such as all or nothing thinking, catastrophizing, perfectionism, and personalization (Figure 6.3). We also discussed thought patterns—for example, not all our thoughts are facts. We identified triggers for both boys and created a list of about 30 people, places, and things that are/were triggers; however, the list had so many items, it was virtually impossible to avoid all triggers. We also worked on taming the flight-fight-freeze response, based on Seigel and Bryson's (2012) work. The boys viewed Dan Siegel's video (2012) on "flipping your lid" and reviewed the Wheel of Awareness. The Wheel of Awareness is a visual metaphor of our consciousness and the focus of our attention. We utilized positive affirmations and created a deck of cards with the message "I will thrive, I am a good person, and I can make good decisions."

Figure 6.3 Angela, I will leave all of my fears and questions here—art journal

Figure 6.4 Matt, no mistakes, no success

In treatment, we also worked on not letting the traumatic experiences define the identity of the boys. We calculated the number of times the abuse occurred and the amount of time spent with the abuser. Based on their current ages, we determined that 1% of their lives had been lived in those traumatic experiences. Also, as they become older each year, that percentage gets a little smaller. The boys were encouraged to not allow the 1% to dictate their happiness in life or the future. This form of CBT reframed their thinking (Figure 6.4).

Matt and I worked to create a feelings deck (Figure 6.5), which helped him identify the variety of emotions he was feeling. This intervention also

Figure 6.5 Matt, feelings deck, love card

helped him to acknowledge that he was able to experience several positive emotions, such as love. These cards were 5" x 11.5" cardstock, with a hole punched in the center of the top of the card. We placed the cards on a snapping ring. Matt viewed several magazines and found pictures and words to collage on each card.

How the Mind, Body, and Spirit Responds to Trauma: Male Gender Role Stress

Both boys were trained by their abusers to dance or pose in dramatic ways. The parents, Angela and Edward, were concerned that these movements were more feminine in nature and provocative. Angela and Edward were also concerned that their sons would be gay as a result of the same-sex abuse and the lengthy grooming process the boys experienced. I share more about this topic in the "Sex and Human Development" section of this chapter.

Henry enjoyed dancing and singing. Rather than squash that passion, Henry became involved in musical productions at his school. This provided him with a healthy outlet for his interests. Matt struggled with provocative poses, such as swinging his hips when he walked or standing with one hip out and his arm behind his head. Matt stated he had been taught to pose and walk like this by his abuser. When the sex trafficking occurred, he would be selected from a line of other boys posing in a similar fashion.

I also determined in the early stages of treatment that the boys were struggling with male gender role stress. In particular, the older boy, Henry, felt the abuse was a sign of weakness and a source of shame. Henry struggled to manage the intense negative emotions he felt related to the traumatic events. Male gender role norms in the United States include a mind-set that emotions are feminine, and males should be tough and emotionless. While the boy's parents did not make statements such as "suck it up" or "men don't cry," the boys certainly felt the pressure from society (Jakupcak, Osborne, Michael, Cook, & McFall, 2006).

Building a sense of identity and raising their level of self-esteem was important in working with the boys. Their sense of who they are was skewed for three years, while they were leading a double life as abused trauma survivors and "typical" children. In session, we created pieces of art that utilized the first letter of their names, thus building on their sense of personal identity and raising their self-esteem. The letters were approximately 8" x 4" and made of hard board. Acrylic paint and collage made decorating easy. The boys hung the initials in their respective rooms and brought pictures of the art hangings to show me. The boys were proud of their work, and their growing confidence was visible. Other activities that focused on self-esteem and identity included snowy landscapes in the winter. We based our artwork on the theme each of us is unique, like a snowflake.

The abusers were primarily men in the case. There were a few women involved; however, they were more supporting players in the "club." The abuser sold the sexual services to adult men in hotels and various homes in the area. The boys were also instructed to perform sex acts with other boys their age. This behavior created difficulty for both boys in terms of interacting with grown men and boys their own age. Grown men often were triggers for the boys. Any similarity, like a beard, hair color, or ethnic nationality could trigger the boys' memories of abuse and shame. Peers their own age also created internal conflict. Henry did not want to put himself in a position to harm other boys, so he avoided boys his age. Initially, Henry chose to be friends mainly with girls, as he felt safer with girls. Over time, we were able to work through those feelings, and Henry now maintains good relationships with both male and female peers.

How the Mind, Body, and Spirit Responds to Trauma: Disclosures

The boys made many detailed and difficult disclosures of their abuse. Memories would arise, and many details would pour out that they had not remembered before. I utilized expressive writing and drawing to capture the data around each reported incident. Individually, in session, the boys would disclose their recent memories. Both boys became skilled at writing down the details when they would come up, at home or in the counseling office. Here is a sample of one of the boy's writing and the details he recalled:

> So how they hurt me is they put numbing spray on my penis, so it wouldn't hurt so much. They made me smell their hands. Then the main part was they pinched me in my penis. I only saw, I didn't feel it. It was cold. Then they gave me a shot in my rectum. They took a picture of my butt and showed it to me, it was pink.
>
> (Drosdick, 2017)

Hundreds of disclosures created quite a pile of data to organize. I needed to communicate this information to the police and CPS, so I developed a system to keep things organized. In this situation, the best system seemed to organize the disclosures by the site where the abuse occurred (e.g. Main Street House or Public Library). From there I created a form which captured the who, what, why, when, where and how of each disclosure (see below). We also captured sensory details with questions like what did you smell? What did you feel? What did you see? If additional details came up later for specific disclosures, I could add the new information to that sheet.

Incident/Memory Report

Location— ______________________

Date revealed	
Who was involved?	
What happened?	
Where did it happen?	
Why?	
When—date/ time?	
How?	

Five senses	
Reported to CPS	
Reported to detective	
Other	
CPS #	
Spoke to @ CPS	
Date reported	

Due to the number of reports made to CPS and the police, the authorities were only interested in new sites of abuse details—not additional details to disclosures already reported. However, the authorities were aware that I had additional details and knew they could review my information as needed. The parents of the boys and I felt the details were of importance, but the authorities did not. As the clinician, I had to come to terms with my ethical responsibility for reporting harm. The reports were made on a regular basis and the details methodically tracked.

How the Mind, Body, and Spirit Responds to Trauma: School, Home, Friends

Often, children who have experienced traumatic events show behavioral symptoms at home, as well as at school. Both boys did well academically in school, and they were enrolled in different schools due to age. The parents had decided not to tell the teachers of the sexual abuse their sons had endured. The parents wanted to make school a safe place where the boys did not have to deal with sexual abuse or its residue. This was a good plan until the CPS social worker began show up unannounced to interview the boys at school. Fortunately, the social worker only arrived at school three times during the school year, and the school was able to arrange for meetings in a private conference room where each boy could be isolated. After the first social worker's visit, the parents signed a release for this therapist to speak with the principal. The principal was somewhat cooperative during our conversation but was clearly unsure how the school could best support the children. The need for more trauma-informed training in the school system became apparent.

How the Body Responds to Trauma: Drugs and Bathroom Problems

Both boys reported being given a white powder to ingest and being injected with other substances. Sometimes the injection was in the rectum (possibly a numbing agent to reduce pain) and other times in their arms or chests. With the reports of drug use by the brothers and changes going on in their normal development, doctor visits were scheduled. Henry was developing breasts, larger than other 12-year-old boys. There was also some concern with the small size of Henry's testicles and blood in his stool. The boy's pediatrician made referrals to urologists and endocrinologists. Many tests were completed, and everything came back normal. There was no evidence of a sexually transmitted disease or damage to the rectum. The parents were very good at following through on everything recommended in terms of medical tests and support.

Both boys experience issues concerning bowel movements. While the abuse was ongoing, Matt had bouts of constipation. This is not unusual for children who experienced trauma. Matt continues to have ongoing issues with bowel elimination and will avoid toilet use. Some of the avoidance comes from the fact that a bathroom was often one of the rooms in which Matt was abused. Henry also experienced issues with bowel movements. He was overly concerned about cleaning himself after going to the bathroom and would insert baby wipes into his rectum, a practice that caused irritation and eventually bleeding. The doctor and I worked together to discuss this delicate topic and address Henry's behavior using CBT methods.

How the Mind, Body, and Spirit Responds to Trauma: Vicarious Trauma and Burnout?

Five months into to our therapeutic relationship, I hit a low point. The magnitude of the abuse was affecting me, and I was concerned about my own ability to continue working with the family. I was more tired than usual; I had difficulty sleeping; I would wake up in the middle of the night thinking about the traumatic memories revealed that week in session with the boys. I began to increase my self-care significantly. The family took a few weeks of vacation, during this time, I was able to focus on my own care. Help that benefited me included massage twice a month, weekly Reiki, craniosacral therapy treatments, scheduled vacations, creating my own artwork, and seeing a therapist myself. I also sought outside clinical supervision to ensure I was keeping a good perspective on treatment

Figure 6.6 Drosdick, self-care painting

goals. I am a firm believer that therapists who work with victims of abuse need to have a high level of self-care. Within a few weeks, I began to feel better and was able to continue with treatment for the youngsters with renewed energy (Figure 6.6).

A Brighter Picture Emerges

About six months into our work, I noticed changes in the brothers' artwork. The angular, phallic symbols became softer and more organic. The colors shifted away from red and black to brighter colors, like purple and blue. I also noticed their work was becoming neater, more detailed, and they both handled frustration with the materials better. Henry's artwork is representative of the gang age, according to Lowenfeld's Stages of Artistic Development (1974). Henry began to utilize shading in his artwork, and he would often become very critical of his artwork. Matt's artwork was representative of the dawning realism stage. Matt's artwork showed the start of the use of spatial relationships; however, he often used a strip of green for the grass and a strip of blue for the sky.

Figure 6.7 is Henry's vision board from a January session. He was given a 16" x 24" canvas board, several magazines, and a pile of ephemera to sort through and create his vision for the upcoming year. Henry was very careful in crafting his background, which was a soothing blue. At the early stages of treatment, Henry would have been messy with his application of the paint, and a large amount of paint would have been on his hands and clothes. We learned over time to wear two smocks, instead of just one! The finished piece is organized, symmetrical, and close to what an adult might complete. There are also many positive statements in his creation (Figure 6.7).

Figure 6.7 Henry, vision board

How the Body Responds to Trauma: Sex and Human Development

During our psychotherapy sessions, the brothers frequently discussed homosexuality, human growth and development, and sexuality. Both boys were concerned about being "gay," particularly Henry, the older brother, did not want to be "gay." I encouraged the parents to foster an accepting attitude toward their sons regarding gay lifestyles (we don't know yet if either boy is), with the caveat that a homosexual experience does not predict either will be gay adults. In no way can a person's sexuality be determined by sexual abuse. Human growth and development were important to discuss with the older brother, as he began to go through puberty while in treatment. For instance, when his penis became aroused, he would often think there was a trigger of some sort, and he was acting inappropriately. In therapy, we worked to build the understanding that sometimes he would be aroused, and this had nothing to do with the trauma he experienced. Physiological responses such as an erection are involuntary, and he has no control over them. The younger brother, Matt, was concerned more about sex acts and often stated he would get married but "never have sex." The parents and I continue to work to encourage a healthy attitude about sexuality as a part of a relationship when the brothers are mature enough to handle such a relationship.

How the Mind Responds to Trauma: Neurobiology of Trauma

Due to the length and extent of the abuse (three years), the boys often discussed concern over whether they "liked" the abuse. There was a grooming process involved with a "trusted" adult. I found talking about their physical responses during the abuse provided evidence that the boys did not "like" the abuse. For instance, both boys experienced tonic immobility and collapsed immobility during the sexual abuse acts. Tonic immobility means the body went rigid, and the victim could not move. This is caused when the amygdala detects an attack and signals the brain to freeze (Seigel, 2012). Collapsed immobility is when the individual feels faint and the body goes limp or passes out.

"Why didn't I fight back?" This question came up frequently during treatment. Both boys stated they recalled saying "no" at first but were persuaded by their abuser to proceed with the sexual abuse acts. I found the work of Jim Hopper (2017) to be helpful in discussing what happens to the brain during a reoccurring calculated sexual trauma; the materials specifically address talking with sexual abuse survivors about how the brain is impacted. Other lingering questions included the following: Why can't I just get over it? Why am I so jumpy? Learning about the brain and how the brain reacts to trauma helped both boys understand their feelings and the progress of recovery.

Henry expressed concern frequently that he would grow up to rape someone. We discussed the difference between rape and child sexual abuse or pedophilia. Rape is generally rooted in anger. Child sexual abuse is typically not rooted in anger but in a sexual deviance. We discussed Henry's control over his choices and the fact that he was sexually abused is not an indication that he will grow up to commit the same harmful acts on children.

How the Mind Responds to Trauma: Hyperactive and Inattentive

Nine months into our treatment sessions, I diagnosed the younger brother, Matt, with ADHD. Within a month, the parents had taken him to a child psychologist specializing in ADHD diagnosis and treatment. The psychologist confirmed my diagnosis, and Matt began taking a stimulant medication. The family noticed some improvement in Matt's behavior, better focus and concentration, less impulsivity, and decreased fidgeting during times when he should be still. Henry was also evaluated and found to have ADHD as well but more of inattention and lack of focus symptoms. Henry started a stimulant also. Both boys also started seeing an ADHD specialist who helped them work on executive function and impulsivity. The addition of the ADHD specialist to the treatment team allowed me to continue to focus on the trauma work with the brothers.

Building Resiliency and Friends

In the current stage of treatment, we continue to focus on healing from the trauma, resiliency, and positive emotional development. We have also added social skills development to the treatment plan. Both boys feel different among their peers. Their peers do not know about the traumatic events these boys have experienced, which increases the traumatic isolation. The family continues to keep the trauma private. One of the interventions we completed was titled "I Am Like a Seed." The first step was to write down ways in which the boys felt they are like seeds. Each boy came up with items such as "I am still growing," "I need love and care to grow," "I need someone to make sure the weeds (problems in life) are taken care of and with care," and "I will bloom." The second portion of the intervention included decorating a terra cotta flowerpot with paint.

The family participates in art therapy groups twice a month, which give them a safe, supportive, compassionate group of people with which to practice their social skills. The members of the group are all clients from my practice but not all survivors of trauma. Some members struggle with anxiety, depression, or other diagnoses. One group is an acrylic painting group, and the other is art journaling. In January, the brothers each created personal vision boards using acrylic paints and mixed media. In March, each boy selected an Irish blessing and created a piece of art around the blessing. In November, we worked on creating a painting based on gratitude. Connecting the theme of the group to the time of year helped to orient the boys to current place and time. The weight of the trauma was often so great at times, the boys would forget that they could enjoy mindful moments and holiday celebrations.

The family developed a love of painting, and the boys responded well to learning new creative ways to paint. Brayers, printmaking techniques, fluid art, layering stencils with painted backgrounds—the boys were like sponges eager to learn more and more.

Henry is an active middle schooler now, and he struggles with conflict with peers. He finds himself saying mean things to peers when he is stressed, which creates hard feelings with peers. For instance, in the early stages of treatment, it would have been expected that Henry would tell a peer he did not "like" their artwork or that Henry could "do better." However, 15 months later, we are making progress with approaching others with positive feedback. I utilize the Golden Rule (Vogel, 2004) and the Buddhist Filter for work on social skills. The Golden Rule, if you don't have something kind to say, don't say it. The Buddhist Filter, is it kind, is it helpful, and is it true—if it is not all three, we don't say it (Krishnamurti, 2018). With this philosophy, we are working together, and we are working on helping Henry to treat others with compassion and kindness.

The boys have many factors in their favor, which should improve their ability to recover from the trauma they endured. For instance, the parents sought help as soon as they learned of the abuse; the boys are currently in a safe environment; the family has resources to continue to provide a safe, nurturing environment; and the family is committed to providing the boys with mental health care if they need it.

How the Mind and Body Respond to Trauma: Video Games and Technology

As the boys worked to develop friendships, video games and technology became more of a presence in their lives. Henry enjoyed watching videos on YouTube and playing Fortnite with friends. Eventually, we noticed a hyperfocus on the games and a decrease in efforts toward other healthy habits. The parents and I worked to set limits and boundaries on the technology both boys utilized. Dan Seigel's (2011) Healthy Brain Platter was used as a guideline for daily activities. The platter includes seven areas of concentration: focus time, playtime, connecting time, physical time, time in, down time, and sleep time. This guideline could be of benefit to many parents; it gave Matt and Henry's parents a concrete formula for judging their sons' daily activities and ensuring that healthy habits were included.

Cultural Sensitivity

The parents of the boys are a blend of European American and Hispanic cultures. The family practiced the Greek Orthodox religion, but mom was also Catholic in her upbringing. Respecting the family's values was an important factor in working with them closely. Both mom and dad came from families where everyone was close. There were lots of extended family dinners, holiday celebrations, and participation in day-to-day life. Once the abuse was revealed, 50% of their family network disappeared. The entire family went through a grief phase with this loss of family connection. We spent time in session talking about selecting friends to be a chosen family, instead of a family through blood relation.

The boys had been made to participate in satanic rituals during their abuse. Mom, whose upbringing was Catholic, relied on her spirituality frequently during treatment. Mom went to the local Catholic church and picked up gallons of holy water with which she scrubbed the entire house. She also arranged for Matt to participate in an exorcism, to cast out demons residing within him. Those demons, in theory, moved into Matt when he participated in the satanic rituals. My role was to discuss mom's decision prior to the exorcism and express concerns. I was worried that the exorcism process would be scary for Matt and possibly retraumatizing. Mom felt strongly about the need for the exorcism because of her faith, so she proceeded with the ritual after our discussion. After the exorcism, I worked with Matt and his mother to discuss what happened and process it.

Conclusion

While the work is demanding, depressing, draining, and complex, trauma-informed care is also rewarding. Clinicians are helping children move past horrific events and positioning them to thrive in their lives. In this instance, art therapy was crucial for the boys and their parents in recovering from this unbelievable tragedy and for myself in guiding them on their journey.

In closing, I would encourage therapists working with survivors of trauma to implement the following best practices: you should stay abreast of evidence-based practices in trauma treatment, continue educating yourself on as deep a level as you can, and commit to taking care of yourself. "If you hear a voice within you saying, 'You are not a painter,' then by all means paint, boy, and that voice will be silenced" (van Gogh, 1883). This was good advice to share with the boys. They learned to gain control of their decisions and lives through art therapy. They learned to paint and subdue the pain of their pasts and, with healing, look forward to painting their future lives.

References

American Psychological Association. (2008). *Children and trauma*. Washington, DC: APA Press.

American Psychological Association. (2013). *Diagnostic and statistical manual of mental disorders* (5th ed.). Arlington, VA: American Psychological Publishing.

Bonier, A. (2016). *Psychology: Essential thinkers, classic theories, and how they inform your world*. Berkley, CA: Zephyros Press.

Child Sexual Abuse Statistics. (2018). Retrieved from http://victimsofcrime.org/media/reporting-on-child-sexual-abuse/child-sexual-abuse-statistics

Davidson, R. (2012). *The emotional life of the brain*. New York, NY: Penguin Street Press.

Drosdick, C. (2017). Psychotherapy notes.

Ferrell, D. (2015). Creativity and change in psychoanalysis: Jungian perspectives. *The Psychoanalytic Quarterly*, *84*(1), 175–207. https://doi.org/10.1002/j.2167-4086.2015.00008.x

Growing Minds. (2018). Retrieved from www.growingmindstoday.com/our-mission.html

Heitzler, M. (2013). Broken boundaries, invaded territories: The challenges of containment in trauma work. *International Body Psychotherapy Journal, the Art and Science of Somatic Praxis*, *12*(1), 28–41.

Herman, J. (2015). *Trauma and recovery: The aftermath of violence—From domestic abuse to political terror*. New York, NY: Basic Books.

Hopper, J. (2017). *Neurobiology of sexual assault trauma: Supportive conversations with victims*. Retrieved from www.jimhopper.com

Jakupcak, M., Osborne, T. L., Michael, S., Cook, J. W., & McFall, M. (2006). Implications of masculine gender role stress in male veterans with posttraumatic stress disorder. *Psychology of Men and Masculinity*, 7, 203–211.

Krishnamurti, J. (2018). *What are you doing with your life?* New York, NY: Penguin Press.

Levine, P. (2015). *Trauma and memory: Brain and body in a search for the living past: A practical guide for understanding and working with traumatic memory.* Berkeley, CA: North Atlantic Books.

Lowenfeld, V. (1947). *Creative and mental growth.* New York, NY: Macmillan.

Malchiodi, C. (2011). Trauma informed art therapy with sexually abused children. In Paris Goodyear-Brown (Ed.), *Handbook of child sexual abuse: Prevention, assessment, and treatment.* New York, NY: Wiley.

Nassif, T., Norris, D., Soltes, K., Sandbrink, K., Blackman, M., & Chapman, J. (2015). *Using mindfulness meditation to improve pain management in combat veterans with traumatic brain injury.* War Related Illness and Injury Study Center, Georgetown University School of Medicine, Washington, DC.

National Human Trafficking Hotline. (2019). Retrieved from https://humantraffickinghotline.org/state/wisconsin

Saraswati, S., & Ashram, S. (1984). *Yoga nidra.* Sydney, Australia: Gosford, N.S.W.

Seigel, D. (2011). Retrieved from www.drdansiegel.com/resources/healthy_mind_platter/

Seigel, D. (2012). Retrieved from www.youtube.com/watch?v=G0T_2NNoC68

Seigel, D., & Bryson, T. (2012). *The whole brain child.* New York, NY: Bantam Books.

Shapiro, F. (2017). *Eye movement desensitization and reprogramming (EMDR) therapy.* New York, NY: Guilford Press.

Ulman, E. (1975). *Art therapy in theory and practice.* New York, NY: Schochen Books.

Urena, J. C. (1997). Este son [recorded by Urena, J. C.] On Music from the Coffee Lands [CD].

van der Kolk, B. (2005). Developmental trauma disorder: Toward a rational diagnosis for children with complex trauma histories. *Psychiatric Annals, 35*(5), 401–408.

van der Kolk, B. (2014). *The body keeps the score: Brain, mind and body in the healing of trauma* (1st ed.). New York, NY: Viking.

van Gogh, V. (1883). Retrieved from www.webexhibits.org/vangogh/letter/13/336.htm

Vogel, G. (2004). Behavioral evolution. The evolution of the golden rule. https://doi.org/10.1126/science.303.5661.1128

SEVEN

Use of the Expressive Art Therapies to Bring Healing From the Trauma of Commercial Sexual Exploitation in Kolkata, India

Smita Singh and Mary K. Kometiani

Introduction to Our Children

Ehan (pseudonym) was 6 years old. His mother was a prostituted woman living in the notorious *red-light* (sex trade) area of Songachi. Every evening when his mother was "working," Ehan was forced to leave their room and wander around the streets until around 11 p.m. when he was allowed to come home. He had many times seen men in his room through a half opened door, and they seemed to be beating his mother and torturing her. He would become very afraid and run away. The sounds of his mother's screams used to haunt him in his sleep. As he wandered around the streets, some of the men would give him small packages to hand over to other men/women in exchange for money. Unknown to him, he was running drugs for these men. Sometimes they would buy him some food if he said he was hungry. Then one night, one of these men took him into a dark alley and asked him to take off his shorts. Ehan was raped. Experiencing extreme pain, he screamed out, and he was consequently beaten by this man. When he went home that night, he saw that there was a lot of blood on his shorts and thinking his mother would scold him, he quietly washed his shorts. This abuse continued for months. His mother saw him becoming more and more quiet and not wanting to go out, and she asked him what was going on. It was then that he told her.

His mother approached our aftercare home for placement to keep him safe. Once he was brought to the Mahima Homes, Ehan was always very quiet and would not speak much. He was shaky, nervous, and used to stammer. However, when he engaged in drawing, Ehan was able to articulate what had happened and how he felt. Through expressive arts therapy (EXA), he was able to communicate much better, and he was even able to verbalize more. This progression allowed Ehan to express his fears, experience stabilization, and slowly heal.

Our Country and City

Every day, children experience abuse in India. Among the other children introduced in this chapter, Ehan was rescued from maltreatment and brought to the Mahima Homes, a project of Jatiyo Kristiyo Prochar Samity (JKPS), and benefited from the expressive arts program. A Christian nongovernmental organization, JKPS' mission is a holistic transformation for the poor, marginalized, and oppressed. At JKPS, staff members have adopted a *we culture*, caring for children as if they were their own. JKPS is located in Kolkata [Calcutta], the capital of West Bengal, on the central, eastern side of India close to Bangladesh.

India has the world's largest population living in slums and the second-largest urban population (Child Rights and You [CRY], 2013). India has the largest population of children in the world with 39% of the population below 18 years of age, yet children's rights are ignored, and they are the most neglected group in the country (Child Line India Foundation, 2011; CRY, 2013). In this country, we are constantly bombarded by the news and media of the various kinds of atrocities that children, especially the female child, are subjected to and the trauma that they endure. That means that JKPS has a vast number of at-risk children who require our care. Some disheartening examples include the following:

- Fetal sex determination and female feticide (abortion of female fetus) are widespread and have contributed to skewed gender ratio and selling of females into marriage (United Nations International Children's Emergency Fund [UNICEF], n.d.).
- Number of child marriages continue to increase (CRY, 2013).
- About half of the 220 million school-aged children in India do not attend school with 60% as females (Kelso, 2008).

Complex, complicated issues prevail in India, and there are many causes and obstacles to its problem with sex trafficking. Sex trafficking contributors in India include

- economic factors such as poverty, unemployment, and lack of employment;
- environmental calamities, like droughts, cyclones, floods, and tsunamis;
- cultural influences, such as domestic violence and lack of respect for women's and children's rights, caste discrimination, customary

prostitution, coerced early marriages, notion of gender discrimination that women are a burden and should not have the same access to education and economic opportunities; stigmatization of females who have been raped, abandoned, or divorced, and the belief that having sex with a virgin will cure STIs (sexually transmitted infections);
- government flaws of wars and conflict, drug trafficking, laws that ignore exploitation of children by their own families; and
- family circumstances exemplified by indebted generations of poverty, children of trafficked women, and street children (Joffres et al., 2008).

It is important to briefly explain India's caste system. Accepted to be more than 3,000 years old, the complex caste system provides order to life through classification and segregation; although recent influence of this practice has declined, caste identities endure (BBC News, 2017). The castes divide Hindus into four categories including Brahmins (scholars), Kshatriyas (leaders), Vaishyas (traders), Shudras (menial employment); outside of the caste system are the oppressed, the scheduled caste, previously known as the untouchables.

There are many statistics that demonstrate the tragedy our children undergo and how they suffer in a multitude of ways:

- The *Hindu* (2019) reported that every 15 minutes, one female child is sexually abused in India.
- Every eight minutes, a child goes missing in India (Every 8 Minutes, 2014).
- Kidnapping, abduction, and rape are the most prevalent crimes against children; crimes against children have increased 500% in the last 10 years (CRY, 2016).
- In India, more girls and women go missing than boys and men; of 2.90 *lakh* (Indian number unit equal to 100,000)/ 290,000 people missing of whom 1.74 lakh/174,000 were female and 24% or 7,250 of these were girls below the age of 18 years (National Crime Records Bureau, 2016).
- Tiwary (2016) recounted that in 94.8% of the cases, children were subjected to rape by someone known to them according to National Crime Records Bureau (NCRB).
- West Bengal topped the list in missing children and has one of the highest incidents of child abuse (NCRB, 2016).
- An estimated 40% of India's children are victimized by violence, lack adequate adult care, and are vulnerable to exploitation (CRY, 2013).
- One in every three child brides in the world is a girl in India (UNICEF, 2014).
- In the tribal area of Visakhapatnam, 57% of female youth were forced into child marriage (The *Hindu*, 2019).

- According to Pandit (2018), a newspaper report cites over 3.4 crore (Indian number unit equal to 10 million or 100 lakhs)/34,000,000 calls were received at Childline (toll free helpline for children in distress) between April 2015 and March 2018 that were silent calls. While the background sounds were audible, the caller remained on the phone but did not say anything; this was received as a muted call for help. The number of calls per year increased from 27 lakh/2,700,000 in 2015 to over 53 lakh/5,300,000 in 2017–2018 (Pandit, 2018).

Sex Trafficking in India

Most sex trafficked survivors are identified in Asia (Global Slavery Index, 2018), and millions of individuals are sexually exploited in India (United States Department of State, 2018). According to the Indian government, almost 5,000 individuals were rescued from sex trafficking in 2016 (Dasgupta, 2018). India is a source, transit, and destination country for commercial sexual exploitation (United States Department of State, 2018). India is an international provider for the trafficking of women and children to the Gulf States in addition to serving as a destination country for females from Nepal and Bangladesh (Joffres et al., 2008).

In India, sex trafficking occurs in these forms:

- exploitation from false employment opportunities, debt bondage (selling child to pay for debt), and arranged marriage of young, deprived, marginalized females;
- religious prostitution, pre-pubertal females who are concubines with temple priest, from the scheduled castes of Devadisi, Jogini, Nailis, Muralis, and Theradiyan;
- tribal prostitution (sex with ranked members of tribes) involves young females from different tribes such as Bedia and Nats; and
- sex tourism exploitation of children by international and national tourists (Joffres et al., 2008).

Most of India's trafficking problem is internal (United States Department of State, 2018). In India, many individuals are trafficked as minors by people who are known to them, and family disruption, such as violence, marital separation, or abandonment is directly associated with trafficking in India (Silverman et al., 2007). A woman grows up treated as a commodity of the family and after getting married, she becomes a commodity of her husband's family (Epatko, 2017). Poverty and gender-based oppression of females increases the risk of sex trafficking (Silverman et al., 2007). Those indebted from previous generations, the lowest scheduled caste *Dalits*, tribal communities, religious minorities, and females from excluded groups are most vulnerable (United States Department of State, 2018). Environmental calamities such as the tsunami in 2004 orphaned 35,000 children, making them especially vulnerable for sexual exploitation (Huda, 2006). In 2015, the earthquake in Nepal made women who traveled through India at high risk for trafficking, and refugees are still considered at risk for sex trafficking (United States Department of State, 2018). Economic, environmental, cultural, governmental, and familial influences impact sex trafficking in India, making this a complicated and multifaceted domestic issue.

Kolkata

Kolkata is known as the center of the trafficking industry in India due to its size and population. It is the source, destination, and transit point for the trafficking of girls and women. Kolkata has 29 red-light areas, including Sonagachi, Kidderpore, Kalighat, Rambagan, and Bowbazar (Joffres et al., 2008). Kolkata's Sonagachi (Golden Tree) is known as one of the largest red-light areas in all of Asia. Sonagachi has existed for at least 150 years and services about 20,000 clients a day (Joffres et al., 2008). The busy, crowded labyrinth of alleyways lined by brothels extend a half kilometer in square area and contain more than 10,000 sex workers (Dasgupta, 2018). Kolkata's brothels usually consist of several rooms divided by curtains into booths with beds (Joffres et al., 2008). Kolkata is also a transit point for many individuals who are initiated into exploitation before being resold (Joffres et al., 2008).

Aftermath of Sex Trafficking

Survivors of sex trafficking experience intense physical, emotional, psychological, and spiritual consequences. Chapter 2 described the typical diagnosis for survivors, including depression, anxiety, posttraumatic stress disorder (PTSD), and complex trauma. Complex trauma in youths is defined by chronic and consecutive exploitation, maltreatment, neglect, and violence; complex trauma results in impairment to relationship attachment, development, affect regulation, dissociation, behaviors, cognition, and self-worth (National Child Traumatic Stress Network, n.d.). Survivors in India also experience additional diagnosis of asthma and bronchiolitis due to high pollution of areas, dwellings that are ridden with mold, poor quality of air, and smoke exposure in addition to poor nutrition (Joffres et al., 2008). Not only do India's sex trafficked survivors face compounded consequences due to complex trauma, they are also exposed to further health risks from the environment.

Our Mahima Story

Because of the setting of sexual abuse, violence, and trauma against children, JKPS has been supporting the work of healing and restoration of children since 1976. Our story started with helping the children and women who have faced intense trauma resulting from the oppressive culture.

We began our journey exactly nine years ago in 2010 when we received our first seven girls. Our hope was to work on a model of care that allowed children who had been brutally abused and exploited to find a place to heal, find hope, and transform their lives. We wanted to return these children to the community as strong and empowered young women who saw themselves as worthy advocates against injustice. We receive funding from churches and foundations in the United States and Canada, as well as internal sources.

Our first home, Mahima Umang (Glory Exaltation), opened for minor female survivors of commercial sexual exploitation. Offering 20 beds, it employed 16 staff members, including a counselor, social worker, case-worker, and part-time teacher. In 2012, we fulfilled a need for a second home with 15 beds for adult women survivors who willingly want to leave the sex trade—Mahima Udaan (Glory Flight).

Many children whose mothers were prostitutes and were living in the red-light areas around the city were in a very vulnerable position, and they were placed by government child services in our homes. Some of these children had already been abused as young as 6 and 7 years old. Our homes for such children, Premanand Boys Home (Joy of Love) and the Mahima Umeed (Glory Hope) for girls, were set up in 2014. Umeed (20 beds) has the mission to prevent second-generation prostitution and encourage the mothers to leave the sex trade. All the girls in Umeed were also victimized by abuse. Mahima Premanand Boys Home offered 20 beds for boys whose mothers are in the sex trade.

From 2015–2016 onward, we realized the need to look toward the preventative aspect as well. This came about when we started working in the community within the high at-risk districts of North and South 24 Parganas (district of West Bengal and Murshidabad) that are highly prone to sex trafficking cases. We educate the families on keeping the children safe as well as provide information about how to report abuse to the public justice system. In India, access to the public justice system is challenging but not impossible. The government provides the public prosecutor to defend the victims, and free legal aid services are available. The law also requires the police to take cognizance of any complaint of abuse through the Juvenile Justice Act, children in need of protection as well as in conflict with the law, and the Prevention of Children from Sexual Offences Act, POCSO, which provides more stringent protection for children who have been sexually abused (Government of India, 2017; UNICEF, 2017). However, due to a lack of information, resources, and knowing what their rights are, common people find it difficult to access the system. In addition, much government corruption complicates this process.

Currently, we are awaiting licensing before opening Mahima Upasana (Glory Worship), a preventative home for female children of commercial sex workers who are vulnerable to getting trapped in the trade. This home is in the South 24 Pargana and will be for 20 girls, with space to accommodate up to 50 beds.

Mahima Homes also provides a community center at the heart of Sonagachi. We provide medical care to underprivileged individuals, especially those with HIV and other STIs. Every evening, we have about 100 children registered to come after school and learn computers, conversational English, and attend life skills classes. We offer music therapy for children in the area as well as a mother's support group where we discuss many issues and share with the mothers avenues of alternative employment should they wish to leave the sex trade. Approximately 40 women come every Thursday to experience community and sharing.

Our Approach to Healing From Trauma

The Mahima Homes, a project of JKPS, are passionate about protecting children, India's most vulnerable individuals, and improving their quality of life. JKPS' main goals are to empower women, raise children into leaders, and help families out of poverty; bring change to impoverished children and encourage them to dream; and restore hope and self-worth for commercial sex trafficking survivors. Our work with survivors focuses on health initiatives for individual and personalized treatment through psychiatric care, intensive psychological therapy for trauma, trauma-focused expressive therapy (art, music, and dance/movement), weekly medical intervention, providing avenues for education, vocational training according to interest and skills, job preparation and placement, encouraging justice initiatives of speaking against abusers in court, and connecting them with their families and, finally, returning them home—be it here locally, nationally, or internationally to Nepal and Bangladesh. Our hope is that these young girls and women will be advocates for progressive change in society.

Humans are resilient; however, trauma experiences do leave traces, whether large scale, such as cultural, or smaller, as in our families of origin, and these are passed down intergenerationally (van der Kolk, 2014). Even when trauma is resolved, it affects an individuals' emotions, thoughts, relationships, immune systems, and biological levels of functioning (van der Kolk, 2014). The trauma of sex trafficking and the abuse that ensue continues through generations, and we witness this in our children every day. The goal of trauma therapy is rebuilding an individual's wholeness (Levine, 1997), and EXA offers a nonthreatening and effective approach to treat trauma and repair an individual in entirety.

Framework

The Mahima Homes program started without any model to follow. During this initial time, the government homes, and some nongovernment organization (NGO) homes were only able to provide safe housing; they did not offer any plans or programs for survivors. The government home did not have any counselors or social workers, and the NGO homes had one part-time social worker for about 120 girls. The counselors were not trained in trauma, and no specific plan was followed for each female survivor.

The lack of professional training available for trauma in Kolkata meant that we had to follow the conventional methods of client-centered therapy and cognitive behavior therapy (CBT). Client-centered therapy allows individuals to tell their stories at their own pace; the therapist's goal is to understand the perspective of the client through an empathetic, congruent manner that communicates positive regard (Harvard Medical School, 2006). CBT is a form of therapeutic treatment that focuses on changing thought and behavior patterns, and it has demonstrated improved functioning and quality of life with various mental health diagnoses (American Psychological Association [APA], 2019). In 2011, we availed of a training in trauma-focused CBT (TF-CBT), because we felt this approach would work well with the survivors. TF-CBT is a model for treatment that uses trauma-sensitive interventions with CBT; this approach is recommended for children and adolescents who have significant emotional issues resulting from the experience of trauma (National Child Traumatic Stress Network, 2012).

However, we quickly came to see that a CBT-based framework of therapy was not effective with all our clients. Many of them were not comfortable with verbalizing their feelings. Others, due to their trauma, were unable to understand the abstract concepts of CBT. The children were unable to perceive errors, connect emotions to thoughts and actions, or understand cognitive restructuring. We were struggling to get the clients to open up about their experiences and help them to reintegrate their trauma to move forward in their recovery. It was a frustrating time as we groped around to find ways to reach them, but we learned from observing the children what helped them best.

We witnessed that survivors tended to pick up paper and art supplies, and they would draw or paint when they were emotionally disturbed or had trauma flashbacks. They played instruments like the piano and ukulele and were easy to engage in music. Dance/movement therapy was introduced twice a week, and the EXA program was initiated. Since many of the girls responded well to this alternative treatment, this proved to be a successful addition to the program. In 2016, art therapy was offered once a week in all three minor homes. Then in 2017, music therapy was added once a week, and girls from three homes could access the music therapist for extra support as needed.

We saw noticeable progress from EXA, as the children were able to express their emotions and their experiences in a safe and non-threatening manner. The first improvement noted was in attention and concentration; although the children were usually restless, after engaging in EXA, they were able to focus on topics for an extended time.

The children began to utilize art and music as tools to self-sooth when they were anxious or angry. Later on, we realized that they were less depressed and anxious and more social and engaged with the other programs in the home. The children were also less conflicted with the other residents and had fewer aggressive outbursts. We also saw that they felt some peace when they were involved in EXA of music, art, and dance/movement.

EXA

Although the EXA is an established profession in other countries, it has extremely limited availability in India, and there is no regulation or requirement for professional licensure or credentialing. There are a few universities that offer diploma courses or a certificate program for the separate therapies—art, music, and dance/movement—but there is no advanced degree available. Training for music therapy is a certificate or diploma course and only available online and through distance learning (Mir & Sharma, 2016). Most therapists who practice EXA in India are trained by a trainer, meaning an expressive arts therapist provides training and education. As exemplified through Kolkata Sanved (2017), the "training of trainers" (TOT) dance/movement therapy program teaches survivors to lead the groups independently. Kolkata Sanved has trained 64 individuals to become trainers since 2005, and in 2015, Kolkata Sanved trained 26 girls; 30 of those who trained are practicing dance/movement therapists (Rise Learning Network, 2015). This illustrates a growing need for trainers for dance/movement therapy.

The EXA staff at Mahima includes a dance/movement therapist who has training in dance/movement therapy and has been working with survivors of various shelter homes in Kolkata for the last 20 years, a music therapist who has completed music therapy training, and an art therapist who has a master's level of training (previously employed). The other trained staff members have master's degrees in social work or psychology and have been trained by both certified art and play therapists from the United States and Europe.

The program at JKPS' Mahima Homes applies EXA as a resource-oriented and solution-focused process. EXA accentuates expression of the body through making music, creating art, dancing, and singing (Levine, 2009). Using a multimedia approach in EXA to emphasize the mind/body relationship, survivors of human trafficking are more likely to share their trauma narratives as compared to traditional therapy (Morita, 2006; Rafferty, 2017). The goal of EXA is to increase the survivor's span of expression and expand her dreams to minimize the perspective of limitations. The process of EXA provides healing, while the final product provides insight, and the entire process makes transformation possible (Rogers, 1999). This requires the therapist to remain open and sensitive to what emerges in EXA.

The role of the EXA therapist becomes the guide for the individual seeking recovery (van Lith, Schofield, & Fenner, 2012). In the therapeutic relationship, the survivors are the experts in their lives. The therapist is affected by personal hindrances toward the therapeutic relationship through awareness, opinions, history, and countertransference. If a power dynamic is expressed in the therapeutic relationship where the therapist is *all knowing*, a change in the outcome for the client may not always be in their best interest (Brown, 2015). Instead, the art therapist is viewed as an equal who assists the client to find the best personal solution.

EXA is a promising practice used with survivors to help process trauma and reconnect with their bodies; during EXA, there are four areas of expected therapeutic impact, including communication, imagination, dynamic engagement, and mind-body connection (Sanar Wellness Institute & Polaris, 2015) Alternative approaches, including EXA, are the preferred approach when working with trafficked survivors due to the benefits achieved through a safe, creative, and open approach to expression. Through play, laughter, and connection, survivors of sex trafficking engage in the healing process and visualize their future via the expressive arts (Hopper, Azar, Bhattacharyya, Malebranche, & Brennan, 2018). Art, music, and movement interventions externalize trauma in a sensory experience, reduce distress and regulate affect, and enhance connections in relationships (Malchiodi, 2015). Hence the United States Department of Health and Human Services (2008) recommends art, music, and drama therapy as alternative therapies that provide opportunities to increase self-worth, experience empowerment, and reconnect with the self.

EXA Case Examples

Nargis (pseudonym) was 14 years old and living in Dhaka, Bangladesh. Her father was a poor rickshaw puller who barely made any money and what money he did make was spent every night on alcohol. Her mother worked hard as domestic help but was suffering from tuberculosis and soon was unable to work. Her younger brother needed to go to school because education was prioritized for males. Nargis grew up in a violent home. Her father beat her mother and her almost every day. She quickly realized that she had to be the one to earn money, and so she started working at a garment factory, lying about her age. After 12-hour shifts, her hands were sore, her body was exhausted, and she returned home to the same violence and poverty. Whatever she made seemed to go into a "bottomless pit" because of her father's alcoholism.

She met a distant relative at the factory who was very supportive and sympathetic toward her. The lady told her that she could help her find a job in Kolkata, India, in a jeans factory where she could earn a lot of money. Nargis was intrigued by this promising opportunity. She agreed to go to Kolkata without informing her family. Her relative handed her over to a young man who brought her across the border illegally where she was handed over to three other men. These men took her to a building where girls were dressed in skimpy clothes and men would come at all hours of the day. She cried that she wanted to go home, and the more she cried, the more she was beaten. She was kept locked in a room and not given more than two meals a day. There were a couple of men who would come every day and violently rape her. She was left in pain and bleeding, and nobody cared. The beatings continued. Soon she gave up hope and became a body to be abused daily.

Once she was brought to Mahima Homes, Nargis was extremely hostile and angry. She was involved in a lot of conflict with her peers and staff. Not having any other way to cope, she would self-harm frequently. Repeatedly, she cut her hands with whatever she found—plastic, pins, and lipstick covers. When she first started attending the EXA sessions, she drew bleeding hearts, human figures with blood coming out of the private parts, and bleeding knifes. Whenever she remembered the cousin who trafficked her, Nargis would get violently angry and dissociate. She was prescribed antipsychotic medication due to her vivid visual and auditory hallucinations. Burdened by her suffering, drawing and listening to Bangladeshi music seemed to relieve her the best. Through EXA sessions, she learned how to manage her pain and to self-soothe by using art and music. By the time she left and was repatriated to Bangladesh, she was healthy and completely functional. Although she still has more healing to do, she was in much better condition when she returned to her family. She continues to do well, has a job working in a garment factory, and she is living with her family.

Art Therapy

India offers a vibrant culture where art has a significant role in not only holidays and tradition but also everyday life. Artistic expressions, images, and symbols are universal communications (Morita, 2006), and the arts connect us to meaning beyond ourselves (van Der Kolk, 2014). The creative approach of art therapy offers an unspoken form of expression of feelings, thoughts, and experiences for survivors who are experiencing shame, guilt, and anger. Art therapy is not only a valuable way to attain awareness, more importantly, it is a way to process sexual abuse and trauma (Pifalo, 2002). Especially for those who cannot find the words, art becomes the vehicle for what cannot be spoken for many reasons. Art therapy provides an opportunity for survivors of sex trafficking to communicate what cannot be verbalized and to find meaning beyond the trauma, pain, and anguish.

The art therapy sessions take place within a safe, noninterrupted, and quiet space. A choice of art supplies including drawing and painting materials are available. The art therapy program is focused on providing experiences of control to the survivors who lost this sense during their traumatic pasts. Art therapy with abuse survivors provides empowerment through the goals of trauma processing, emotional catharsis, and future visualization (Pifalo, 2009).

In a typical art therapy session at JKPS, the art therapist facilitates a check-in process, a warm-up exercise, and then the creative intervention. Check-in is a time for show and tell of creative art journals and for the art therapist to connect themes and address progress through images. For survivors of violence, creative arts journaling demonstrated power to improve resiliency, symptom, and relationships (Ikonomopoulos et al., 2017). The art journals are blank books that the girls can use during sessions and keep with them outside of the group. When they feel sad or angry, the girls use this as a tool to calm themselves and to process what is going on with them. They are encouraged to use the space for writing and drawing their thoughts, feelings, and reactions. Sometimes they are given prompts and exercises to follow, and spontaneous creation is encouraged a well. Creative arts journaling is a safe and convenient method for expression.

Art Therapy Example

In a particularly notable art therapy group session, a warm-up exercise facilitated a mindfulness exercise regarding future wishes of what the girls wanted most in the world. The four girls, all minors under the age of 18, present in the group were a mix from India and Bangladesh. All had been rescued following the trauma of being trafficked and held against their will. Preya (pseudonym) connected with the mindfulness example, and she shared that she wanted to go home, and she wished for love from her family. Her drawing reflected the enjoyment of expressing herself safely through color and symbol. Maalai (pseudonym) was resourceful with her use of coloring and symbolism, and she shared with the group that she wished to be a nurse. Although she did not appear comfortable with the others in the group, she was still able to express her future wish for a career. Although survivors struggled to articulate their thoughts and emotions verbally with the non-EXA counselor, in the EXA sessions, while feeling safe and creating together, Maalai and Preya felt free to share their feelings without any reservations. They shared future goals, wishes, and their hopes to go home and reconnect with their families. This allowed them to feel a sense of connection to each other and further reduce personal isolation. Art therapy assisted survivors in finding support in shared experiences, work through their pain, and begin to feel empowered for their futures.

Following the life skills sessions on child rights, the girls were asked to paint a message they would like to give society. Preya engaged with expressing her hopes for education and a future career (Figure 7.1). She shared that she felt imprisoned by her lack of education and how society does not value her education. She painted the word Kanyashree, which is

Figure 7.1 I don't want to be imprisoned by illiteracy

Figure 7.2 I want to study and not be a bride

a government program offering annual scholarships for female children in order to promote higher education, encourage well-being, and prevent child marriage (Chief Minister's Office, n.d.). Preya knew receiving an education would give her freedom in her future. Maalai engaged with painting about her hopes and dreams to return to school and someday attend college. She knew so many other young females who became child brides, and she did not want that life for herself. Maalai's image is representative of her future choices, and her dream to become a nurse and help care for others. Her painting boldly emphasizes, "I want to study and not be a bride" (Figure 7.2).

Art Therapy Example

Farida (pseudonym) was born into a middle-class Muslim family. She was sent to an English medium school (where English is the primary language of instruction) and was studying in class IX/high school. When she was 11 years old, she opened a Facebook account. She was happy to take pictures of herself and post them on social media, and the attention she received from others made her feel popular. She accepted friend requests from random people as she wanted to have many "friends." So when she received a request from a girl, Annie (pseudonym) who was one year older, she "liked" her profile and accepted Annie as a friend. Farida saw that this girl had very expensive clothes, went to a lot of parties, and was seen with boyfriends and expensive cars. Farida started bunking (skipping) school and spending time with her. Since Annie was introduced to her family as a friend, Farida was permitted to stay over at her home. Annie lived with her mother, and her mother did not have any problems with her daughter going to nightclubs or prostituting herself at 17 years of age because she was contributing financially to the household. Farida started going to nightclubs and parties where she was introduced to drugs and alcohol and soon became dependent on marijuana and inhalants. Then under Annie's direction, she entered the business of prostitution. Annie collected the money and gave Farida funds to buy drugs and clothes.

Finally, Farida was rescued by the police during a raid in a private apartment, and Annie was arrested. Once Farida was brought to Mahima Homes, her addiction to drugs and the exploitation of her body led her to sexually act out, lose complete control over her emotions, and experience extreme negativity. Art became the door to her recovery. Farida was able to use painting as a way to cope with her pain, addiction, and exploitation and, ultimately, to heal from her trauma. Art therapy assisted in her recovery by providing her with the means for expression, reflection, and empowerment. Farida's quality of life drastically improved at Mahima, and she achieved a deeper sense of awareness and personal growth as a result of art therapy. Initially, Farida's paintings were very dark, as she used a lot of black in her paintings. However, with her stabilization, she started using brighter colors, and she was able to express more verbally through the expressive arts (Figure 7.3). Farida continues to paint, and this has become a source of income for her.

Music Therapy

Music is something that stirs the soul of every person, especially with our young clients who suffer from the effects of complex trauma. Listening to music, singing, and dancing are ways they have coped with their trauma over time. Music is relaxing for the survivors, particularly at times when they are very disturbed by symptoms of PTSD; music is one way that they are able to ground themselves and self-soothe. For survivors who have

Figure 7.3 Farida's painting as a way to heal

difficulty with verbalizing feelings, music therapy allows the girls to use various instruments, rhythms, songs, and sounds to express pain, anger, and stress, as well as experience peace. Music therapy uses both active engagement and listening to attune to one another.

Research also proves the additional benefits to self-expression in music therapy for survivors. Music therapy offered a healing approach for youth survivors of sex trafficking through encouraging interaction, relaxation, and a nonthreatening way to confront the trauma (Schrader, 2012). Survivors of sexual abuse may also benefit from the open communication, increased awareness of trauma feelings, improved self-esteem, validation of emotions, and strengthened social interaction from music therapy (LaVerdiere, 2007).

Music Therapy Example

Golap (pseudonym) was a minor client who was trafficked from Bangladesh and was awaiting repatriation (the legal process of returning home) to Bangladesh as per government norms. She had waited 1.5 years because the process involves multiple government and police agencies on both sides of the border and getting all of the documentation in place is a challenging, arduous task.

Due to her traumatic exploitation, she was under psychiatric treatment for severe symptoms of PTSD, depression, and excessive self-harm and cutting. She was on medication for depression. However, Golap was easy to engage with music, and she attended music therapy regularly with interest. At the end of her treatment, she found it hard to focus on anything except her approaching departure date. During music therapy, she expressed and communicated feelings regarding her transition and was even able to process her personal progress.

The music therapist was concerned with her depressed mood during the waiting period, and she encouraged Golap by engaging in song and improvisation. By engaging with the instruments, she was able to focus in the session and experience relaxation to enhance her resilience, thus improving her distress tolerance and depressive symptoms. In talking about her upcoming transition, Golap was asked about what she had learned from music therapy. She acknowledged the improvement she'd made, reflected, and stated the following:

> It's been helpful to express the pain that I feel. I learned patience from the hard time of waiting. . . . I have realized that my love for her family is deeper that I knew. I have enjoyed the calming effect of music and as well as the energizing affect of music.

Golap had undergone TF-CBT, but despite this treatment, she continued to struggle with her depression. Music therapy was the treatment that helped her to feel calm and to refocus on the positives in her life. Golap was repatriated to her home in February 2019 as a much healthier person, as evidenced by the decrease in her symptoms and her ability to maintain safety and experience peace.

Dance/Movement Therapy

Dance/movement therapy focuses on mind/body connection for survivors to process traumatic memories both cognitively and physically, experience relaxation through breathing, and create a trauma narrative to experience empowerment and regulate the sympathetic nervous system (American Dance Therapy Association [ADTA], 2013). Movement offers an emotional, thoughtful, and reflective language; using movement in therapy allows the physical, mental, and emotional aspects of a person to reconnect (Halprin, 1999). Furthermore, dance/movement therapy allows survivors to access their inner power and make meaning from their trauma (ADTA, 2013). Through a six-month pilot study, dance/movement therapy demonstrated rewarding benefits for trafficking survivors in Kolkata and Mumbai by using classical Indian dance to help survivors overcome trauma; decrease anxiety, depression, and anger; and develop confidence and positive body image (Chandran, 2016). Indian dance is especially suited to dance/movement therapy; the energetic footwork from the classical dance *Kathak* releases anger, the eye movement from the area of Tamil Nadu assists in emotional expression, and traditional folk dancing increases connection (Chandran, 2016).

Dance defines identity (Halprin, 1999). India has a strong culture of music and dance, especially in Kolkata; the Bengali people are especially oriented to music and dance. In the red-light areas, dance is used in a very negative way to seduce the clients. The survivors have learned to use their bodies in ways that are highly sexualized. When they are rescued, the trauma of having their bodies abused leads to a rejection of their bodies, low self-image, and shame. For many, there has been much self-harm and cutting that leads to permanent scars on their bodies. Therefore, it is imperative for the girls to learn to love their bodies and love themselves, and dance has proved to be an important tool in this regard. Following a distressing trauma, dance/movement therapy is beneficial in reconstructing an individual's sense of self and experiencing a sense of wholeness (Gray, 2001), and one of the fundamental goals of dance/movement therapy with survivors of sexual trauma is body acceptance (Valentine, 2007). Additionally, group sessions of dance/movement therapy aid in expression, empowerment, and solidarity (Valentine, 2007).

The dance/movement therapist facilitated group sessions for the girls to become more comfortable with their bodies. This also helped in building self-control, self-confidence, and cooperation among the group members. Survivors, who had come into the home as broken shells of themselves, bloomed in the dance/movement therapy sessions. They smiled, laughed, giggled, and swayed with the beat of the music. Observers could witness the freedom they experienced during this time. This was often the first time the girls felt free and in control of their bodies since their exploitation. They began to feel a sense of acceptance of their physical space in a community again (Figure 7.4).

Figure 7.4 Dance therapy session

Out of the dance/movement therapy sessions emerged the use of drama. Utilizing drama in the EXA, survivors expressed themselves through role-playing, interactions, symbolization, and storytelling (Silverman, 2007). Many Mahima Homes clients felt more comfortable in expressing the emotions of a "character" rather than identifying with their own experience. Initially, this active engagement in drama helped them to understand different emotions, their manifestations, and how they are expressed. This EXA process gradually helped them to identify and regulate their own emotions in a healthy manner.

The utilization of drama has been documented to educate communities on important issues, such as human rights, health, and safety (UNODC, 2012). In addition, drama is a powerful way to inspire change, suggest solutions to a problem, and address misconceptions (UNODC, 2012). For example, Banglanatak.com identifies a vulnerable community, performs a study of the problem, and provides resources and helpline numbers, followed by an open discussion to address the issue in greater depth and building community support through presentations (UNODC, 2012).

At Mahima, the girls have performed before large audiences to sensitize the community about the impact of trafficking, rape, and sexual abuse. Those who were afraid to speak to more than one person at a time performed on stage with a confidence and energy of seasoned performers. Drama helped increase self-confidence and empowerment and reduce fears. Performances were given for public awareness on sexual violence. Mahima Homes' dance/movement therapist conceptualized, choreographed, and directed the performance that subsequently helped heal and rebuild the survivors' lives (Millennium Post, 2018).

Dance/Movement Therapy Example

Suhana (pseudonym) was 13 years old and lived in Kolkata. Her father had passed away, and she lived with her mother and younger sister in a slum area. Her mother worked as domestic help. Soon Suhana noticed her mother had more money and was dressing better. She did not pay too much attention to the change in her mother's appearance because she was busy going to the local government school. One day, her mother told her that she would have to drop out of school and start working as domestic help in the house of a very nice lady. Suhana's mother took her to a new home to live with a couple with their young child. She started looking after the baby and doing household chores. Then one night, the man of the house came into the place she was sleeping and raped her. She cried out and went to tell his wife. The wife only laughed and said that Suhana could be a co-wife to her husband. Following this incident, Suhana was raped every day. Her mother came each month to take her salary. When Suhana told her mother she wanted to leave, her mother did not believe her and said she must stay.

After about six months of this sexual abuse, Suhana was taken by this couple to another house, and there she saw other girls come and go as men would take them into separate rooms. Suhana was forced into prostitution and made to service 10–12 men each day. At 14, she became pregnant and was taken to a private hospital for an abortion. She rested one day and then returned to work as usual. Suhana realized that she had been sold as her mother continued to appear and collect money from the couple every month. Every night, she was left in a huge two-story house, which had one dog for security and a door locked from outside. Suhana was very afraid and locked herself inside one room until the next morning when the oppressive ordeal began again. She was also taken to various hotels in tourist spots around the city, and men would rape her day after day.

After a year of this abuse, Suhana, who was very traumatized, was rescued. At Mahima Homes, Suhana had many nightmares, was very shaky, and anxious, but she slowly responded to expressive arts program. Dance/movement therapy helped Suhana gain control of her body, her shame, and her fear. With practice, she became more confident, happy, and was able to put her fears and pain behind her. As a 13-year-old who was taken out of school to be sold by her mother into slavery for profit, repeatedly and violently raped, and endured pregnancy and abortion, Suhana responded to the arts to overcome her trauma and recover her life.

Conclusion

Abuse of children is relentless in India due to many factors, including acceptance of an outdated class system of segregation, a cultural preference for male children, a country with pervasive indigent economic levels, and ineffective government protection for women and children. In response to modern India's "black hole" of abuse, the Mahima Homes, a project of JKPS, have assisted many of the young sex trafficked survivors through their journey back to health and well-being. Seeing that conventional methods of counseling were not working, Mahima therapists and counselors saw the girls react to art, music, and dance. New methods to help these traumatized children were created by the workers, and the EXA program was initiated and housed within the shelters. A proven and effective form of treatment around the world for survivors of trauma (van der Kolk, 2014), EXA made an encouraging impact toward healing some of the most vulnerable and destitute people in India. EXA allowed survivors to feel acceptance of themselves and each other. An integral part of the programming, art therapy gave communication to unspeakable memories and expressed lost lives, lost dreams, and future hopes. Dance/movement therapy gave confidence, freedom, and joy the power to overtake and replace fear, pain, and trauma. Music therapy provided relaxation, mental focus, and a unique form of catharsis and cultural expression to the girls. Along with the other EXA, art therapy increased stabilization, managed pain, and increased the ability to self-soothed. As isolation was reduced, reflection, communication, and empowerment grew and increased. Personal growth, a higher sense of awareness, and improved quality of life were witnessed as results of the EXA in a traumatized and deprived population of abused youth in India. Art therapy enabled these survivors to find support in shared experiences, work through their pain, and feel empowered for their futures.

References

American Dance Therapy Association. (2013). *Dance/movement therapy: A healing modality for women who have been subjected to violence*. Retrieved from https://adta.org/wp-content/uploads/2015/12/DMT-A-Healing-Modality-for-Women-Who-Have-Been-Subjected-to-Violence-English.pdf

American Psychological Association. (2019). *What is cognitive behavior therapy?* Retrieved from www.apa.org/ptsd-guideline/patients-and-families/cognitive-behavioral

BBC News. (2017). *What is India's caste system?* Retrieved from www.bbc.com/news/world-asia-india-35650616

Brown, A. (2015, November). *What do the arts have to offer women who have been traumatized by a variety of experiences? Can art interventions be implemented in a time limited frame and still be effective?* Unpublished master's thesis. European Graduate School, Switzerland.

Chandran, R. (2016, February 24). Classical Indian dance helps trafficking victims to heal, study shows. *Thomas Reuters Foundation News*. Retrieved from http://news.trust.org//item/20160224085927-9ns5w/

Chief Minister's Office. (n.d.). *Kanyashree*. Government of West Bengal. Retrieved from http://wbcmo.gov.in/kanyashree.aspx

Child Line India Foundation. (2011). *CHILD protection & child rights*. Retrieved from www.childlineindia.org.in/child-in-india.htm

Child Rights and You [CRY]. (2013, November 10). *Status report on child rights in India*. Retrieved from www.cry.org/resources/pdf/Status-Report-on-Child-Rights-2013.pdf

Child Rights and You [CRY]. (2016). *CRY media release: Crime against children 2016*. Retrieved from www.cry.org/wp-content/uploads/2018/01/CRY-Media-release-Crime-against-Children-2017.pdf

Dasgupta, S. (2018). Indian bill to "protect" trafficking victims will make sex workers less safe. *The Conversation*. Retrieved from https://theconversation.com/indian-bill-to-protect-trafficking-victims-will-make-sex-workers-less-safe-104535

Epatko, L. (2017, December 29). Sex traffickers target poor communities in India. This groups aims to stop them. *PBS News Hour*. Retrieved from www.pbs.org/newshour/world/sex-traffickers-target-poor-communities-in-india-this-group-aims-to-stop-them

Every 8 Minutes. (2014, November 24). *Know the facts*. Retrieved from www.every8minutes.org/?p=1235

Global Slavery Index. (2018). *India*. Retrieved from www.globalslaveryindex.org/2018/findings/country-studies/india/

Government of India. (2017). *POCSO introduction*. Retrieved from www.ncpcr.gov.in/index1.php?lang=1&level=1&&sublinkid=14&lid=607

Gray, A. E. L. (2001). The body remembers: Dance/movement therapy with an adult survivor of torture. *American Journal of Dance Therapy*, *23*(1), 29–43.

Halprin, D. (1999). Living artfully: Movement as an integrative process. In S. K. Levine & E. G. Levine (Eds.), *Foundations of expressive arts therapy: Theoretical and clinical perspectives* (pp. 133–150). London, UK: Jessica Kingsley Publishers.

Harvard Medical School. (2006). Client-centered therapy. *Harvard Health Publishing*. Retrieved from www.health.harvard.edu/newsletter_article/Client-centered_therapy

The Hindu. (2019, January 25). One girl child is sexually abused in every 15 minutes, says experts. Retrieved from www.thehindu.com/news/cities/Visakhapatnam/one-girl-child-is-sexually-abused-in-every-15-minutes-say-experts/article26083518.ece

Hopper, E. K., Azar, N., Bhattacharyya, S., Malebranche, D. A., & Brennan, K. E. (2018). STARS experiential group intervention: A complex trauma treatment approach for survivors of human trafficking. *Journal of Evidence-Informed Social Work*, *15*(2), 215–241. https://doi.org/10.1080/23761407.2018.1455616

Huda, S. (2006, July 17). Sex trafficking in South Asia. *International Journal of Gynecology & Obstetrics*, *94*(3). https://doi.org/10.1016/j.ijgo.2006.04.027

Ikonomopoulos, J., Cavazos-Vela, J., Vela, P., Sanchez, M., Schmidt, C., & Catchings, C. V. (2017). Evaluating the effects of creative journal arts therapy for survivors of domestic violence. *Journal of Creativity in Mental Health*, *12*(4), 496–512. https://doi.org/10.1080/1540138.2017.1328290

Joffres, C., Mills, E., Joffres, M., Khanna, T., Walia, H., & Grund, D. (2008). Sexual slavery without borders: Trafficking for commercial sexual exploitation in India. *International Journal for Equity in Health*, *7*(22). https://doi.org/10.1186/1475-9276-7-22

Kelso, C. M. (2008). Child labor and the trafficking industry in India. In O. N. I. Ebbe & D. K. Das (Eds.), *Global trafficking in women* (pp. 67–78). Boca Raton, FL: CRC Press.

Kolkata Sanved. (2017). *From survivors to healers*. Retrieved from http://kolkatasanved.org/training-of-trainers/

LaVerdiere, E. M. (2007). The use of music therapy with children who have been sexually abused. In S. L. Brooks (Ed.), *The use of creative therapies with sexual abuse survivors* (pp. 207–217). Springfield, IL: Charles C. Thomas Publisher, Ltd.

Levine, P. A. (1997). *Waking the tiger: Healing trauma*. Berkley, CA: North Atlantic Books.

Levine, S. K. (2009). *Trauma, tragedy, therapy: The arts and human suffering*. London, UK: Jessica Kingsley Publishers.

Malchiodi, C. A. (2015). Neurobiology, creative interventions, and childhood trauma. In C. A. Malchiodi (Ed.), *Creative Interventions with traumatized children* (pp. 3–23). New York, NY: The Guilford Press.

Millennium Post. (2018, April 21). Abuse victims to enact drama to spread awareness. Kolkata, India.

Mir, S. A., & Sharma, S. (2016, July). Music therapy education & its training in India. *Sangeet Galaxy*, *5*(2), 2–11. Retrieved from www.sangeetgalaxy.co.in/admin/manufiles/12327850022-Music_Therapy_Education_and_Training_in_India_-Current_State.pdf

Morita, A. (2006). Expressive arts therapy applied research method. *Asian Breeze*, *48*, 6–9.

National Child Traumatic Stress Network. (2012). *Trauma-focused cognitive behavioral therapy*. Retrieved from www.nctsn.org/interventions/trauma-focused-cognitive-behavioral-therapy

National Child Traumatic Stress Network. (n.d.). *Effects*. Retrieved from www.nctsn.org/what-is-child-trauma/trauma-types/complex-trauma/effects

National Crime Records Bureau (Ministry of Home Affairs). (2016). *Crime in India: Statistics*. Mahipalpur, New Delhi: Government of India. Retrieved from http://ncrb.gov.in/StatPublications/CII/CII2016/pdfs/NEWPDFs/Crime%20in%20India%20-%202016%20Complete%20PDF%20291117.pdf

Pandit, A. (2018, August 25). 1.36 crore "silent" calls received by child helpline in 3 years. *The Times of India*. Retrieved from https://timesofindia.indiatimes.com/india/1-36-crore-silent-calls-received-by-child-helpline-in-3-years/articleshow/65536656.cms

Pifalo, T. (2002). Pulling out the thorns: Art therapy with sexually abused children and adolescents. *Art Therapy: Journal of the American Art Therapy Association*, *19*(1), 12–22. https://doi.org/10.1080/07421656.2002.10129724

Pifalo, T. (2009). Mapping the maze: An art therapy intervention following disclosure of sexual abuse. *Art Therapy: Journal of the American Art Therapy Association*, *26*(1), 12–18. https://doi.org/10.1080/07421656.2009.10129313

Rafferty, Y. (2017). Mental health services as a vital component of psychosocial recovery for victims of child trafficking or commercial sexual exploitation. *American Journal of Orthopsychiatry*, *88*(3), 249–260. https://doi.org/10.1037.ort0000268

Rise Learning Network. (2015, September 23). *Kolkata Sanved's dance movement therapy*. Retrieved from https://riselearningnetwork.org/resource/kolkata-sanveds-dance-movement-therapy/

Rogers, R. (1999). The creative connection: A holistic expressive arts process. In S. K. Levine & E. G. Levine (Eds.), *Foundations of expressive arts therapy: Theoretical and clinical perspectives* (pp. 113–132). London, UK: Jessica Kingsley Publishers.

Sanar Wellness Institute & Polaris. (2015, November). *Promising practices: An overview of trauma-informed therapeutic support for survivors of human trafficking*. Retrieved from https://polarisproject.org/sites/default/files/Sanar-Promising-Practices.pdf

Schrader, E. (2012). Music therapy programming at an aftercare center in Cambodia for survivors of sexual exploitation and rape and their caregivers. *Social Work & Christianity*, *39*(4), 390–406.

Silverman, J. G., Decker, M. R., Gupta, J., Maheshwari, A., Patel, V., Willis, B. M., & Raj, A. (2007). Experiences of sex trafficking victims in Mumbai, India. *International Journal of Gynecology & Obstetrics*, *97*(3), 221–226. https://doi.org/10.1016/j.ijgo.2006.12.003

Silverman, Y. (2007). Drama therapy with adolescent survivors of sexual abuse: The use of myth, metaphor, and fairytale. In S. L. Brooks (Ed.), *The use of creative therapies with sexual abuse survivors* (pp. 250–260). Springfield, IL: Charles C. Thomas Publisher, Ltd.

Tiwary, D. (2016). NCRB data: 25 percent of children raped were targeted at work by employers and co-workers. *The Indian Express*. Retrieved from https://indianexpress.com/article/india/india-news-india/ncrb-data-rape-child-minor-workplace-by-employee-crime-3005142/

United Nations International Children's Emergency Fund. (2014). *Ending child marriage: Progress and prospects*. Retrieved from www.unicef.org/media/files/Child_Marriage_Report_7_17_LR.pdf

United Nations International Children's Emergency Fund. (2017). *Juvenile Justice Act 2015: A handbook for administrators*. Uttarakhand, India: National Gender Centre. Retrieved from http://megpolice.gov.in/pdf/child_protection/JJ%20Act%20Handbook%20for%20Administrators.pdf

United Nations International Children's Emergency Fund. (n.d.). *Fact sheet on commercial sexual exploitation and trafficking of children*. Retrieved from www.unicef.org/indonesia/Factsheet_CSEC_trafficking_Indonesia.pdf

United Nations Office on Drugs and Crime. (2012, July.). *India: Bringing the curtain down on human trafficking*. Retrieved from www.unodc.org/southasia/frontpage/2012/july/bringing-the-curtain-down-on-human-trafficking.html

United States Department of Health and Human Services. (2008, March 15). *Treating the hidden wounds: Trauma treatment and mental health for victims of human trafficking. Core components of trauma informed and specific services*. Retrieved from https://aspe.hhs.gov/report/treating-hidden-wounds-trauma-treatment-and-mental-health-recovery-victims-human-trafficking/core-components-trauma-informed-and-specific-services

United States Department of State. (2018). *Office to monitor and combat trafficking in persons*. 2018 Trafficking in Persons Report. Retrieved from www.state.gov/j/tip/rls/tiprpt/countries/2017/271205.htm

Valentine, G. E. (2007). Dance/movement therapy with women survivors of sexual abuse. In S. L. Brooks (Ed.), *The use of creative therapies with sexual abuse survivors* (pp. 181–195). Springfield, IL: Charles C. Thomas Publisher, Ltd.

van der Kolk, B. (2014). *The body keeps the score: Brain, mind, and body in the healing of trauma*. New York, NY: Viking.

van Lith, T., Schofield, M., & Fenner, P. (2012, November). Identifying the evidence-base for art-based practices and their potential benefit for mental health recovery: A critical review. *Disability and Rehabilitation*, *35*(16), 1309–1323. https://doi.org/10.3109/09638288.2012.732188

EIGHT

The Women's Transformational Program

An Art Therapy, Life Skills, and Reproductive Health Program in Nepal

Atira L. Tan and Tiffany M. Moore

Introduction

Sex trafficking is a complex, global issue and a rapidly growing problem in Nepal. According to the 2012 Global Slavery Index, Nepal is one of the five worst countries with regard to modern slavery, and an estimated 86% of those trafficked are girls and women (United Nations Office on Drugs and Crime [UNODC], 2012).

When a trafficked girl or woman is rescued by police or social workers, the reintegration back into the community typically begins at a non-government organization (NGO) shelter program. This period ranges between six months and two years. During this time, the survivor is provided vocational education, medical, and mental health treatment in order to reintegrate into mainstream society. Researchers and practitioners question the effectiveness of the present rehabilitative process (Gozdziak, 2016), which is hamstrung by the deeply rooted cultural conditioning that causes women's feelings of hopelessness, helplessness, and disempowerment. Survivors of trafficking and commercial sex exploitation often face magnified desolation and exclusion and cannot envision their own identities as more than a sexual object (Chatterjee, Chakraborty, Srivastava, & Deb, 2006). This experience leaves the survivor unable to separate and remember the person they once were (Robinson & Paramo, 2007). Coupled with the stigma of their experience, it often results in survivors returning to the sex trade (Frederick & Kelly, 2000).

Cultural Conditioning and Gender-Based Violence in Nepal

> "*Choriko jamma, hareko karma.*"
>
> Nepali Proverb: To be born a daughter is a lost destiny. Educating a daughter is like watering your neighbor's garden.
>
> (Kondos, 2004, p. 11)

In the predominately Hindu culture of Nepal, patriarchal values espouse female inferiority; girls are seen as a burden on society (Niaz & Hassan, 2006). This cultural perception permeates much of South Asia, where the subordinate position of women is perpetuated socially and economically and fosters the widespread violence against women. The Nepalese law 48/104 defines violence against women as any act "that results in, or is likely to result in, physical, sexual, emotional and psychological harm or suffering . . . including threats of such acts, coercion or arbitrary deprivation of liberty" (General Assembly Resolution, 1993).

Globally, gender-based violence "remains the largest single cause of morbidity and mortality among women aged 15–49 years, claiming more lives than cancer, malaria, traffic accidents and war combined" (Murthy & Smith, 2010). Women in South Asian countries face the threat of multiple forms of violence, including "sexual violence by family members, strangers and agents of the state; domestic abuse including spousal murder; being burned; disfigured with acid; beaten and threatened, ritual honor killings and custodial abuse and torture" (Niaz, 2003, p. 173).

A World Bank report from 2016 stipulates that South Asia has the highest global rate of female-to-male mortality, child marriage, and intimate partner violence. Interpersonal, ideological, sociocultural, and religious norms are the ultimate determinants of their pervasiveness and the key reason legislative interventions have had little impact. For example, *karma*, the idea that previous good or bad actions determine prosperity or suffering, plays a vital role in the trauma inflicted on girls and women. This mind-set infers that women have been less pious than men in previous lives, consequently rendering them deserving of the injustices and abuse currently inflicted upon them (Kohrt & Hruschka, 2010). As women are regarded as subservient to men, this attitude translates to less access to education, citizenship, and civil rights (Crawford, 2010). Sons are prized, while mothers are praised for birthing them. Consequently, mothers who give birth to daughters are chastised—verbally and physically abused for the perceived drain on the community (Crawford, 2010). In 2011, the State of the World's Children Report found that 23% of Nepali women between the ages of 15 and 49 considered their husbands justified in beating them if they argued back, burned the dinner, or neglected the children. Many girls and women remain in the sex trade in order to "pay back" their "karmic debt" and provide financially for their family members to offset their burden. This mind-set is normalized by centuries of agricultural debt bondage and the practice of servitude that continues to endure in South Asia (Gozdziak, 2016).

Throughout South Asia, sex trafficking forms a web known as the "wicked problem." The wicked problem is defined as one without a single solution, residing in an "un-ordered domain, non-linear in nature with a multiplicity of agents that defy conventional analysis" (Beurden, 2011, pp. 83–84). Sociocultural influences affect the interplay of religion, superstition, tradition, societal hierarchy, inconsistent legislative enforcement, and access (or lack thereof) to resources, services, support, and opportunities, which, in turn, perpetually stigmatize and harm those victimized. In short, no simple problem, no quick fix.

Menstrual Discrimination

Menstruation is a source of stigmatization in many cultures throughout the world (Adhikari, Kadel, Dhungel, & Mandal, 2007). The idea of menstruation impurity is prevalent throughout the Hindu community, with religious rituals used to sanitize and conceal menstruation. The concept of "untouchable being," or *Chhaupadi*, requires complete segregation of a menstruating woman. Some ethnic groups within Nepal ritualize menarche with the custom of *gupha basne*, or "staying in the cave," where the menarcheal girl is required to remain in isolation for up to 12 days (Crawford, Menger, & Kaufman, 2014). It is estimated that as many as 95% in Nepal's mid- and far-reaching western regions observe this practice. Women live outside the home, often in a shed-like dwelling (Ranabhat, Kim, Ayral, & Ah, 2015; Taracena, 2018), and are prohibited from consuming dairy, having access to public water, entering temples, or touching any male (including their husbands) out of fear of contamination (Crawford et al., 2014; Ranabhat et al., 2015). Many risks are attributed to this observance, including poor sanitation, poor ventilation from the dwellings, malnutrition, infectious diseases, sexual assault, animal attacks, and death (Taracena, 2018). As a result, many women harbor negative feelings and shame toward their bodies and reproductive cycles.

Sex Trafficking in Nepal

The Nepalese authorities do not accurately track the number of sex trafficked survivors but estimates top as many as 200,000 annually (Sangroula, 2001). Nepali girls and women are trafficked from remote villages to urban centers for prostitution, including within *dhabas* (highway hotels), dance bars, cabin restaurants, and massage parlors (United States Department of State, 2011). Victimhood often results in permanent injury or death. Victimized individuals are frequently denied access to education, health care, and proper nutrition, and they are often subjected to violence, starvation, and addiction to drugs administered by traffickers (Stallard, 2014).

During times of natural disasters, especially the earthquakes in April and May of 2015, activists become increasingly concerned for vulnerable populations—i.e., orphaned children, young women, widows, and persons who lost their livelihoods. News outlets report that after the earthquakes, authorities rescued 160 Nepalese children trafficked to northern India. Kamal Saksena, home secretary for Uttar Pradesh state in India, indicated that as many as 60 arrests for sex trafficking were made in his district alone (The ABC News, 2016).

It has long been argued that "the global sex trade is not unitary and cannot be simply reduced to one monolithic explanation of violence to women" (Kempadoo, 2001, p. 28), so it's important to understand the ongoing complexities surrounding the global sex trade in order to combat it (Kempadoo, Sanghera, & Pattanaik, 2016). Trafficking also needs to be understood in the context of "the realities, contradictions and intersections of various global relations of power" (Kempadoo, 2001, p. 28).

Art to Healing

Art to Healing (2018) is an Australian grassroots charity providing trauma-informed care and mental health support to girls and women directly impacted by gender violence, trafficking, and commercial sex exploitation and sexual abuse specifically throughout Southern Asia and the Pacific. Founded by Atira Lydia Tan in 2005, the organization has worked with thousands of individuals and over 40 partner organizations, including local agencies, clinical services, government bodies, and anti-trafficking NGOs. The agency provides direct psychological support for survivors, capacity building, professional development, supervision for staff and organizations to improve their trauma-informed care, and evidence-based qualitative research. Art to Healing harnesses its approach from the expressive art therapies (EXA), Somatic Experiencing™, Neurosequential Model of Therapeutics™ (NMT), and theories focused on developmental and attachment trauma; sexual and reproductive health education; and awareness-based practices of yoga and meditation. The Women's Transformational Program (WTP) is one of the programs that Art to Healing created as part of their therapeutic modalities.

In 2016, Atira Tan created an art therapy, life skills, and reproductive health program named the WTP in conjunction with three local anti-trafficking organizations, Asha Nepal (Asha meaning *hope*), Center for Awareness Promotion (CAP) Nepal, and Chorri Nepal (Chorri meaning *daughters*), to work closely with adolescent girls undergoing the rehabilitative process. All three organizations provide shelter, food, vocational, formal and nonformal education, and medical services for girls and women who have been rescued from sex slavery and exploitation. Asha Nepal focuses on helping girls who have an aptitude for formal education, supporting them to finish high school, while CAP has an emergency short-term shelter and a long-term residence shelter.

WTP: Life Skills, Reproductive Health, and Art Therapy

WTP was created after five years of delivering trauma-informed programs to women and girls who experienced sex slavery and exploitation in Asia. A powerful theme emerged among the data collection linking the somatic ailments and challenges in prioritizing self-care, the disconnection between survivors' bodies and feelings, and the influence of negative, self-hatred about their bodies and identity as a woman. Many participants shared similar physical reproductive health issues: HIV/AIDS, sexually transmitted infections, polycystic ovarian syndrome, menorrhagia, dysmenorrhea, amenorrhea, and uterine and ovarian cysts. Although these girls and women were given adequate medical assistance, the support for their physical ailments did not adequately address the important psychological and emotional dimensions of their well-being.

The WTP is a six-week reproductive health and life skills program, utilizing EXA as an approach to explore and understand the subjective experiences of trafficking and commercial sex exploitation. This program seeks to improve the knowledge of female participants in their psychological, physical, and emotional well-being, including education regarding reproductive and menstrual health. Through a high-quality delivery of therapeutic and educative arts-based interventions, the program works to heal, empower, cultivate resilience and self-regulation, and create positive changes in how they see themselves and their gender.

The WTP also functions as a research tool to gather quantitative and qualitative data about participant experience to aid program efficacy, determine impact, and promote the process of change. Its unique delivery allows for a rich assortment of emergent data, which helps us understand the unique experiences of Nepalese girls and women who have experienced trafficking and commercial sex exploitation. As participants dive into their personal narratives, the WTP uses creative methods, such as EXA and the formation of artwork, to act as a "container" for powerful emotions: rage, pain, and shame. Positive change can occur when one is able to tell his or her story through art and introspection—by reframing how one feels to produce a deliberate response to an event or experience. The art represents something distinct and separate from a person to allow for perspective, healing, experimentation, and rehearsal of a desired change. In working with tangible objects that can be manipulated, the process also allows for concretization of thoughts and feelings (Malchiodi, 2012). Capacity for change depends on the variants of a client's capacity and willingness to engage in the appropriately selected processes (Waller, 2006). Research echoes the positive impact of EXA as a transformative tool in dealing with marginalized and traumatized populations within the clinical and nonclinical fields (Bird, 2018; Coemans & Hannes, 2017; Frohmann, 2005; Green, 2015; Kapitan, Litell, & Torres, 2011; Kozlowska & Hanney, 2001; Tsutsumi, Izutsu, Poudyal, Kato, & Marui, 2008; Wood, 2012).

Themed-based art therapy thrives when adhering to a specific focus or intention and can unite a group through shared experiences (Liebmann, 1986; Thornton, 1985). The WTP adheres to the approach of theme-based art therapy, where participants connect for a common purpose: to explore an area of interest and experience. In this case, women's reproductive health and the experience of being a woman (Liebman, 1986). The group began with an introduction and warm-up with the selection of a theme and then time to engage in art making; this was followed by optional sharing and a group discussion (Barber, 2002; Campbell, 1997; Liebmann, 1986; Ross, 1997).

An example of sharing came from Goma Rai (consent was provided for the use of her real name), the director and founder of Shakti Milan Sahaj, an NGO assisting the recovery of sex trafficked survivors diagnosed with HIV/AIDS and their children. Goma Rai herself was sold into sexual slavery at the age of 13 and later rescued by Child Workers in Nepal Concerned Center. In addition to forming Shakti Milan Samaj, she was also the founding member of Shakti Samuha, a survivor-led nonprofit organization in Nepal fighting the trafficking and enslavement of girls and women. Goma Rai attended the WTP in 2016 and shared her experience:

> I was sold into sex slavery when I was 13 years old. Because of my past, I hated being a woman, I hated my period and I hated my reproductive organs because I felt that these were the reasons why bad things, like getting HIV/AIDS and being sold, happened to me. I even went to the doctor to request for a hysterectomy, so that I could take my womb out, and stop my period because I hated having my period. I was told by my doctor that I was still young so they could not do the operation.
>
> After participating in this training program [with Art to Healing], I have realized that I deserve to be loved for being a woman, and my reproductive organs and my womb deserve to be loved as well and they are important to me. I have realized the importance of self-care and loving myself. I am now proud to have been born a woman, and I can't wait to share this information I have learned with my community. I will now continue to love myself and care for my body, and I know that being born female is a thing to be valued.
>
> (G. Rai, personal video communication, November 19, 2017)

Art to Healing ran the first WTP in 2010 with 26 trafficked survivors in Nepal. The format was a five-day workshop. In follow-up sessions, many participants reported that the therapeutic theme-based art therapy exercises and reproductive health education helped them overcome some reproductive health symptomology. Many reported an increase in self-awareness, empowerment, confidence, and self-worth—along with an improved understanding of the value and importance of self-care.

One WTP participant reported in a follow-up interview that when she was trafficked three years before, her menstruation stopped completely. But after finishing the program, her periods have become regular again. She has become a counselor for sex trafficking survivors, passing on what she learned about herself to other sex trafficked survivors. She shared that her own transformation has helped other survivors find greater self-awareness, self-care, and self-esteem.

As a result of the effectiveness of the previous program, Art to Healing resumed offering WTP to sex trafficked survivors in 2016 and responded to the requests of partner organizations to include a "Training of Trainers" (TOT) program. The TOT program is a continuation of WTP, training women leaders to facilitate the program in their own communities. So far in 2019, there have already been over 2,000 participants who have benefited from the WTP across Nepal.

Participants and Setting

To deliver WTP in Nepal, Art to Healing partnered with three local anti-trafficking NGOs: Asha Nepal, CAP Nepal, and Chorri in Kathmandu. These agencies operate programming and shelters for girls and women 11 to 35 years of age who have experienced trafficking or commercial sexual exploitation. They are provided temporary accommodations, food, vocational training, medical assistance, and psychosocial counseling. The WTP also included a three-hour workshop each week for six weeks. Participants were familiar with each other from cohabitating in the residence, and most of them were survivors of the 2015 earthquake. The rehabilitative process ranges from six months to two years prior to reintegration into their communities.

Framework and Methodology

The goal was to adapt the tenants of the creative arts in order to research projects and tap into the "unique capabilities of the arts as a way of knowing" (Leavy, 2017, p. 191). So a phenomenological stance was adopted that emphasized participants' perception of their social reality—a common practice when working in an arts-based context to help participants make sense of their experience. In this framework, the stance was as follows: What it is like to be a woman in Nepal (Hesse-Biber & Leavy, 2011).

In addition to the planned conclusion, the program included the exploration of six key themes:

1. What it means to be a Nepali woman
2. Preovulation and the relationship with your thoughts and goal setting
3. Ovulation and the relationship with your inner and outer resources
4. Premenstruation and the relationship with emotions
5. Menstruation and the relationship to body and body image
6. Summary, completion, and celebration, with the initial theme "what it means for you to be a Nepali woman" explored again to measure change within participants' attitudes and beliefs.

The structure remained consistent each day, providing continuity—and safety—for participants. EXA was a way to illicit responses from participants through the modalities of visual artwork, poetry, songs, and descriptive storytelling. Responses doubled as research data for evaluation in helping to document participant change from the outset to program completion. A mixture of mediums was used based on participant comfort. Magazines were available for cutting, easy-to-use drawing, and painting materials (i.e., paint, oils, chalk pastels, color pencils, and pens) were offered to aid in the creation of images. Collages were suggested for those new to, or reluctant to, making art as an easy and accessible way to express themselves (Leavy, 2009).

The art materials were chosen from experience and based on Art to Healing's wider practitioner cohort with various groups over the past few years. The key was to assist participants in deepening their understanding of each theme through their own subjective experiential lens. At the beginning of the program, the facilitator explained that making art is not about skill or about producing something to be critiqued; rather, it's a means of personal expression that encourages both playful curiosity and enjoyment. Participants were invited to share their artworks and responses with the larger group, aiding in personal reflection and fresh insight. Facilitators made use of their personal stories, challenges, and visions to communicate key messages and inspire hope among participants. Meditation, creative visualization, and ritual were employed across program delivery. Each workshop focused on an educational theme through understanding and managing emotions; resilience and resource building, self-awareness and self-regulation, the menstrual cycle, and reproductive health; and demystifying beliefs/behaviors set about by *Chaupaudi* and the cultural stigma of menstruating women.

It was important to create a psychologically safe environment for the program. Each participant acknowledged the sharing of their story with the understanding that their identities would not be disclosed with similarly themed artwork. The setting was a training room within the shelter, behind closed doors, and took place without interruption. Translators and cofacilitators were also either psychosocial counselors or social workers in the organization and familiar with the positive, nonjudgmental approach from prior workshops.

The themes of the stories and narratives that the participants shared during the process are presented next, as well as intersubjective artworks created by the facilitator in response to the themes that emerged in each week. An intersubjective arts response is artwork created by the art therapist in response to the material that arises in the therapeutic space. Traditionally, art therapists use intersubjective response art to contain difficult material, express and examine their experiences, and share their experiences with others. The intersubjective arts response further protects the clients' stories and identities.

Art Therapy Process, Themes, and Results

Week 1: What It Means for You to Be a Nepali Woman

The workshop began with an introduction of the program and the facilitator/cofacilitators and was followed by group agreements about safety and confidentiality. Then, to warm up, participants created a name tag and were asked to identify themselves and answer a question: If you were an animal, which animal would you be and why.

The objective for week one concentrated on building safety and rapport among participants and facilitators. The menstrual cycle was then introduced through a discussion on reproductive health with a video exploring gender and self-identification. Participants were invited to begin exploring art therapy by creating an image to describe what it meant for them to be a woman in Nepali society. Themes that emerged included everything from the struggle of gender equality, to being female, to the experience of trafficking.

The intersubjective art response reflects the themes of the stories that were shared (Figure 8.1). In the previous image, there is a woman who

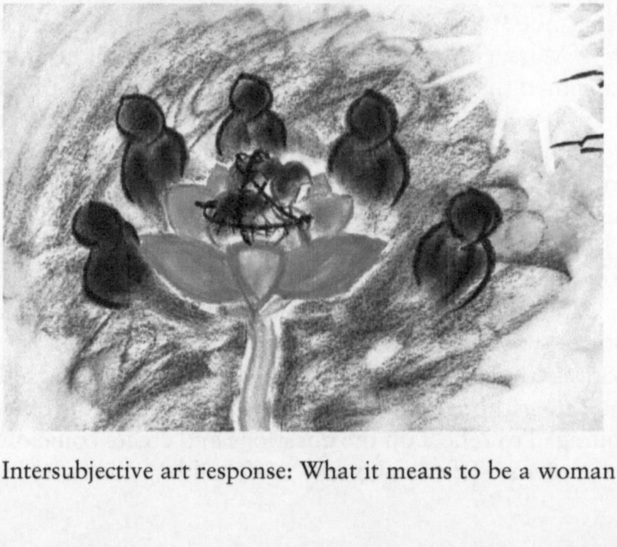

Figure 8.1 Intersubjective art response: What it means to be a woman in Nepal

is burdened with many bags on her back. She is chained up in barbed wire and surrounded by people and a culture that are is suppressing and pressuring her. The woman is curled up in a flower, and there is a sun in the background with birds flying overhead—symbolizing a common theme among participants that women in Nepal need to be able to fly but often face heavy burdens from bad experiences. Many of the participants also drew flowers, signifying that being a Nepalese woman is like being a flower trying to grow but unable to because they lack the chances to do so. Since the women so often have to deny their own thoughts and feelings because of what others think, the central figure in the image is surrounded by people. Some participants also shared that they experienced a happy childhood, but as they grew up, life became more difficult and unhappy.

Week 2: Preovulation and the Relationship With Our Thoughts and Goal Setting

The objective for week two involved education on reproductive health, preovulation, and hormonal health. It also included the psychological and emotional toll of adolescence in addition to life skills through self-awareness, mindfulness, relationships with our thoughts and beliefs, goal setting, and exploring our future dreams. But first, the workshop began with a warm-up of scribble drawing with dry/oil pastels and colored markers. Participants were guided through a mindfulness exercise by observing their thoughts in a nonjudgmental way for five minutes, and they were invited to draw their "here and now," which they were also invited to share (if they wanted). This exercise was adapted from the mindfulness practice of Jon Kabat-Zinn's Mindfulness-Based Stress Reduction program. Mindfulness has been defined as "the awareness that emerges through paying attention on purpose, in the present moment, and non-judgmentally to the unfolding of experience moment by moment" (Kabat-Zinn, 2003, p. 145). Since the concept was first launched at the University of Massachusetts Medical School in 1979, thousands of studies have documented the physical and mental health benefits of mindfulness. This includes an increased awareness and acceptance of affect, which in turn assists in both the emotional and cognitive processing of trauma in a nonjudgmental way (Briere, 2012). The facilitator shared the importance of becoming aware of our thoughts and their relationship with our emotional and physical well-being.

The reproductive health theme of preovulation, hormonal health, and adolescence in a woman's life was linked with goal setting and planning for the future—how positive thoughts can influence what we create in life and support us to reach our goals. This was explored through the art therapy activity: their thoughts, goals, and wishes for the future. Participants were encouraged to reflect on the questions and create coinciding artwork based on the theme. Those who felt comfortable were invited to share.

Figure 8.2 Intersubjective art response: My hopes and wishes for the future

A primary theme emerged around the loss of family and the unresolved sadness and grief predominant in their lives while residing in the shelter. For many, their wishes for the future were connected to their families and their desire to return home; however, many did not have any homes to go back to because of the trafficking and exploitation.

The previous image reflects the primary theme that emerged from the artwork and stories (Figure 8.2). All of the participants said their wishes for the future involved taking care of their families. They also shared their grief and loss about their families, as many of them were unable to return home because they were too afraid of being discriminated against by their families and village members. And all of them said that their primary motivation for staying in the shelter home was to do something good, get a job and take care of their families, and help others.

The grief and loss of family is something all the survivors expressed. One participant confided that although she once felt close to her family, it would never be the same after her trafficking experience. However, some of the girls also acknowledged how much being in the shelter home brought them hope and a relief from their isolation. One girl said that when she arrived there, she met other girls and knows now that she is not alone in her experiences. She also said that in the future, she wants to travel to remote villages like her own and teach women about the perils of sex trafficking, teach them that women are not weak—that they are strong.

In one of the shelters, a participant shared her dream of being an international model to change her situation and help her family. After sharing, she began to cry, expressing her unhappiness and her feeling of helplessness of her situation. The sadness she felt in not being able to return to her family was echoed by many others in the group who also became emotional. They, too, experienced the same feeling of despair about their situations: unable to return to their families and villages because of the shame they acquired from their trafficked experience. Many believed their families would not take them back because the dishonor would extend to their families—all because of them.

This is a major barrier to recovery. The loss of family and the development of attachment trauma experienced prior to being trafficked is an important issue that requires psychosocial care, especially in the recovery phase within the shelter setting. Additionally, participants felt a deep sense of shame and guilt about their experiences, hindering full emotional recovery. For the girls who ran away from their families in search of work in the cities, their exploitation and sale into slavery incurred a fear that their families would find out about their experience. One girl spoke about being afraid of walking in the streets of Kathmandu or going to the hospital to receive treatment. Even in her distress, she was terrified that someone from her village would recognize her.

Week 3: Ovulation and the Relationship With Inner and Outer Resources

The objective for week three involved reproductive health education on ovulation, fertility, sexual health, and psychological and emotional phases of motherhood; life skills for self-awareness and regulation; and exploring strengths, self-care, and inner and outer resources. The facilitator spoke about being aware of our emotions, how that affects our physical well-being, and the importance of regulating those emotions. Affect regulation is the capacity to tolerate intense emotions or affect (positive and negative) without using avoidance strategies, such as dissociation, substance abuse, or other defenses (Thompson, 1994). The themes of ovulation, fertility, sexual health, and motherhood were linked with how we "mother" ourselves and the importance of resiliency.

The main art therapy activity focused on personal strengths and resources. Participants were encouraged to reflect on the following question of exploring their strengths and resources to create their artwork, and they were invited to write a short story/poem from their reflections. Group sharing was available for those who felt comfortable. Many needed guidance in reflecting and expressing themselves since they had never been introduced to the concepts of self-care or self-love before. Despite initial challenges, most participants were able to identify many resources and strengths in their lives.

The intersubjective image shows the themes of this art therapy exercise—and more of the participants' stories (Figure 8.3). Many of the participants could identify their outer resources of activities and items that helped them self-regulate. Many of these external resources included their relationship with nature and their environment, such as the shelter home, as well as their love for music, singing, dancing, and being with friends as coping strategies. However, most of the girls found it

Figure 8.3 Intersubjective art response: My inner and outer resources

challenging to identify their inner resources and strengths. Among their inner resources was actively helping others and personal qualities, such as love, kindness, and helpfulness. Many of them also shared that the shelter home was a great resource for them.

For example, one girl said the shelter provided her with support when she was in trouble or feeling hopeless. She also talked about the challenge of not having the support of her mother, which made her feel orphaned. Another girl could recognize her inner strengths as kindness and love in her heart. She could see that when her friends were sad, she tries to make them happy using humor and laughter. She added that she's a good listener and enjoys singing and dancing as ways of calming herself down when she feels sad.

The facilitator closed the workshop by linking the importance of self-care with how we can self-regulate through the use of these strategies. The finale was singing and dancing to a popular Nepali song about the empowerment of women, which the participants loved.

Week 4: Premenstruation and the Relationship With Our Emotions

The objective for week four involved reproductive health education, premenstruation, hormonal health, and the psychological and emotional phase of menopause. Continuing the theme from the week before, the discussion focused on life skills and how to respond to challenging emotions, identify needs, and ask for help and support. Many participants reported an increase in moodiness, anger, and irritability during premenstruation, so the facilitator stressed the importance of becoming aware of their emotions, affect regulation, and the different ways of responding to their emotions. The facilitator also emphasized the importance of paying attention to the emotions of others who are experiencing the same thing and caring for others.

The main art therapy activity was my emotions and that emotions are our friends. This exercise was adapted from the research of Shaver, Schwartz, Kirson, and O'Connor, who identified six "basic" emotions (Shaver, Schwartz, Kirson, & O'Connor, 2001). This research was modified in this art therapy exercise. Participants were encouraged to create an image to explore five primary emotions, including happiness, love, sadness, anger, and fear.

After the artwork activity, participants were invited to group the artwork of each emotion. The artwork to express happiness was gathered together, and participants were invited to stand around with the cofacilitators, who guided participants in a phenomenological art therapy discussion that encouraged the sharing of themes in the art. This technique was adapted from Betensky's 1995 work as a way to investigate the full subjective experiencing of worldly things as they present themselves in consciousness and immediate experiences. Betensky (1995) emphasized the importance of *seeing* and suggests that this is "art therapy's most important contribution to general therapy and even to phenomenology itself, because art therapy pays attention to the authentic experience in a two-fold way" (p. 5). There is the direct experience of creating art and then the experience of looking at the art (Betensky, 1995).

After a discussion of the themes, participants were asked to reflect on the quality of each emotion: what happens when each emotion arises, what each emotion needs in order to feel better, and how we can ask for what we need when we feel this emotion. This exercise helped the participants to identify, understand, and normalize their emotions, building up awareness about what they needed to feel better and how to communicate their needs.

The intersubjective image illustrates the collective themes that appeared in the artwork (Figure 8.4). Many of the participants drew their homes and returning to their villages with their families as a representation of their happiness. Most of them also shared memories of family members who loved them—and said they felt most loved being with other people. There were discussions about how the participants felt when they were

Figure 8.4 Intersubjective art response: My emotions and emotions are our friends

sad and their sense of isolation when they were depressed and afraid. The exploration also addressed what they needed when they were feeling angry, sad, or scared in life and how to ask for help when they needed.

Participants were evaluated six months after the end of the program. Many of them shared how much they learned about emotional regulation and its impact on daily life. One participant said that prior to the workshop, she felt upset if anyone showed emotion. After the workshop, she accepted the emotions of others and herself—a testament to its effectiveness.

The workshop concluded with a small ritual of participants writing down an emotion or experience they wanted to release. A candle was lit in the middle of the circle and the participants were guided to burn the paper with the emotion on it and the corresponding experience, symbolizing its release. Many participants affirmed how much more relaxed and "lighter" they felt after the closing ritual.

Week 5: Menstruation and Our Relationship With Our Bodies and Body Image

The objective for week five was reproductive health education relating to menstruation, exploring cultural beliefs and conditioning around menarche and menstruation, and psychology and emotions of menarche. It also included education on self-care during menstruation, awareness of bodily sensations, self-care, and health of a woman's body, cycle, nutrition, and rest. The facilitator emphasized the importance of becoming aware of our body's sensations and honoring what it needs. The theme of menstruation, self-care, self-love, and menarche was linked with the practice of awareness to different reproductive body parts and how to care for our bodies.

The main art therapy activity was womb bowls. This activity was adapted from Focusing Oriented Expressive Arts (FOAT®) by Eugene Gendlin in 1981 and further developed by Rappaport in 2010. The idea is that focus comes from both mind and body and involves self-directed listening and the inner felt sense of experience. The process can access the body's innate wisdom and potential to heal, helping the client find new ways of recovery (Rappaport, 2006). FOAT® integrates Gendlin's focus with art therapy (Rappaport, 2010) and may culminate in a relationship that can offer the client an "experiential knowing of the self that is whole" (Rappaport, 2010, p. 140).

The exercise began with mindfulness as the group was instructed to hold a ball of clay in their hands and focus on breathing into their uteruses. The breath and intentional focus assisted the sensory experience in the corresponding area of the body. When they felt ready to begin, they were guided in creating a pinch bowl with the ball of clay. The womb bowl exercise allowed for the group to connect the importance of self-care to their bodies. The themes that emerged centered on the importance of self-care, rest, and empowerment.

Figure 8.5 Intersubjective art response: Womb bowls

The image is an example of the womb bowls artwork with clay (Figure 8.5). The primary theme seemed to be that the participants now better understood the connection between their uteruses and the importance of self-care throughout their cycle, especially during menstruation. One of the participants also expressed that her womb felt like a fire in her body. She felt a deeper connection to her womanhood and a greater desire to understand her womb and body more. She felt her womb as a source of power, able to produce life and protect a child. She shared her pride in being a woman.

In the six-month follow-up to the program, many participants shared how this exercise was integral to their recovery. One girl opened up about her previous shame and resentment for not being born a man. This workshop allowed her to connect with her power because of her ability to produce life. As a result, she began to take better care of herself. Another participant said she now fully grasped the importance of self-care and has begun to incorporate it into her daily life.

The workshop concluded with women sharing stories and poems from the exercise—and naming one self-care activity they could continue during menstruation. And, finally, a short ritual for the girls to honor and celebrate being women. This ritual was very important because many had shared the conditioning and stigma of *Chaupaddhi* in their daily lives. This ritual provided another way of experiencing themselves as equal, powerful, worthy, and most, importantly, enough.

Week 6: Summary, Completion, and Celebration

The objective for the final week was to revisit "what it means to be a Nepali woman," thus coming full circle and reminding participants to integrate the information of the program into their daily lives. The main art therapy activity centered on the initial idea of Nepali female identity. After discussion, participants were encouraged to create a collage and write a story/poem about their artwork reflecting back. From these stories, themes of pride in womanhood, empowerment, self-responsibility, and motivation emerged.

This intersubjective image represents the themes we saw during the last week of the program (Figure 8.6). The image shows a woman with a Nepali flag on the top of Mt. Everest, the tallest mountain in Nepal and in the world, and conveys a sense of pride and importance. On the right, the sun shines brightly with birds flying in the sky. Many of the participants expressed the feeling that they were proud of being born female and verbalized their appreciation of themselves. One participant shared that she is proud to be a daughter and that she loves herself because she is a daughter of Nepal.

Another girl wrote that she now understood the importance of womanhood and recognized that men and women are equal. They felt a better understanding that this equality would bring about respect and peace in the world. Yet another participant shared her pride of being a woman and the importance of positive thinking—because a strong mind is the vehicle to do anything that she wishes. She also said she appreciates creating life as a woman. All the girls felt they could more easily recognize the beauty in this world.

The workshop concluded with an optional sharing of artwork and poems with a celebration of dancing, singing, and food. The girls appeared relaxed, happy, and grateful for their experience with the program and were at ease with each other and the facilitators.

Figure 8.6 Intersubjective art response: What it means for me to be a Nepali Woman

Implications and Psychological Benefits

The WTP helped participants gain a new understanding of gender equality and identity, process unresolved emotions and experiences related to their past, and increase self-esteem, emotional affect regulation, self-awareness, self-care, and resiliency. In addition, the program provided participants with important women's reproductive health information often overlooked or lacking in their lives.

Six months later, Art to Healing returned to the shelters and conducted a follow-up, evaluating 15 girls from the program. Participants shared how the program had supported them to increase their confidence, hope for the future, and self-esteem. They also reported an increase in understanding and acceptance of themselves and others, a greater sense of community, and a decrease in menstrual health issues.

Increased Confidence, Hope for the Future, and Self-Esteem

One participant explained how she feels empowered to make positive changes in her life. Hoping to share the information she learned in order to help others, she even led a menstrual education workshop in her school with her teacher. Another girl spoke of now knowing that she is able to do more with her life—and that this is a vital attitude that will stay with her.

In addition, the psychosocial counselors in the shelter homes also reported that the participants' self-esteem had improved. Before the program, one of the girls found it difficult to make eye contact, had closed body language, and avoided looking in the mirror at herself. After the program, her body language became more open—and she started to make more eye contact with her friends in the shelter, as well as the workers. They also found that she was no longer avoiding looking at her own reflection in the mirror.

Change in Reproductive Health Issues

There were also reports of a change in reproductive health issues, both physically and in their attitudes toward menstruation, body image, and self-care. One girl shared that now that she is honoring her menstruation, she feels fresh during her period rather than negative. Another participant stated that she no longer suffers from the same physical symptoms during her period.

Another girl reported that before attending the program, she suffered from acute pain during menstruation and even had to take medication to ease her pain. However, after the program, she stopped taking medication and has been pain free for three months. Yet another participant said her physical ailments could be directly traced back to her emotions. This connection has helped to lessen the menstrual pain.

Affect Change, Regulation, and Greater Community Cohesion

Many of the participants expressed that the program—especially the emotion art exercise in Week 4—helped them to accept their feelings more. One participant shared that now she remembers that emotions are her friends and that she does not need to suppress or reject them anymore. She has also learned to be more understanding toward her friends who show feelings, such as sadness, anger, or fear. She said that when her friends in the shelter are menstruating, she will help them by getting them a hot water bottle and listening to their feelings.

Another girl reported that after the program, she was able to manage her negative feelings—especially anger, which she was struggling with before the program. She also demonstrated an increase in self-awareness, and although she cannot control her anger completely, she is more aware about how she feels and about how to ask for what she needs.

Increase in Self-Awareness and Resiliency

Many of the participants and the counselors in the shelter homes reported a greater sense of self-awareness and reflection in the participants. One girl shared that before the program, she had no awareness of her body during menstruation, or even of premenstrual symptoms. After the training, she now recognizes the changes in her mood and can communicate to her friends and the counselors about what she needs. She said she feels more confident in her understanding of the mind/body connection—and more empowered to self-regulate her emotions.

Another girl shared that now she understands she is responsible for her feelings and no longer blames others for her emotions. She also explained how the program taught her skills like self-reflection and evaluation, and she now takes time to reflect on her actions and feelings. One participant reported that before the training, she felt confusion about her body and feelings but that now she understands so much more about both her body and how to manage her emotions.

Art Making and Art Therapy

At times, it is difficult to find the language to describe the process and emotions of traumatic experiences. Art therapy allows for this expression and understanding through a nonverbal lens. Our emotions and experiences are encoded in nonverbal imagery pathways to the brain (Breat & Ostroff, 1985). Making art is an effective tool to express a deeper understanding as well as a deeper meaning within their lives.

Evidence of this was abundant in the six-month, follow-up workshop. One girl reported that art has helped her express herself and helped her understand the information she learned through the workshop. She enjoyed the art making and felt that if the content had been taught in other noncreative ways, she wouldn't have understood the information as well as she did.

Another girl said she enjoyed the process of art making and realized in the process that she was not able to share her feelings without the artwork. She found that expressing herself through art was easier than speaking about her feelings, and now her artwork speaks for her—and is rich with personal meaning.

In addition, through making art and sharing their stories, many of the participants realized that they were not alone in their experiences and suffering and felt a kindred connection with the others in the group, gaining a sense of community, solidarity, and strength in that they became aware of the feelings of others and are now able to respond thoughtfully. Prior to this workshop, many felt isolated, ashamed, and discriminated against by the larger society. Understanding that others felt similarly lessened their own sense of isolation and fear.

Informing Intervention Therapeutic Models in Shelter Care and Future Recommendations

Sex trafficking in Nepal is deeply connected to cultural and gender-based conditioning—critical elements to be considered when helping survivors and establishing self-esteem, self-care, and self-compassion. Psychoeducation around female sexual health—and life skills through creative art therapies—can be helpful on the road to recovery and are essential to future psychosocial intervention models and policies.

The WTP has demonstrated that it can serve as psychological and emotional intervention for trafficked girls and women in Nepal. The process has empowered the gender attitudes, mental health, and lives of its participants by helping connect them to a more profound sense of self-awareness of their bodies, thoughts, and emotions. Through the creative process, participants were able to process their suffering and traumatic experiences in a safe environment. Findings from the program also provided valuable insight into the emotions participants were facing, which, in turn, created the ability to adapt to the group and all the experiences, challenges, and unresolved feelings of grief and shame they shared about the past and their families.

It is also important to note that psychosocial counselors present at the workshop did not know how to effectively respond to the strong emotions arising among the group. Counselors are typically trained in solution-focused therapy. Although this can be helpful at times, it is not effective in the recovery from grief, loss, shame, fear, and behavioral problems participants often struggle with. Psychosocial care needs to be trauma-informed, specifically with assisting survivors with affect regulation, processing unresolved emotions, and helping with recovery from development and attachment trauma.

Most psychosocial counselors in the shelters in Nepal undertake a six-month training that focuses on practical solutions through talk therapy, but they lack essential knowledge and training in trauma. Treatment plans are unstructured in many of the anti-trafficking shelters, creating challenges in the recovery process. Solution-focused approaching has its benefits; however, it is ineffective for the deeper developmental and attachment trauma that sex trafficked participants face during their developmental years. Positive psychological models build resources and strengths that foster the compassion, connection, and courage so critical to the recovery process. These models also encompass understanding and utilize a body-based approach to building resilience, self-regulation, and affect change as demonstrated in the program. EXA can be an effective tool for recovery, supporting the participants to heal and express themselves in a gentle, noninvasive way.

Art to Healing hopes to expand the WTP further for other cultural settings and approaches to recovery. We hope the qualitative information will be used to advocate for more psychological and emotional support, including art therapy, in treatment and shelters for sex trafficked survivors. Policy makers are often not informed about the mental health struggles plaguing survivors during the rehabilitative process. Through similar research projects, policy makers can understand at a deeper level the suffering these survivors face and raise the standard of effective treatment. These brave girls and women deserve nothing less.

References

The ABC News. (2016, February 14). Nepal earthquake: More than 160 trafficked Nepalis rescued by India in aftermath of quake. *The ABC News*. Retrieved from www.abc.net.au/news/2016-02-15/nepal-earthquakes-cause-spike-in-human-trafficking/7168398

Adhikari, P., Kadel, B., Dhungel, S., & Mandal, A. (2007). Knowledge and practice regarding menstrual hygiene in rural adolescent girls of Nepal. *Kathmandu University Medical Journal*, *5*(3), 382–386.

Barber, V. (2002). *Explore yourself through art*. New York, NY: Plume.

Betensky, M. (1995). *What do you see? Phenomenology of therapeutic art expression*. London, UK: Jessica Kingsley Publishers.

Beurden, E. V., & Kia, A. (2011). Editorial—Wicked problems and health promotion: Reflections on learning. *Health Promotion Journal of Australia*, *22*(2), 83–84.

Bird, J. (2018). Art therapy, arts-based research and transitional stories of domestic violence and abuse. *International Journal of Art Therapy*, *23*(1), 14–24.

Breat, E. A., & Ostroff, R. (1985). Imagery and PTSD: An overview. *American Journal of Psychiatry*, *142*, 417–424.

Briere, J. (2012). Working with trauma: Mindfulness and compassion. In C. K. Germer & R. D. Siegel (Eds.), *Compassion and wisdom in psychotherapy* (pp. 265–279). New York, NY: Guilford.

Campbell, J. (1997). *Creative art in groupwork*. Abingdon-on-Thames, UK: Taylor & Francis.

Chatterjee, P., Chakraborty, T., Srivastava, N., & Deb, S. (2006). Short and long-term problems faced by the trafficked children: A qualitative study. *Social Science International*, *22*(1), 167–182.

Coemans, S., & Hannes, K. (2017). Researchers under the spell of the arts: Two decades of using arts-based methods in community-based inquiry with vulnerable populations. *Educational Research Review*, *22*, 34–49.

Crawford, M. (2010). *Sex trafficking in South Asia: Telling Maya's story*. Abingdon, UK: Routledge Research on Gender in Asia Series.

Crawford, M., Menger, L., & Kaufman, M. (2014). This is a natural process: Managing menstrual stigma in Nepal. *An International Journal for Research, Intervention and Care*, *16*(4), 426–439.

Frederick, J., & Kelly, T. (Eds.). (2000). *Fallen angels: The sex workers of South Asia*. New Delhi, India: Lustre Press, Roli Books.

Frohmann, L. (2005). The framing safety project: Photographs and narratives by battered women. *Violence Against Women*, *11*(11), 1396–1419.

Gendlin, E. T. (1981). *Focusing* (2nd ed.). New York, NY: Bantam Books.

General Assembly Resolution 48/104. (1993). Retrieved November 7, 2018 from www.un.org/documents/ga/res/48/a48r104.htm

Gozdziak, E. M. (2016). *Trafficking survivors returning home: Case study of Nepal*. Washington, DC: Georgetown University. Retrieved from www.researchgate.net/publication/305640027_Traffiking_Survivors_Return_Home_Case_Study_of_Nepal/download

Green, A. (2015). Art and music therapy for trauma survivors. *Canadian Art Therapy Association Journal*, *24*(2), 14–19.

Hesse-Biber, S. N., & Leavy, P. (2011). *The practice of social research* (2nd ed.). Los Angeles, CA: Sage.

Kabat-Zinn, J. (2003, Summer). Mindfulness-based interventions in context: Past, present, and future—Commentary. *Clinical Psychology. Science and Practice*, *10*(2), 145.

Kapitan, L., Litell, M., & Torres, A. (2011). Creative art therapy in a community's participatory research and social transformation. *Art Therapy: Journal of American Art Therapy Association*, *28*(2), 64–73.

Kempadoo, K. (2001). Women of color and the global sex trade: Transnational feminist perspectives. *Meridians: Feminism, Race, Transnationalism*, *1*(2), 28–51.

Kempadoo, K., Sanghera, J., & Pattanaik, B. (2016). Preface. In K. Kempadoo, J. Sanghera, & B. Pattanaik (Eds.), *Trafficking and prostitution reconsidered: New perspectives on migration, sex work and human rights* (2nd ed.). Abingdon, UK: Routledge.

Kohrt, B., & Hruschka, D. (2010). Nepali concepts of psychological trauma: The role of idioms of distress, ethnopsychology and ethnophysiology in alleviating suffering and preventing stigma. *Cult Med Psychiatry*, *34*, 322–352.

Kondos, V. (2004). *On the ethos of Hindu women*. Kathmandu, Nepal: Mandala Press.

Kozlowska, K., & Hanney, L. (2001). An art therapy group for children traumatized by parental violence and separation. *Clinical Child Psychology and Psychiatry*, *6*(1), 49–78.

Leavy, P. (2009). *Methods meets art: Arts-based research practice*. New York, NY: Guildford Press.

Leavy, P. (2017). *Research design: Quantitative, qualitative, mixed methods, art-based and community-based participatory research approaches*. New York, NY: Guildford Press.

Liebmann, M. (1986). *Art therapy for groups: A handbook of themes and exercises* (2nd ed.). London, UK: Routledge.

Malchiodi, C. (2012). *Handbook of art therapy*. New York, NY: Guildford Press.

Murthy, P., & Smith, C. L. (2010). *Women's Global health and human rights*. Burlington, MA: Jones and Bartlett Learning.

Niaz, U. (2003). Violence against women in South Asian countries. *Archives of Women's Mental Health*, *6*, 173–184.

Niaz, U., & Hassan, S. (2006). Culture and mental health of women in South-East Asia. *World Psychiatry*, *5*(2), 118–120.

Ranabhat, C., Kim, C. B., Ayral, A., & Ah, Y. (2015). *Chhaupadi* culture of reproductive health of women in Nepal. *Asia-Pacific Journal of Public Health*, *27*(7), 785–795.

Rappaport, L. (2006). *Clearing a space: Expressing the wholeness within using art*. Retrieved from www.focusing.org/pdf/rappaport_clearing_a_space_expressing_the_wholeness_within_using_art.pdf

Rappaport, L. (2010). Focusing-oriented art therapy: Working with trauma. *Person-Centered and Experiential Psychotherapies*, *9*(2), 129–142.

Robinson, R., & Paramo, P. (2007). Juvenile prostitution and community rehabilitation: An exploratory analysis of beliefs and values. *Journal of Community and Applied Social Psychology*, *17*(3), 237–247.

Ross, C. (1997). *Something to draw on: Activities and interventions using an art therapy approach*. London, UK: Jessica Kingsley.

Sangroula, Y. (2001). Trafficking of girls and women in Nepal. Building a community surveillance system for prevention. *Kathmandu School of Law*. Retrieved from www.childtrafficking.com/Docs/sangroula_2001_trafficking_.pdf

Shaver, P., Schwartz, J., Kirson, D., & O'Connor, C. (2001). Emotional knowledge: Further exploration of a prototype approach. In G. Parrott (Ed.), *Emotions in social psychology: Essential readings* (pp. 26–56). Philadelphia, PA: Psychology Press.

Stallard, R. (2014). *Child trafficking in Nepal: Causes, consequences and education as prevention*. Childreach. Retrieved from www.scribd.com/

Taracena, K. N. (2018). *Her space: Design explorations for menstrual hygiene management in western Nepal*. Doctoral thesis, University of Buffalo. Retrieved from www.womenepal.org/about-us/about-us/

Thompson, R. A. (1994). Emotion regulation: A theme in search of definition. *Monographs for the Society for Research in Child Development*, *59*, 25–52.

Thornton, R. (1985). Review of Gerry NcNeilly's article, Directive and non-directive approaches in art therapy. *Inscape Journal of Art Therapy*, *4*, 23–25.

Tsutsumi, A., Izutsu, T., Poudyal, A., Kato, S., & Marui, E. (2008). Mental health of female survivors of trafficking in Nepal. *Social Science and Medicine*, *66*, 1841–1847.

United Nations Office on Drugs and Crime [UNODC]. (2012). *Global report on trafficking in persons 2016*. Vienna, Austria. Retrieved from www.unodc.org/documents/data-and-analysis/glotip/2012_Global_Report_on_Trafficking_in_Persons.pdf

United States Department of State. (2011). *Trafficking in persons report*. Retrieved from www.state.gov/documents/organization/164457.pdf

Waller, D. (2006). Art therapy for children: How it leads to change. *Clinical Child Psychology Psychiatry*, *11*(2), 271–282.

Wood, L. (2012). How youth picture gender injustice: Building skills for HIV prevention through a participatory, arts-based approach. *South African Journal of Education*, *32*(4), 349–366.

PART III

CLOSURE AND CONCLUDING REFLECTIONS FOR ADVOCATES

NINE

Entrusted With Trauma

Advocacy and Human Trafficking

Kathryn Farmer and Leigha Shoup

> Life is a hard battle anyway. If we laugh and sing a little as we fight the good fight of freedom, it makes it all go easier. I will not allow my life's light to be determined by the darkness around me
>
> —Sojourner Truth (Editors of Peter Pauper Press, 2018, p. 30).

The Art of Advocacy

Survivors of human trafficking are often isolated after they leave their trafficking situation due to a lack of support and resources, mental health issues, separation from loved ones, stigma from trafficking, and full reliance on the trafficker (White & Lloyd, 2014). They do not always know whom they can trust or where to turn for comfort. Creating a safe and supportive environment is vital as the survivors heal through the trauma of their situation (Shelley, 2010). The role of the advocate is to provide a survivor-centered, strengths-based approach while walking alongside survivors in their journey to help combat those feelings of loneliness and isolation (Ladd & Weaver, 2017).

For the purposes of this chapter, advocates are specially trained professionals equipped to support survivors of crime (United States Department of Justice, 2017). The meaning of advocacy, in its purest form, is a verb; advocacy is action. Advocacy means actively listening, completely and objectively, to a person's truth—to that person's hopes and fears. It means responding in the middle of the night to a crisis at the hospital, connecting survivors with necessary resources, walking with them in their day-to-day struggles, and, in some cases, accompanying survivors to court (Ohio Family Violence Prevention Center, 2010). Advocacy means creating an environment where survivors recapture their inner power, which has been ripped from them, as they heal through the trauma of their experience.

Limited literature exists that discusses the impact of trauma-informed care on advocates who work with human trafficking survivors. However, there is substantial literature describing self-care for advocates who work with sexual violence survivors, and it will be utilized, as there is significant overlap in the two fields (Baird & Jenkins, 2003; Carmody, 1997; Wasco, Campbell, & Clark, 2002). Advocates who repeatedly engage with trauma survivors are vulnerable to experiencing symptoms of trauma as well. This type of secondary or vicarious trauma experienced by advocates can look similar across fields of work. Self-care, self-nurturing, a balance in life activities, and connection to self and others can play a key role in managing vicarious trauma (Merchant & Whiting, 2015). Understanding and attending to one's own triggers can help to guide advocates through any secondary or vicarious trauma when providing services to survivors.

When survivors engage with advocates, the survivors are entrusting the advocates with their story and the trauma of their experience. This connection places the survivor in a vulnerable position; the advocate is tasked with ensuring that the survivor's needs and wishes are respected to encourage self-determination. The experiences and situations that survivors have encountered and then share with advocates can impact advocates in ways this field is still discovering. This chapter will pull from personal experiences of advocates who previously worked or are currently working at Crime Victim Services in northwest Ohio and discuss how the work has impacted them both as professionals and as human beings.

Human Trafficking in Rural Ohio

Crime Victim Services' main office is located in Lima, Ohio, within Allen County. Lima is a small city surrounded by rural communities with a population of approximately 37,149 individuals (U.S. Census Data, 2017). While Lima and the surrounding area have an array of resources, programs, and agencies, the rural makeup of the communities offers fewer resources than would be present within a metropolitan setting.

Crime Victim Services' mission is to help victims prevail over the trauma of their victimization by assisting and advocating for safety, healing, justice, and restitution. Crime Victim Services is a United Way–affiliated victim support program. Since 1981, the agency has recognized that crime is not just breaking a code or law, but that consequential deeds affect people in significant ways as well. Crime Victim Services' Advocates strive to ensure that survivors have safety information and advocacy with offender release information through Victim Information and Notification Everyday, sex offender registration, protection orders, emergency shelter, transitional housing, and separate waiting areas at court. Survivors are able to gain access to emotional healing assistance, such as crisis counseling, spiritual ministry, support groups, victim offender dialogue, 24-hour crisis line, employer and creditor intervention, accompaniment to court/interviews, and advocacy for social services. Crime

Victim Services easily allows survivors and their families to participate in the justice process by attending hearings, providing input, and receiving case information; examples include investigation through possible parole hearings and receiving money from offender restitution from Ohio's Victim Compensation Program years after the crime was committed and from Crime Victim Services' emergency financial assistance.

As a comprehensive "one-stop" victim service agency in Allen and Putnam Counties, Crime Victim Services typically works with over 4,000 victims annually, including all types, ages, genders, ethnicities, physical and cognitive abilities, language proficiencies, and people with various sight and hearing levels. Crime Victim Services assists victims through its Day One (rape crisis, antihuman trafficking, and prevention), Domestic Violence, Court Appointed Special Advocates, Child Advocacy Center, Elder Victim Ministry, Court Advocacy, Counseling, Victim Offender Dialogue, and Special Victims Unit programs.

The term "Day One" was developed by the Survivor Advocates at Crime Victim Services and represents that our program is there with survivors from the *first day* of their victimization and represents the prevention work we do in the community—individuals can step up *today* and help prevent these types of crimes from occurring in the first place. Survivors who are assisted by Day One have a multitude of different backgrounds, experiences, and pathways. Since Day One began serving survivors of human trafficking 2014, the program has served 25 survivors of labor trafficking and 134 survivors of sex trafficking. Day One has provided services to survivors between the ages of 4 and 65; however, most survivors fall within the age range of 18–24. These demographics follow national data that shows individuals generally start being trafficked as young adults (Polaris, 2015). Day One advocates work with survivors by meeting them where they are in their trauma recovery journeys. Advocates provide survivors with options to help them recapture the power and control over their lives that was previously taken from them. The goal of the Day One Program is to assist survivors in meeting their basic needs, work with them to recover through the trauma of what happened to them, equip them with life skills, and help them transition to live independently and safely in the community.

Crime Victim Services is the fiscal agent of the Northwest Ohio Rescue and Restore Coalition (NWORRC). The NWORRC was formed in 2012, and its mission is to end sex and labor trafficking through public education, survivor recovery, and justice response. The Coalition is made up of survivors, medical professionals, mental health agencies, law enforcement, the faith-based community, children services, boards of developmental disabilities, colleges and universities, and nonprofit agencies. The Coalition provides training and technical assistance to approximately 1,000 people each year. The two white dots in Figure 9.1 signify both of Crime Victim Services' office locations; however, the survivor advocates work out of the Allen County office in Lima.

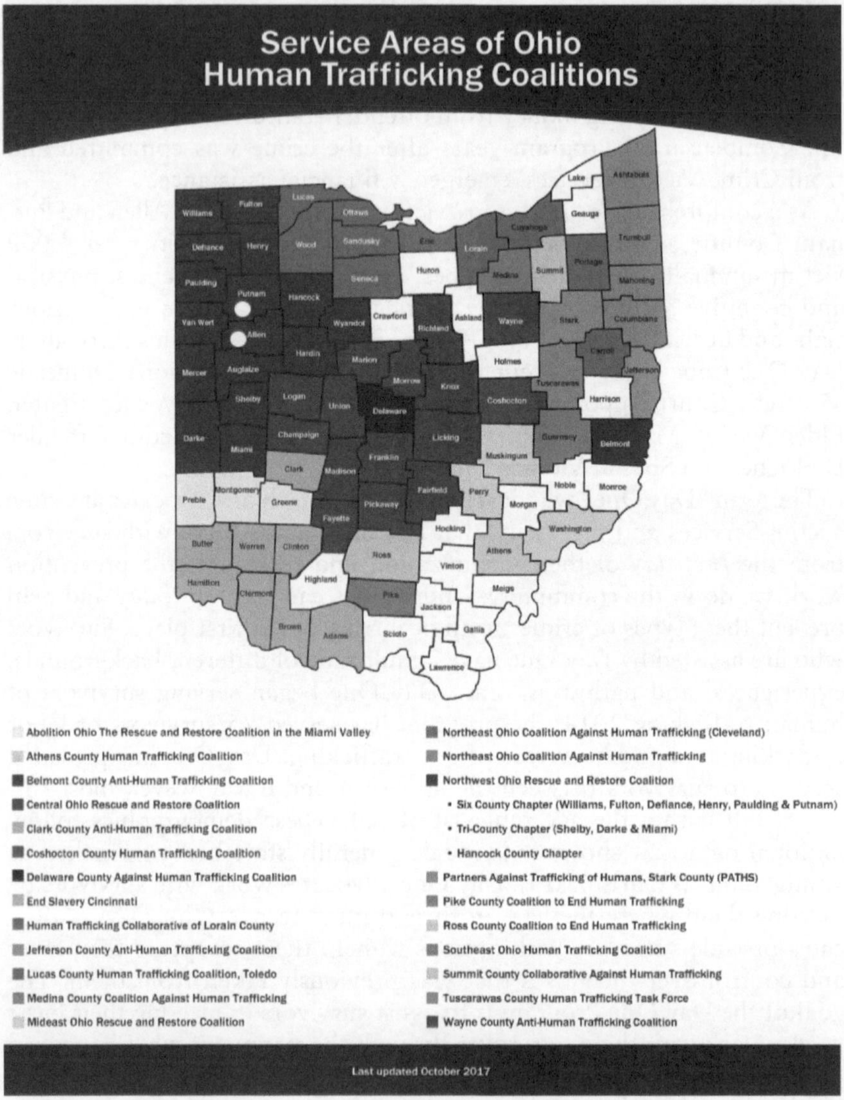

Figure 9.1 NWORRC covers the largest geographic region in Ohio and can be identified by the darkest counties in northwest Ohio on the map.

When poverty rates are high, resources are limited, and at-risk individuals feel that they have no one to turn to, their vulnerabilities are more easily preyed upon by traffickers. The rural area and environment of northwest Ohio creates barriers and gaps in services for survivors. Survivors tend to be very transient and may end up in multiple areas of Ohio or surrounding states in one day (Ohio Human Trafficking Task

Force, 2013). This alone can make it difficult for survivors to access needed medical, mental health, and advocacy services. A comprehensive local community can offer a holistic response to human trafficking where multiple agencies work together to address, prevent, and intervene when survivors seek assistance for themselves or are identified by a community partner. It is necessary for these supportive agencies to maintain a certain level of connectedness to survivors and, at times, that can be difficult due to limited funding, resources, and large client caseloads assigned to advocates.

Trauma and Trauma Initiatives

Trauma Response

Due to the difficult and traumatic situations that advocates are faced with every day, they can become overwhelmed and start to experience burnout, secondary trauma, or vicarious trauma (Bober & Regehr, 2006; Campbell & Wasco, 2005; Craig & Sprang, 2010; United States Department of State, 2017). While multiple factors have contributed to turnover in the field, two common themes are the lack of the importance of self-care and the possibility of burnout that comes from vicarious trauma (Sprang, Clark, & Whitt-Woosley, 2007). Research suggests that advocates thrive in work environments where supervisors facilitate true self-care, promote mental health wellness, and actively help staff identify and address burnout and the effects of vicarious trauma (Sprang et al., 2007). Supervisors can improve retention by prioritizing connection, cooperation, flexibility, and innovation. This helps advocates better meet the challenges of advocacy and its burdens (Merchant & Whiting, 2015).

Van Dernoot Lipsky and Burk (2009) describe vicarious trauma as "trauma exposure response" (p. 4). These authors explain the cyclical nature of vicarious trauma and the ways advocates and clinicians can take care of themselves. They describe this process as trauma stewardship and define it as "the entire conversation about how we come to do this work, how we are affected by it, and how we make sense of and learn from our experiences" (van Dernoot Lipsky & Burk, 2009, p. 6). Other terms for trauma exposure response are provider fatigue, compassion fatigue, and/or secondary trauma. The words refer to the experience of having exhausted hearts, minds, bodies, and souls from helping survivors process through their painful experiences. Trauma exposure response develops as the advocate emotionally takes on the survivor's experiences. Vicarious trauma can impact the advocate physically, including a change in appetite, physical activity, and nightmares, which impact sleeping patterns. Lack of collaboration, trust, control, hypervigilance, and intimacy issues in relationships are other ways that advocates experience vicarious trauma. Advocates may experience anxiety, decreased joy, and avoidance of job duties. They also might experience low motivation or changes in worldview (Bober & Regehr, 2006; Jenkins & Baird, 2002; McCann & Pearlman, 1990).

Established Self-Care Initiatives

The National Child Traumatic Stress Network (2012) identifies several self-care strategies for service providers, including

- strategies to evaluate secondary stress,
- cognitive behavioral interventions,
- mindfulness training,
- reflective supervision,
- caseload adjustment,
- informal gatherings following crisis events,
- change in job duties, and
- referrals to employee assistance programs or outside agencies.

These collectively point to the agency's role in reducing trauma exposure response rather than allowing the advocate to remain solely responsible for self-care. An agency actively engaging in trauma-informed practices not solely for survivors, but also for employees, can create an environment of healing, self-care, self-nurturing, and a balanced work and personal life balance. Bober and Regehr (2006) found that individual self-care strategies did not protect against symptoms and the solutions should focus on structural changes rather than individual practices. An agency that promotes self-care practices builds the importance of it holistically within agency culture. Self-care, structurally speaking, is a standard of practice. It is built into the workday through team meetings, supportive supervision, and inclusive policies and procedures. Employees come to depend on an agency with a trauma-informed culture that allows for advocates to prevent and address vicarious trauma, if it occurs. This trauma-informed culture is a benefit to the agency, because employees remain healthy and continue the work that survivors depend on.

Crime Victim Services' Initiatives

The Day One Department at Crime Victim Services focuses on work with sexual crimes, including human trafficking. This program has experienced a high turnover rate of advocates within the anti-trafficking team over the past several years due to vicarious trauma. Advocates who interact with traumatized survivors face the impact of vicarious trauma from their work. Advocates have the potential of experiencing burnout without proper self-care; thus, some choose to leave their direct service roles. Retention of advocates who work with trauma survivors is low with an average work life of two to three years (Merchant & Whiting, 2015). Vicarious trauma, long hours, large caseloads, violation of both perceived and real emotional and physical safety, and employee advancement may be causes for why direct care staff do not remain in their positions long term (Massachusetts Council of Human Service Providers, 2007).

Self-care comes in many different forms, styles, amounts, and frequencies. There is no "right" way to practice and implement self-care techniques (The National Domestic Violence Hotline, 2014). Service providers can find it difficult to help advocates implement self-care; however, assisting advocates in identifying ways to help includes brainstorming and discussing what advocates enjoy doing in their free time, what helps them relax or stay calm, and ideal work environments. Self-care is viewed as a unique journey of looking inward and assessing how the work environment has impacted the advocates' sense of self and view of the world.

Based on funding priorities from several federal grants and the leadership's shared value of taking care of employees, Crime Victim Services has implemented and continues to develop cultural changes within the agency that assist advocates from the onset of hire, including new staff orientation, a comprehensive onboarding process, and continuing education on trauma and self-care. This allows new employees to experience and learn the trauma-informed culture of the agency. Crime Victim Services also engages in cultural awareness and understanding of diverse staff needs and creates a supportive workplace environment. The agency actively engages in acknowledgment of how historical and institutional trauma can impact the trauma responses of staff.

Crime Victim Services creates and maintains protocols to ensure the physical safety of staff and has an open-door policy for employees to express concerns in a safe and appropriate manner. Departmental practices of Day One include providing

1. trauma-informed, supportive supervision;
2. appropriate caseload balances;
3. regular team meetings;
4. art therapy in a group setting; and
5. utilization of paid time off.

These practices actively address vicarious trauma experienced by advocates. Recognizing and managing vicarious trauma can be the difference between an advocate becoming overwhelmed and unable to complete daily activities of life and an advocate remaining mentally and physically healthy in both work and personal life.

One of the key aspects of creating an environment where advocates thrive is regular supervision. Trauma-informed supervision is crucial when it comes to providing holistic services. Supervision can be utilized to support staff by promoting problem solving, developing creative free-thinking, enhancing self-care, and coordinating services. It can also be used to promote best practices through increased accountability; review of policies, protocols, and procedures; and examination of ethical considerations. Incorporating trauma-informed supervisions can help to address self-care and secondary and vicarious trauma of staff. Documentation is an extremely useful key to regular supervision. This allows for ideas and information to be recorded but also keeps both the supervisor and supervisee on track with how and when services are being implemented (U.S. Department of Health and Human Services, 2014). When advocates feel actively supported by their supervisor, the emotional load of the work is lessened.

Research Methodology

Background Information

Crime Victim Services is a nonprofit agency that offers multiple programs. One of the many programs is Day One, which encompasses human trafficking, sexual violence, and violence prevention. The Anti-Trafficking Team has three full-time advocates who provide case management and crisis intervention through a trauma-informed care lens. The program is funded by the Victims of Crime Act federal grant and covers 16 counties in Ohio with support from the Northwest Ohio Rescue and Restore Coalition. The coalition and the department work hand in hand to provide services to northwest Ohio.

Research Design

This case study examines one anti-trafficking program as a preliminary look into how working with survivors of human trafficking impacts advocates. It also explores individual and agency-implemented, self-care techniques to help the advocates stay grounded. The topics include whether the work has changed them and their worldview, if the agency could better support them, what self-care techniques they implement, why self-care is difficult for people in general, and if art therapy has impacted their work as an advocate. Giving voice to this population is important since there is limited research regarding advocates who work with human trafficking survivors. Consent was obtained prior to the interviews, and the interviewers reiterated the voluntary and confidential nature of their participation at the time of the interview. There was a potential for psychological risk from participating in the interviews due to the topic of trauma. The advocates were instructed that they could leave the interview at any time if they were not comfortable sharing their experiences or if they became overwhelmed. There were no payments or direct individual benefits from participating in the study.

Sample

The sample for the interviews was a nonprobability, nonrandom, purposive sample. A purposive sample is used when the interviewer wishes to study a particular type of population. The rationale behind this type of sample is that the population needs to be homogeneous in nature so that advocates of human trafficking are the variables under study (Neuman, 2007). Advocates at Crime Victim Services are all in their 20s and 30s. The advocates, all identifying as female, were five white, two Asian, two Latinx, and two African American. A total of four semistructured interviews were held with advocates who no longer work at the agency and current advocates who are still employed. The ages ranged from 24 to 37 years old (M = 29). The names of the advocates were changed to protect their identities.

Instrument

The semistructured questionnaire consisted of seven to nine questions depending on the type of interview. All advocates were asked the primary questions, and two questions were added specifically about the art therapy session offered in August, 2016, if the advocates were present during that session. All of the interviews lasted approximately an hour long. Three of the interviews took place at Crime Victim Services, and one of the interviews took place over video chat. The authors provided the questioning for all of the interviews.

Data Analysis

The interviewers digitally recorded the information shared by participants during the interviews. Subsequently, the interviewers transcribed the data into a word processing document and analyzed it for common themes and patterns.

Findings

Qualitative Analysis

Initially, the data was analyzed using a low-inference coding method after each interview was transcribed. Key answers were highlighted from the transcriptions and labeled with words or short phrases. For example, answers to the question related to self-care techniques would be coded as "accountability," "taking a walk," "talk to someone," "tapping," "trust," "grounding," "saying no," "running," "crying," "yoga," "cleaning," "cupping," "family," "church," "taking a break," "eat better," "organizing," "turn off phone," or "snacks." Those codes were placed into Microsoft Excel and coded into broader categories: "running," "taking a walk," "yoga," and "eat better" were placed into a category title "physical health." This process of coding, through the creation of categories, subcategories, and further subcategories, developed the higher-level coding of analysis.

Field notes with observations of the advocates were also referred to throughout the process as a way of adding depth to the results. Furthermore, key quotes from each question were also placed into Microsoft Excel to aid in the process of analysis. Eventually, this progression led to the overall themes that emerged from the study. The original codes and quotes from the advocates were referenced throughout the entire process to ensure accurate representation and to safeguard the integrity of the data from the original interviews.

Summary of Findings

The results from the interviews produced four main themes: 1) intentional practice, 2) agency culture, 3) incongruent expectations, and 4) humans not machines. These themes relate directly back to what advocates reported about their experiences working with survivors at Crime Victim Services. Their stories serve as a foundation for future recommendations to Crime Victim Services as to how advocates can be better supported and what further work needs to be done to ensure their well-being.

Intentional Practice

The theme of intentionality emerged throughout the entirety of this research. Intentional practice is the concept that advocates must be purposeful in practicing self-care to experience a better integration of themselves and the world while working in this field. Several factors are contained within this theme. The first of these factors is mindfulness. The advocates had varying ideas of what mindfulness meant, whether it was yoga, breathing, taking a walk to clear their heads, or going to a nearby salt cave. Leo said, "I excuse myself from meetings sometimes if I just need a minute to breathe or to feel like I need to kind of shake off all of the stress." Jessica said, "I do a lot of tapping, so bilateral stimulation and you can do that in meetings, you can do that by walking." While not all of the advocates utilized mindfulness techniques in the traditional sense of the word, all of them referenced using a self check-in process. Zara stated, "Taking intentional pauses. I think that's the best way to frame it . . . doing the intentional work, taking the intentional pauses to really get what you need."

The second factor was having the self-awareness to know themselves and recognize when they needed rest or when to seek out support. Jessica reflected back on when she first started the work and recalled, "I would want to learn more about myself and who I am before I try to help other people learn who they are." Zara said, "Reach out if you need help, or even if you don't think you need help. Reach out and make sure you have that go-to person." While thinking about how their own care impacted client care, Zara went on to say,

> You can't give from an empty cup. You've gotta fill up your cup or you're just depleted. Once you are depleted, filling that cup back up is going to be that much harder. You can't give someone else something to drink if you don't have anything to drink yourself. So it's important to find resources to fill that back up.

All the advocates indicated that they want to be helpful to their clients but that sense of being helpful often carries over into their personal lives. Maria said, "I feel horrible saying no . . . but people still call me after work—friends, you know. They are dealing with their problems. But I'm like, I'm sorry, but I can't and feel bad." Being intentional in practice means that there isn't a quick fix for those who are struggling. It is a lifelong endeavor. Zara expressed that by saying, "Self-care is another one of those always *a work in progress* sort of deal where you can always get better and always strive for more sort of a thing. I don't think anyone is perfect at self-care."

The third factor was using art as a form of intentional practice. After a scheduled art therapy session for advocacy support facilitated by a registered, board certified art therapist in 2016, they saw the benefits for themselves and how it can positively impact their clients. In reference to her collage regarding her personal meaning of resilience, Zara said, "For once we had to think about ourselves when we were doing that. At first, it's kind of awkward, but then as you go through the magazines, you are like, oh! This describes me." Leo said, "It was a reflection time for me to be able to think about what keeps me going in my job." She went on to say, "Art therapy . . . doing it at work was just a validation for things I was already doing in my own life. But also it gave me more ideas about something I was already interested in anyway." Zara stated,

> I know that art is important, not just for the advocates, but also for the clients. Once you see the client start getting involved in something, whether it is drawing, or color, or putting stuff together, it's like they forget for a moment all the things that they are going through and focus on that.

Figures 9.2–9.4 show a representation of three of the pieces of work completed by advocates who participated in the art therapy session. Art created during this session focused on team support demonstrated through the words "connection" and "sisterhood" (Figure 9.2), and mindfulness activities that bring balance to the minds of the advocates (Figure 9.3), and outside support systems, such as family (Figure 9.4).

Figure 9.2 This piece was created during the group art therapy session and describes how the advocate feels connected to her team. She thinks it is important to be grounded in order to do the hard work. Nature and meditation were areas that emerged as sources of comfort

Figure 9.3 This piece was created during a group art therapy session. The advocate used the word resilience and described it as "strength and hope" to demonstrate how she views the other advocates in this work. She utilized several pictures that represent nature, as it is a source of comfort and healing for her

Figure 9.4 This piece was created during the group art therapy session. The advocate spoke about significant struggles in her life, but noted she practices self-care by going to the movies, spending time with family, listening to music, traveling, and exercising

Another form of creative expression is journaling. In early 2015, at a team meeting, while reflecting on questions provided by the supervisor geared toward vicarious trauma, Jessica wrote the following,

> Inner anxiety levels boil over; each day it feels as if the pot begins on high heat. If I leave the pot on the stove the anxiety quickly begins to flirt with the chance to pass the rim. Thru the day I stop often to remove the pot from the heat of the stove. Anything to take my mind off of all those hurting and the few hurting people who need so much more than I can give. The change of thoughts allows the boiling to cease and simmer for a bit but the heat always returns. Without the heat I yearn for it . . . and sometimes I let the flirtation with the rim go on just long enough that I can still stop it but feel the bubbles getting so close to escaping the pot.

This reflective journaling demonstrates the level to which Jessica was experiencing vicarious trauma. She was intertwined with the work and was close to a breaking point but felt as if she could neither leave nor address the trauma.

Agency Culture

The second theme that emerged was agency culture, which describes how the agency supports advocates and creates a space for them to thrive while working with survivors. The first factor that emerged was the sense of support that the advocates feel within the department at their organization. Zara said, "We have a pretty good team so talking among the team is awesome." Maria stated, "It's draining but it's rewarding too. That's why I stay at this job. I like it. I like the people I work with." Several of the advocates spoke about the importance of their team helping to keep them accountable. Jessica said, "I think we have to hold each other accountable. Like, hey, I'm noticing that you are really exhausted. Having coworkers that are sensitive to that and holding each other accountable." However, some said they keep their feelings of stress inside. Maria said, "I don't tell people when I'm struggling . . . but I feel supported by everyone." Overall, there was a sense that having a cohesive team makes the difficult work manageable and bonds the individuals. Leo stated, "One of the things is having camaraderie with co-workers and being able to rely on them . . . like a sisterhood."

The second factor was the need to have structure within the agency to support the advocates in their work. Leo said, "I think having structure . . . I think consistency is helpful and the ways in which we have policies." Jessica had a similar sentiment,

> I guess my hope is that . . . the roles will be more structured, and there will be more policies and procedures and kind of guidelines even in a world where there are no guidelines in this work or working with this specific population.

They also discussed having protocols that outlined boundaries and the advocates maintaining those boundaries. Zara stated, "Just maintain boundaries so that you don't trip and fall." Jessica mentioned the newness of the program and how it impacted the work. "We were all just doing the best we could with what we had and what we knew. And it being such a new area and like kind of trailblazing." The advocates also spoke about the importance of having a supportive supervisor. In reference to the supervisor, Leo said, "You really encourage that we take time off and flex our time. You care about us and not just the work we are doing." These statements indicated that the environment of the workplace and the people with whom the advocates work make a difference in how they were able to sustain the work. It also points to putting the agency in a responsible place to take appropriate steps to create a workspace where advocates can flourish and does not place all ownership for self-care on the advocates themselves.

Incongruent Expectations

The theme of incongruent expectations describes the advocates' unrealistic expectations for themselves as an advocate. The first factor is the advocates feeling as if they are not doing enough or that they are not good enough. Furthermore, several advocates talked about how those messages often translate into shame for them. Zara said, "I think it all boils down to some of those shame messages that we give ourselves and where we place value." Jessica referenced Dr. Brené Brown (2012), a research professor at the University of Houston, and said, "I think Brené Brown really talks about shame really well and talks about these shame gremlins that kind of sneak up on us when we least expect it." She went on to say,

> Knowing what I know now about shame, um, there have been shame messages that I gave myself as a social worker. I thought shame and embarrassment were the same thing for a very long time. So I didn't realize I was telling my own self, like, you're a bad social worker if you're not doing this. Having that self-care to really reflect and realize that sometimes those shame messages are distorted thinking, and sometimes it's just not a good fit, and that's ok, that it doesn't mean there's anything wrong with you.

Leo tied in self-worth with the work she is doing. She stated,

> And something that I know all too well, is for me, I place a very high value on the work that I do . . . so if I'm not at work, then I'm not valuable. I think a lot of us in the helping profession struggle with that shame of "I could be doing more," "I should be doing more," and "I'm not a good enough social worker."

Maria questioned whether she was actually making an impact on the clients by saying,

> Some days you do feel like, what am I doing, you know? Or like, am I making a difference? So I tell myself that I am. And some days will be harder than others, but just like coming to work is making a difference. And caring, probably too much. But we all do that.

Zara said, "We care more about our clients than ourselves."

The second factor was the expectation that advocates can do it on their own or that they will know when they need self-care rather than making it a daily practice. Maria said,

> It's hard for me to admit or ask for help because I'm supposed to be helping other people. It's not necessarily that I don't know what to do, but I didn't realize that I probably should be doing it every day. That didn't occur to me.

They also discussed how sometimes they see the need for it in others but not themselves. Leo said, "It's always easier to tell other people things that you notice or things that you recommend, and then doing it for yourself is a whole different thing." Zara said, "Self-care is important or you are just going to drown. . . . It's easy to talk about it; it's difficult to implement it." Several advocates spoke about not taking the time for it. Jessica said, "I will come up with every excuse of why I don't have time to do self-care. And I'll do it tomorrow." Maria stated, "I know I need to do it more, but I don't know, not that I don't know how but I just don't make the time for it."

The third factor was how the lack of advocates' self-care impacts survivors when self-care is ignored. The survivors already must deal with their own self-doubt. Leo said, "Every survivor is different. But there are themes of self-blame, and guilt, and feeling dirty, and there are a lot of things that survivors have in common." Maria stated,

> I think that we are hypocrites sometimes because we ask our clients to take really good care of themselves because they've had a lot taken [from them], and we're like asking them to fill themselves back up but maybe we aren't always willing to do that.

When the advocates focus solely on the clients, they isolate themselves, and it can be detrimental to both them and the survivors. Zara stated, "We do things that are irrational and ridiculous, and it hurts us in the end. And it hurts the people we are trying to help in the end." Jessica succinctly reflected about the direct impact on her clients of not taking care of herself and summarized,

> Because ultimately, if we aren't taking care of ourselves, it's rubbing off on the clients and if we are chaos, then they will feel that chaos. And they've got enough chaos to deal with. It's not fair for us to put our own chaos onto them, too.

Humans, Not Machines

The final theme that emerged was humans, not machines. This phrase describes the idea that advocates cannot continually give *of* themselves without taking time *for* themselves because, eventually, they will reach a breaking point. The first factor was how the work physically and mentally impacts them. Maria talked about some of the hardest days dealing with trafficked clients. She said, "When people go back to their trafficker/pimp, I think that can be frustrating . . . I think it affects you more than [you think]." Zara said, "It also makes you hyper-vigilant." Jessica reflected,

> I would say today, almost two years later, there are pieces that get triggered from that work, or memories, or some of those messages that I've given myself, which is my own shit, but it's, I think, kind of driven from the work that was being done and also just the fact that it was new work in a really chaotic population.

Zara simply stated, "If we are constantly giving and never refilling, then there's nothing to give at some point." All these statements describe the toll that work with trafficking survivors can take on the ability of advocates to provide good advocacy and take care of themselves.

The second factor was how it has changed their worldview. Jessica stated, "I don't think I actually fully realized in the moment, how much it actually changed me. Until I was like fully away from that life, and I say life because it was basically a lifestyle, rather than a job." Several also talked about their view of God. Leo stated, "[It] definitely affects the way you see, or the way I see God." Zara said, "So it makes you question whether there is a God or who is this God." Jessica reflected,

> Looking back, there are very few hours where it didn't change me. In ways that I saw kind of the broader world, in the ways that I saw myself, in the ways that I saw my relationships, whether that be with an intimate partner, or with my family, or with friends.

These statements demonstrate that when advocates work with clients who have experienced significant levels of trauma, it can, in turn, negatively impact their personal relationships and worldview due to their steady exposure to the evil underbelly of society that exists in the world.

The final factor was the need for them to rest. One advocate used the analogy of a car to talk about what happens when regular maintenance doesn't occur. In reference to the "humans, not machines" theme, Leo said, "You can't just drive a car and not change the oil. You have to take care of it and maintain it or eventually it will die." Zara said, "Humans have a limited amount of energy to give, and if you operate under the assumption that you are never ending, then you will find yourself at the end very quickly." Both Leo and Zara compared overworking to a freight train. Leo said, "I think our society values running yourself around like a freight train. And it's expected. And if you aren't doing that, then you are failing." Zara stated, "You are doing better than you think. You don't have to run yourself like a freight train in order to be more productive or important or worthy. Also, take more risks. Try more new things. Learning is uncomfortable." These statements indicated that working more hours or working harder without taking time to rest can result in more harm than good.

Discussion

Interpretation and Implications of Findings

This area of study is limited and due to the size and limitations of this exploration, the findings are only considered applicable to Crime Victim Services and do not have a broader application for other agencies. The findings from these interviews reveal the importance of advocates developing their own internal practice but also show how vital it is to have agency support. Working with survivors of human trafficking is taxing and having a setting that provides practical and emotional support and encourages self-care can help prevent secondary or vicarious trauma from occurring. Some of the more seasoned advocates had developed healthy coping techniques over time but still admitted to struggling with how to ensure that they were appropriately dealing with the trauma they faced every day in the stories and lives of their clients. Some of the less experienced advocates shared that they could tell they were struggling but did not know what to do. All advocates spoke with passion about the work that they do and how they wanted to find ways to stay in the field without having the work overwhelm them or experience burnout.

The topic of shame and worthiness arose in every interview. The advocates shared that they struggled with feelings of not being good enough or not accomplishing enough for survivors. The reflections they shared showed that sometimes these feelings were heightened when the survivor returned to their trafficker or began using drugs again. The advocates would blame themselves, even though they fully knew it was not in their control to prevent downfalls from occurring. Those messages played into their ability to take care of themselves because they felt as if they could not rest due to the never-ending client crises, tasks, challenges, paperwork, and referrals that needed to be made.

Another commonality was the practice of advocates isolating themselves from their families and coworkers when the effects of vicarious trauma began impacting them. That isolation created a sense of martyrdom that they portrayed to the world and then started to believe it about themselves. They wanted others to see them do this incredible groundbreaking work, or they felt as if they were the only ones doing it; however, the martyr attitude was damaging, because the advocates could then adopt a sense of invincibility, which led directly to vicarious trauma. In one situation, an advocate carried out their work as if they were the only one who could help the client, taking on a "savior" or "hero complex." This mind-set became apparent when the advocate started dropping everything else for clients and portraying all of the clients' needs as an emergency. This led to the advocate working extremely long hours outside of the typical workday and outside of their role with clients. It became a challenge because the advocate was working in a silo that did not include the survivor's multidisciplinary team, which had service providers devoted to that specific work. It blurred the lines of roles, and the advocate believed they were the only one that knew how to help the client or felt that others did not care as much as they did. In the end, it led the clients to solely rely on one advocate for support rather than utilizing the existing network of providers.

Recommendations and Conclusion

The purpose of the advocate interviews was to explore how this work impacts them professionally, interpersonally, and personally. Advocates of human trafficking have not been widely studied, and it was important to question and analyze their perspectives about their work. The use of interviews, while a small sample size, allowed the advocates' voices to be heard. Once heard, the advocates were able to gain a higher sense of personal and professional awareness. This mindfulness was also able to be translated to a collective cognizance for the advocate community at Crime Victim Services. Two of them expressed that this brief discussion allowed them to think more about their own practices and what they were doing to take care of themselves. One mentioned that she would like to have further regular conversations about how to continue implementing practices within the agency to promote well-being with staff. These interviews provided an opportunity to gather data in an area where research is limited and allowed them to process the difficulty of what they do in a safe, anonymous setting.

While there are significant strengths present within this study, there are also several limitations. The interviewers work directly with the survivor advocates and could have potential bias in how they see the survivor advocates handle and respond to the workload and could influence the findings. Additionally, the instrument for the interviews had not been previously used, thus creating an opportunity for credibility to be questioned. However, the individual queries were presented to peers for feedback and to increase the reliability of the questions. The amount of time to collect data was short; had there been more time, more advocates could have been a part of the process, thus adding depth to the stories presented within this research. This study only examined one program and thus examined a limited sample and should not be generalized to all advocates who work with survivors. Additionally, not all advocates from the agency participated in this study. Crime Victim Services is only one agency in one geographic region of Ohio. Consequently, the diversity of the sample was limited because not all of the agencies that work with survivors were involved in the process. More data gathering and analysis should be conducted with other advocates in order to examine other agencies in similar rural geographic areas.

Through the entire duration of this study, it was our intention that the voices of the advocates remained at the forefront of the investigation. The advocates often felt only empathy and concern for the survivors; the advocates continually challenged themselves to work longer hours and work more effectively. They felt responsible for relapses with survivors who often fall through the cracks. The advocates had to be encouraged to seek support from others while being fully aware that many of their peers leave the field due to trauma fatigue and job stress. Throughout the entirety of the study, advocates often focused on their work with survivors and did not spend significant time speaking about their own lives. This speaks to the altruistic nature of many social workers in this field of work and could have implications for reasons that individuals become burned out or experience secondary or vicarious trauma. To make the situation more complicated, by nature, these advocates are outward focused and want to continually give to others; they may not be open to advice on how to intentionally practice self-care, which may appear counterproductive to them at first. If, however, advocates are able to recognize that they are not tireless machines and would benefit from self-care, their longevity in the field would increase and thus provide a strengthened continuity of care for survivors. The perceptions and voices of the advocates who work with human trafficking survivors truly provided a clearer picture of their experiences, the effects of the interactions of the advocates and their clients, and the dedication and sacrifices these advocates make on a daily basis for survivors.

References

Baird, S., & Jenkins, S. R. (2003, February). Secondary traumatic stress and burnout in sexual assault and domestic violence staff. *Violence and Victims*, *18*(1), 71–86.

Bober, T., & Regehr, C. (2006, February). Strategies for reducing secondary or vicarious trauma: Do they work? *Brief Treatment and Crisis Intervention*, *6*(1), 1–9.

Brown, C. B. (2012). *Daring greatly: How the courage to be vulnerable transforms the way we live, love, parent, and lead*. New York, NY: Gotham.

Campbell, R., & Wasco, S. (2005, February). Understanding rape and sexual assault: 20 years of progress and future directions. *Journal of Interpersonal Violence*, *20*(1), 127–131.

Carmody, M. (1997). Submerged voices: Coordinators of sexual assault services speak of their experiences. *Affiliated Journal of Women and Social Work*, *12*(4), 452–462.

Craig, C. D, & Sprang, G. (2010). Compassion satisfaction, compassion fatigue, and burnout in a national sample of trauma treatment therapists. *Anxiety, Stress, and Coping*, *23*(3), 319–339.

Editors of Peter Pauper Press. (2018). *Revolutionary women: From colonists to suffragists*. White Plains, NY: Peter Piper Press, Inc.

Jenkins, S. R., & Baird, S. J. (2002). Secondary traumatic stress and vicarious trauma: A validational study. *Journal of Traumatic Stress*, *15*(5), 423–432.

Ladd, S. K., & Weaver, L. N. (2017). Moving forward: Collaborative accompaniment of human trafficking survivors by using trauma-informed practices. *Journal of Human Trafficking*, *4*(3), 191–212. https://doi.org/10.1080/23322705.2017.1346445

Massachusetts Council of Human Service Providers. (2007). *Recruiting and retaining the next generation of human services workers in Massachusetts*. Retrieved from www.donahue.umassp.edu/docs/help-wanted-2

McCann, I. L., & Pearlman, L. A. (1990). Vicarious traumatization: A framework for understanding the psychological effects of working with victims. *Journal of Traumatic Stress*, *3*(1), 131–149.

Merchant, L. V., & Whiting, J. B. (2015). Challenges and retention of domestic violence shelter advocates: A grounded theory. *Journal of Family Violence*, *30*(4), 467–478.

The National Child Traumatic Stress Network. (2012). Retrieved from www.nctsn.org

The National Domestic Violence Hotline. (2014, August). *The importance of self-care*. Retrieved from www.thehotline.org/2014/08/08/the-importance-of-self-care/

Neuman, W. L. (2007). *Basics of social research: Qualitative and quantitative approaches*. Boston, MA: Pearson Education, Inc.

Ohio Family Violence Prevention Center, Office of Criminal Justice Services. (2010). *Excellence in advocacy: A victim-centered approach*. Retrieved from www.ocjs.ohio.gov/VictimServicesPublication.pdf

Ohio Human Trafficking Task Force. (2013). *Human trafficking prevention plan*. Retrieved from http://humantrafficking.ohio.gov/links/prevention_plan_10-23-2014.pdf

Polaris. (2015, May). *Sex trafficking in the U.S.: A closer look at U.S. citizen victims*. Retrieved from https://polarisproject.org/resources/sex-trafficking-us-closer-look-us-citizen-victims

Shelley, L. (2010). *Human trafficking: A global perspective*. Cambridge, NY: Cambridge University Press.

Sprang, G., Clark, J. J., & Whitt-Woosley, A. (2007). Compassion fatigue, compassion satisfaction, and burnout: Factors impacting a professional's quality of life. *Journal of Loss and Trauma*, *12*, 259–280.

Wasco, S. M., Campbell, R., & Clark, M. (2002, October). A multiple case study of rape victim advocates' self-care routines: The influence of organizational context. *American Journal of Community Psychology*, *30*(5), 731–760. https://doi.org/10.1023/A:1016377416597

White, S., & Lloyd, R. (2014). *The survivor's guide to leaving*. New York, NY: Girls Education and Mentoring Services.

United States Census Bureau. (2017). *Quick facts Lima*. Ohio. Retrieved from www.census.gov/quickfacts/fact/table/limacityohio/PST045217

United States Department of Health and Human Services Substance Abuse and Mental Health Services Administration Center for Substance Abuse Treatment.

(2014). *Trauma- informed care in behavioral health services*. Treatment Improvement Protocol (TIP) Series, No. 57, Chapter 2, Building a Trauma-Informed Workforce.
United States Department of Justice, Office on Violence Against Women. (2017, January). *Reflections from the field on victim/survivor advocacy*. Retrieved from www.justice.gov/ovw/page/file/936746/download
United States Department of State, Office to Monitor and Combat Trafficking in Persons. (2017, June). *Vicarious trauma*. Retrieved from www.state.gov/documents/organization/272972.pdf
van Dernoot Lipsky, L., & Burk, C. (2009). *Trauma stewardship: An everyday guide to caring for self while caring for others*. Oakland, CA: Berrett-Koehler Publishers, Inc.

TEN

Challenges and Future Considerations of Treatment for Sex Trafficked Survivors

Mary K. Kometiani

This chapter will introduce the myriad of difficulties in providing art therapy treatment for survivors of sex trafficking. Recommendations on how to identify survivors and how to manage multifaceted barriers in therapeutic treatment are provided. Taxing challenges for the practitioner are introduced with a reiterated recommendation for self-care support to combat workplace stress and burnout. This chapter will also discuss future considerations and suggestions for the field. Lastly, the book's final summation and challenge will be delivered.

Hindrances to Identifying Sex Trafficked Survivors

Due to various challenges, identifying individuals as survivors of sex trafficking can be very difficult. Sex trafficking is an unknown and underground crime with little awareness in our society of either its devastating enduring effects on its survivors or its growing expansion in many areas. Obstacles in identifying sex trafficked individuals include

- trafficking methods, such as complete control over the individual's living and working conditions;
- covert online exploitation through coded advertisements that suggest the exploited individuals desire sex;
- habitual mobility and complex trafficking circuits to avoid being discovered and inviting attention;
- law enforcement misreporting, nonreporting, or reporting another crime leads to skewed statistics and investigations;
- secret and masked trafficking sites such as private parties, hotels, and truck stops (Nichols & Heil, 2015);

- distrust of law enforcement and helping professionals that equates to lack of seeking assistance and unawareness of support (Shared Hope International, 2014);
- fear of possible prison sentence or threat of harm or death from perpetrator (Childs, 2018); and
- government bureaucracy, turmoil and corruption that tolerates trafficking (Kara, 2009).

The survivors who are the most difficult to recognize are inhibited and reluctant to confide in others regarding their exploitation; they lacked any control over their trafficking situations and have been repeatedly sold in hidden and transitory places. When enslaved by a family member or manipulated through what seemed like a loving and supportive relationship, an individual may not view herself as victimized or in need of help. Over an extended period of time, the exploited individual uses defense mechanisms and accepts her trauma and abuse as normal (Polaris, 2014). The barriers addressed in Chapter 2, including the concept of the trauma bond to traffickers and the extreme trauma effects, contribute to difficulty of identifying sex trafficked survivors. Trafficking survivors are reluctant to seek help because they have no or limited knowledge about resources, learned to distrust others, and experienced deep and unmitigated shame.

In order for sex trafficked survivors to receive essential resources and treatment toward recovery, proper identification must occur. You are encouraged to use the references regarding the screening assessment and interviewing recommendations provided in the appendix and to become acquainted with available resources specific to your community. Indications of trafficked survivors include

- lack of freedom and unusual restrictions within a living or working environment;
- excessively long working hours, employment without being paid, or being unable to pay off large debt that is owed;
- appearing seriously anxious, fearful, submissive, paranoid, and avoiding eye contact with others;
- neglect, malnourishment, and/or abuse;
- few or no personal possessions and no control of their own money and identification; and
- not able to identify where they are, where they live, and/or what time it is due to frequent mobility (National Human Trafficking Hotline, n.d.).

In addition, some specific suggestions in recognizing survivors of sex trafficking are

- lying about age or identity,
- having tattoos or branding to show ownership,

- using suggestive language and revealing clothing, or
- under the age of 18 and involvement in the commercial sex industry (National Center for Missing & Exploited Children, 2019).

The provided suggestions offer only some common trafficking detectors, and they do not construct an all-encompassing list. Once survivors have been identified, crisis assistance meets the basic needs of the survivor making recovery possible (Muraya & Fry, 2015). However, for trafficked survivors, a typical liberation from their captivity is clouded by flawed criminalization, inadequate support services, and lack of trauma-informed care that, unfortunately, allows for retraumatization (Mehlman-Orozco, 2016). When survivors have been removed from the trafficking situation, a long recovery process and grave challenges lie ahead, especially when only insufficient and/or deficient services are available.

Barriers in Treatment for Trafficked Survivors

Human trafficking is an ever-growing issue, and the particular needs of a survivor must be recognized and addressed foremost. Individuals who are sex trafficked often existed under a level of inferior treatment rendered to animals and repeatedly suffered being violated, isolated, starved, abused, tortured, drugged, silenced, threatened, or harmed to the point of murder. Trauma leaves physical, mental, and emotional scars, affecting an individual's ability to experience well-being, pleasure, and intimacy (van der Kolk, 2014). The resulting trauma caused from sex trafficking is powerfully damaging to its survivors, affecting their worldviews of safety, personal identity, and future relationships. As a result of damaging experiences, survivors may struggle with trauma recovery and future progression after liberation from the trafficked situation. Even after attaining freedom, a survivor can still feel imprisoned because of a lack of safety and/or opportunity to succeed (Kara, 2009).

The needs of human trafficking survivors are complex, requiring comprehensive services and continuum of care that may span from crisis management to long-term treatment. Effective therapeutic treatment may last for years, and the time line for each survivor is unique and can be unpredictable. Often with this population, outpatient group therapy attendance and commitment to reside in shelters fluctuate due to the many obligations and issues that arise while attempting independence (relapse in symptoms, vocational problems, family conflict, struggling with addiction, etc.) There are many challenges to working with survivors of sexual exploitation that are attributable to the intense trauma consequences and arduous transition toward healing and renewal.

Psychological Manipulation/Trauma Bonding

Each individual will respond differently to rehabilitation depending on the age of the survivor, length of exploitation, and forms of abuse experienced and personal trauma history (Leitch & Snow, 2010). In addition, cultural and societal influences also affect the survivor's resilience. By reason of relentless psychological manipulation, survivor hurdles concerning recovery include

- hesitancy to self-identify as a survivor because the individual was led to believe that the trafficker loves her;
- firm belief that she needs to be loyal because of her bond with the trafficker, reliance on him, and fear of reprisal; and
- experiences of substance relapse, re-trafficking, and running away.

Survivors have been made to believe that they have had a choice instead of being victimized by a crime (Vardaman, 2018). They may have conflicted feelings and care for their abuser due to trauma bond (United States Department of State, 2014). Due to the extent of force, fraud, and coercion, the survivor may experience serious challenges in trying to adapt to a new life. Attributable to lowered self-worth, self-destructive thoughts, dependency on the trafficker, addictions, and mental health issues, survivors may experience relapse and return to the trafficker. Research showed that youth are at a higher risk for re-trafficking specifically within the first two years of their liberation (Zimmerman et al., 2008). Survivors may choose to return to their old life, but they do not experience a better outcome. Most freed survivors return to the similar conditions as when they left, including poverty, violence, and lack of opportunity, increasing the high risk for re-trafficking (Kara, 2009). In addition to the many adverse effects from sexual exploitation, survivors have difficulty acknowledging and facing the trauma experiences from their perceived shame.

Shame

Chapter 2 presented the emotional consequences of trafficking, including shame as one of the hardest emotions to endure and one of the most obstinate hindrances to trauma recovery, because it affects one's core views and leads to lowered self-esteem (Marich, 2014). Survivors experience profound shame and may believe that their exploitation was their fault (Shared Hope International, 2014). Shame isolates survivors, making them feel degraded, unaccepted, atypical, and guilty. Individuals who have been exploited usually feel marginalized, stigmatized, alone, and rejected by their loved ones. Conversely, survivors may also glamorize prostitution to mask their shame and weakness (Leitch & Snow, 2010). Because of significant abuse, fear, and coercion, survivors may experience utter shame when telling their trauma story and wrongly assume personal responsibility for being trafficked. When shame is complicated by other transition stressors, survivors face greater obstacles in recovery.

Transition Stressors

Survivors face a multitude of stressors through personal, familial, communal, and societal levels, including

- dealing with family issues, such as estrangement and reunification;
- combating addiction;
- attempting independence;
- legal action against their trafficker;
- stigma of sexual exploitation and lack of support;
- difficulty transitioning to a normal structure and routine;
- overwhelming trauma symptoms and the inability to cope with triggers;
- the same unemployment and problematic financial issues that existed prior to being trafficked; and
- societal and cultural ignorance of blaming the victimized individual rather than the criminal and misunderstanding the effects of trauma.

Survivors who are interested in reestablishing relationships with loved ones may be greeted with blame, judgment, or unresolved issues from past substance abuse and mental health disorders. In the safe house setting, survivors may be emotionally triggered by feeling trapped again or re-experiencing loss of control, and they may struggle in adjusting to a new schedule, expectations, and rules. Herman (1997) revealed that conflicts among survivors enable them to recreate trauma through taking on the roles of trafficker, accomplice, victim, rescuer, and bystander; this discord can lead to failure in recovery. Unresolved trauma can cause distressing situations for survivors who live together in residential treatment or in a shelter. The response of fleeing is also a factor for survivors who are focusing on reintegration of their trauma in treatment. Frequently, survivors experience difficulty staying motivated and maintaining commitment in the prolonged recovery process.

Although legal action can provide restitution for the survivor, it is usually not a timely and straightforward pursuit. Survivors are often tentative to cooperate with authorities in an investigation, testify, or confront their abusers in prosecution (United States Department of State, 2014). Reporting issues that occur from the absence of a full investigation in trafficking cases is a challenge in getting the survivors the assistance they require (Nichols & Heil, 2015). During prosecution, the lawyer might choose a charge that is easier to win in court, and a survivor might not be prepared or emotionally ready to report the full crime and testify (Nichols & Heil, 2015). Survivors may also be treated as less reliable witnesses because of backgrounds with criminal behavior, addiction, and mental health diagnosis (Mehlman-Orozco, 2016). Survivors may struggle with progression due to criminal charges and the lack of opportunity to find employment (Smith, 2018). It can take years to prosecute a trafficking case, during which the survivor becomes frustrated with the lengthy process or disappears (Nichols & Heil, 2015). Flawed legal action in sex trafficking cases is caused by issues in reporting, charging, testifying, prolonged prosecutions, and survivor mistreatment. There are many compounded factors in a survivor's transition to a new way of living, and distrust of others often makes this process even more complicated.

Distrust of Helping Professionals

While navigating complex traumatic exploitation, sex trafficked survivors have learned not to trust anyone. Survivors have been manipulated to believe only in their trafficker, and they can be lied to extensively to ensure this loyalty and reinforce commitment to the trafficker. Survivors of exploitation do not depend on others, and they think that they will be doubted by helping professionals (Shared Hope International, 2014). Some trafficking customers can also be from the ranks of law enforcement or justice system, increasing survivors' doubts that anyone can or will help them (Nichols & Heil, 2015). Often, survivors are convinced that police are always going to arrest them, and all helping professionals will either betray or hinder them. Law enforcement are often the first professionals to respond to a trafficking situation, and they might not have adequate knowledge regarding sex trafficking, the effects of trauma, and education about trauma-informed and survivor-centered approach (Nichols & Heil, 2015). Unaware and inexperienced helping professionals may only consider survivors of sex trafficking as prostitutes and addicts, not realizing the level of abuse, the effects of trauma on their behavior, or the type of support they so urgently require.

Trust in the therapeutic relationship takes time to develop, and trauma healing in therapy is an extended and long-term process. Due to surviving intense trafficking trauma, individuals develop cognitive issues and confusion, and they may experience difficulty telling their story in chronological order or they may appear being suspicious when opening up because the establishment of trust requires time (Nichols & Heil, 2015). Survivors should not be rushed into trauma processing in therapy because hastening the therapeutic process can lead to retraumatization. Rothschild (2000) recommended at least several sessions before trauma therapy techniques are applied to allow for a formation of a more secure relationship between the client and therapist. Trauma recovery does not offer a simple and speedy solution, and not equipping the survivor with the necessary resources to endure can be a further barrier to treatment.

Inadequate Services

Insufficient services and necessary resources are also a major obstacle for the treatment of survivors of sex trafficking. Inadequate assistance for sex trafficked survivors often means that there is insufficient safe housing and ineffective support or what is available does not meet the needs of the critical care required. In particular, male sex trafficked survivors encounter a severe lack of restoration programs (United States Department of State, 2017), and the lesbian, gay, bisexual, transgender, queer or questioning plus (LGBTQ+) community confronts the absence of inclusive safe houses (Gerassi & Nichols, 2018). Due to the complicated trauma bond, when support services are scarce, regrettably, the survivor has a higher chance of returning to the trafficker (Mehlman-Orozco, 2016). Poor services cannot offer effective waiting times or available treatment for survivors; often, these treatment disruptions are a result of technicalities, such as the services are only offered where a survivor currently resides and that locale may be different from the area of victimization (Mehlman-Orozco, 2016). These details result in survivor homelessness, an extended repatriation process, and unavailable critical and timely support for survivors. As a consequence of therapeutic restrictions and accessibility, conventional counseling services may be sorely insufficient for survivors, too.

Traditional therapy is not able to respond to the needs of trafficked survivors through long-term trauma recovery (Clawson, Salomon, & Grace, 2008). In contrast to conventional treatment, therapeutic relationships in survivor care require more patience, time, and building rapport (United States Department of State, 2018). Building a trusting therapeutic relationship takes the duration of time, but insurance can limit the number of sessions, and financial restrictions can make extended therapy impossible. Long-term treatment can take months or years before the survivors are independent (Crawford, 2017). For women leaving the sex trade, connections in relationships and peer support that developed over 18–24 months were most successful in recovery (Oselin, 2014). A recovery-oriented care model that provides long-term care, thorough coordinated services of care management, and intensive support is the only option to meet the complex needs of this population (Gerassi & Nichols, 2018). Although mental health care is highly encouraged for aftercare treatment for sex trafficked survivors regarding their complex trauma, quality services are rare, and many are unable to meet the existing needs and restore individuals (Rafferty, 2017). Sometimes only a crisis response is provided because the long-term care that is required for this population is not accessible. Barriers in treatment for the sex trafficked survivor are also further convoluted by the challenges of the practitioner, who is often not prepared for this population or their extent of trauma.

Challenges for the Practitioner

Mental health professionals may meet trafficked survivors through an array of settings not limited to private practice, homeless shelters, child advocacy and domestic violence centers, foster care, prison and juvenile detention, and health care. Enhanced awareness of the issue of human trafficking and comprehensive trauma-informed training are required for practitioners to be able to provide the best care. If counselors are unaware of the gravity of the survivors' trauma, they may not be able to effectively diagnose or treat trafficked individuals. When therapists are alert to the possibility of sex trafficking as an issue, they can efficiently aid in treating a survivor who has been traditionally disregarded and blamed. In time, experienced therapists can create greater public awareness and better educated communities concerning the pervasive and corrupting effects of sex trafficking.

Assessments and Treatment

Trained mental health providers should use appropriate assessments through available screening tools to identify survivors of sex trafficking. Screenings need to assess safety, employment, and living conditions of an individual (Macy & Graham, 2012), and abuse, family dynamics, and ability to attend school need to be addressed for youth as well (Gerassi & Nichols, 2018). Comprehensive psychiatric assessment is preferred for survivors of trafficking, and psychological evaluation can assess needs based on trauma experiences and presentation of comorbidity of diagnosis (Williamson, Dutch, & Clawson, 2010). Suicidality is necessary to address, too. Due to the many physical effects of sex trafficking, survivors should also be referred for a complete medical assessment to include testing for STIs (sexually transmitted infections) and gynecological examinations (Oram, Stockl, Busza, Howard, & Zimmerman, 2012).

Therapists who treat survivors of sex trafficking may feel challenged to provide treatment as limited research is available, and current treatments follow the evidence-based practices developed for trauma and/or other survivors of abuse and violence. However, without any best practice models to follow for mental health with survivors of sex trafficking, traditional approaches might not be effective for this population (Levine, 2017). Although most research in sex trafficking has focused on health consequences rather than on recovery services (Rafferty, 2017), recommendations clearly demonstrate that therapists need to implement trauma-informed strategies to decrease the risk of retraumatization and promote empowerment and self-worth (Office for Victims of Crime, n.d.; Hemmings et al., 2016; United States Department of State, 2018). Refer to Chapter 4 regarding recommended modalities for treating the sex trafficked survivor.

Increased Risk

Counselors are encouraged to meet the survivors where they are mentally, emotionally, and psychologically and to use their terminology while in therapy. Survivors will rarely, if ever, identify with the term *trafficked survivor* and may struggle with calling either boyfriend or partner by the term *trafficker* (Chesnay, 2013). Survivors may have difficulty verbally communicating their trauma, and art therapy should be a recommended option provided by an art therapist who has the proper education requirements, training, and qualifications to provide trauma-informed treatment. With this especially vulnerable population, art therapists need to consider increased sensitivity and maximum attention to confidentiality when sharing past experiences through art shows or in educational workshops; trafficking survivors should never face another situation in which they feel exploited again (Davis, 2017). In the therapeutic setting, professionals are cautioned to provide the utmost care, protection, and safety with this exceptionally at-risk population, especially since survivors may be more susceptible to further exploitation due to their prior victimization.

Group Therapy

Group therapy sessions, frequently used for art therapy treatment of trafficking survivors, can pose other challenges because clients may only be seen for a limited time. Group participants can change frequently with new individuals arriving without much notice or any time given for transition processing for those who relapsed or ran away. These inherent challenges with survivors affect the pace of treatment; subsequently, introducing emotionally overwhelming topics is not advisable for groups in which the participants have attended only a few times (Malchiodi, 2015). Again, extreme caution is advised when providing treatment to this population to limit the possibility of further risks. Therapists are encouraged to prioritize a safe environment to gradually build security and trust in their relationship with the survivor to encourage recovery.

Survivor Recovery

Trauma-informed care recognizes that recovery is possible for all individuals (Guarino, Soares, Konnath, Clervil, & Bassuk, 2009). With appropriate services and assistance, survivors can move forward with their lives and beyond their distress (United States Department of State, 2014). However, due to the severe trauma that survivors endure and the addiction they face, it is important to acknowledge that slow progression is typical. Recovery is a complicated and unique process for each individual (United States Department of State, 2014). Available support, diagnosis/comorbidity of diagnosis, trauma endured while being trafficked and length of time, and readiness for intervention all factor into recovery (Clawson, Small, Go, & Myles, 2004; Levine, 2017).

Recovery appears different for each survivor. Although there is scarce research on survivor recovery and wellness, the ultimate goal for survivors is to accomplish well-being, despite ongoing challenges (Bintliff, Stark, Brown, & Alonso, 2018). Feeling positive, satisfied, and fulfilled in functioning describes well-being (Centers for Disease Control and Prevention, 2018). For youth, signs of trauma recovery consist of the ability to express one's emotions; respond, solve problems, and make safe choices; maintain appropriate relationships with others; and have suitable sleeping, eating, and hygiene behaviors (Steele & Malchiodi, 2012). Applying these concepts to survivors, recovery is demonstrated through achieving independence, personal wellness, functional status, and satisfying relationships. In summary, therapy's success is defined by improved outcomes of mental illness symptoms, functioning, and quality of life (Williamson et al., 2010).

Responsibility of Therapist

Although survivors are in control of their own recoveries, the therapist may feel a responsibility for therapy's success. Chapter 9 details how professionals who treat survivors of sex trafficking are at risk, and many of the other chapters raise this issue as well. Trauma-informed models seek to support staff to avoid vicarious trauma and enhance resilience (Gerassi & Nichols, 2018). Compassion fatigue, burnout, and vicarious trauma may ensue for mental health-care providers who treat survivors of complex trafficking trauma. As a matter of fact, both vicarious trauma and trauma have been found to stimulate the same area of the brain, implying that vicarious trauma can have similar harmful results (Gerassi & Nichols, 2018). Empathetic professionals may experience an overwhelming emotional burden from the heavy weight of the trauma from working with survivors.

In addition, professionals who are not trained with this population may feel helpless when working with this population and their adversities. Survivors who appear reluctant and combative may be experiencing trauma symptoms, because trauma interrupts thought process and the ability to handle stress and emotions (United States Department of State, 2018). Behavior issues for child survivors of sex trafficking are acting out, sexualized conduct, and self-harm (Rafferty, 2017). Sex trafficked survivors can present as challenging cases to the practitioner—acting defiant, impulsive, and moody—making progress in the therapeutic relationship difficult and slow paced.

In order for the therapist to be effective and develop a safe, trusting, and strong alliance with the client, the therapist must practice humility (Hook, Davis, Owen, Worthington, & Utsey, 2013). *Cultural humility* means maintaining respect and equality when working with a client who is of a different culture (Hook et al., 2013). The therapist is encouraged to be open, curious, and interested in learning about the survivor's belief system, cultural background, personal values, experiences and worldview; the therapist is cautioned to not assume from previous experience, education, or knowledge (Hook et al., 2013). There is a delicate balance for the experienced practitioner to remain humble and open to learning from their clients. Even for the knowledgeable practitioner, treating sexual abuse can be trying.

Therapists may experience difficulty hearing some details from sexual abuse too. Some therapists may struggle with a lack of personal judgment for survivors due to the relationship with their perpetrators and what they were forced to do while being trafficked. In addition, when survivors experience relapse, run away, or are re-trafficked, there may not be an opportunity for professionals to process the individuals' transition, creating an emotional challenge for both the group and therapists. Professionals are reminded to seek supervision, practice self-care, and regularly connect with others to avoid fatigue, burnout, and secondary trauma when working with survivors (Litam, 2017). Self-care is a critical component for those who work with trafficked survivors due to the taxing effects of hearing horrific stories, feeling tested by the unique challenges of working with survivors while providing safe care at a comfortable pace, and limited innovative research regarding best treatment models for this population. Art therapy is a viable option for advocate support.

Future Considerations

The future of art therapy within trauma-informed treatment for sex trafficked survivors must continue to advance in order to meet the demanding needs of this population, especially as we become more aware and experienced with its treatment. Native healing techniques of storytelling, arts, connection to community, and ritual provide therapeutic experiences, leading individuals not only to feel better but also to function better by altering the stress response (Perry, 2015). The arts have always been a part of the healing process, and art therapy offers an integral and vital healing option for those who are sex trafficked survivors to enhance their well-being and, ultimately, live more fulfilling lives.

This book summarizes the powerful benefits of art therapy with sex trafficking survivors:

- Chapter 5 demonstrated that structured art therapy interventions facilitated in a group setting for female adults aided in recovery through providing experiences of empowerment, emotional processing and reintegration of trauma, increasing sense of self-worth, hope, and establishment of a community of support.

- In Chapter 6, art therapy was an integral part of the healing process for male youth who were sex trafficked by family members, as it reduced guilt, shame, symptoms of trauma, depression, and anxiety and provided coping mechanisms for the boys and their parents.
- Chapter 7 confirmed the healing benefits of expressive arts therapy for children in India as an alternative to conventional verbal therapy and a successful way to experience peace, reduce fears, process transition, improve self-image and quality of life, develop self-acceptance, achieve stabilization, and educate the community.
- A creative art therapy and reproductive health program, featured in Chapter 8, helped Nepalese female adolescents experience a deeper sense of self-awareness and appreciation for their bodies, thoughts, and emotions; process their suffering and traumatic experiences in a safe environment; and promote self-efficacy while resolving feelings of isolation, fear, grief, loss, and shame.
- Chapter 9 included art therapy as a form of self-care and grounding practice for professional advocates who work with survivors of human trafficking to prevent and address secondary and vicarious trauma.

Once safety has been established, art therapy is effective for those who have difficulty verbalizing because it allows for empowerment, containment, externalization, and use of symbol (Malchiodi & Crenshaw, 2017). Images created in art therapy are safe vessels for trauma; they can reveal an individual's inner world or represent connection to the future. The expressive opportunities provided in art therapy enable the survivor to regain control and experience empowerment to instill hope, and this is one of the most important aspects in the recovery process.

Future research of art therapy treatment with sex trafficked survivors is a much-needed goal to continue to build awareness and educate society about this crime and its effects. This book contains rich case studies that offer considerable and encouraging results of how art therapy has benefited a globally diverse population of sex trafficked survivors. Case examples of art therapy and expressive arts therapy treatment with children, adolescents, and adults from settings including a shelter, private practice, and nongovernmental organizations were provided. However, since these studies were limited in size, further research is highly recommended for a more comprehensive and precise application. Additional data is needed to explore survivors who have consistently utilized art therapy services, how the treatments have been facilitated, benefits sustained from therapy, and possible improvements to the services that would contribute to a better understanding of the uneven recovery process.

Historically, human ownership has been abolished in many countries, and yet the worst type of slavery continues to exist today in the universal trafficking industry. Unfortunately, unwavering demand fuels the global exploitation machine. In the sex trafficking industry, the consumer is encouraged by the affordable sale of ready sex, and although he might not realize he is purchasing a slave, he is purchasing sex to express his abusive, chauvinistic, pedophiliac behaviors (Kara, 2009). Today, the industry of sexual exploitation continues to expand from limitless demand for buying sex, availability of vulnerable individuals, inequality and substatus of women, and government failure to intervene. When two or more of these factors interface in a society, an unending cycle of exploitation and abuse begins. In spite of this discouraging and cynical perspective, practitioners need to continue to believe that healing and growth are possible for all survivors.

Conclusion

You may be surprised and perhaps reluctant to accept that widespread slavery exists today within the modern world, but sex trafficking is truly slavery, a violation of basic and fundamental human rights. Trafficking is also destructive against society and its values; it is the crime of people who have lost their moral sense. Vicious sex trafficking behaviors can be described as disparaging, deviant, and sadistic. As the crimes of sexual exploitation continue to be a part of the world's story, art therapists need to be aware of the modern implications and how to help the struggling individuals who are either lured, manipulated, or coerced into this destructive lifestyle. This book proves that many individuals are endangered by sex trafficking, including young boys from a middle-class nuclear family, poor and oppressed children and adolescents from India and Nepal, and manipulated and coerced female adults who are led to believe they have no choice. Trauma-informed treatment is not only the recommended option from research, it is the best way for survivors to experience safety. Survivor protection is of utmost concern in treatment, and this resounding theme is interwoven through all of the chapters. Without safety in relationships, there is no way to advance in recovery.

The extent of the trauma of human sex trafficking cannot be overestimated. Every day, survivors will remember their trauma, and they will grieve, but recovery enables the level of the trauma to be less intense and less oppressive in their lives (Herman, 1997). Survivors have experienced a time in their lives when they were treated inhumanely and unworthy, like property or a commodity. In response to their trauma, survivors existed and adapted by embracing dissociation, numbness, self-destruction, and addiction. After living through exploitation, survivors need to experience their humanity again. In other words, survivors need to relearn life, experience positive and negative emotions, cope and adapt to a new life with its many transitions and establish a meaningful identity again. Survivors are forever changed, but there is hope for recovery now and in the future.

Survivors of sex trafficking cannot deny or forget the horror they have lived through. Haunting and distressing fears are always part of their histories, but they have endured, and they can continue not only to live but also to heal and prevail. Like survivors of natural disasters, war, and terror, these individuals struggled simply to exist—to be alive—in spite of unspeakable horror and despair. Trafficked individuals lost their voices for a period of time; they may have forgotten what being heard involves, what it is like to be accepted and to feel understood. Through art therapy, survivors have an opportunity to reclaim what is missing in their current life, what was lost through their trauma, and what was taken during their trafficking terror. Art therapy provides expression and purpose, hope and empowerment, and it guides the way to recovery and healing. Healing begins when the voice is reclaimed, shared, recognized, and honored. Through art therapy, the trafficked person again learns how to speak through the safety and richness of color, line, image, design, and symbolism. Art therapy allows honest portrayals of personal chaos to translate into beauty. The survivor experiences the power of being heard and acknowledged through the collective strength of peers when communication and connection are regained. Supportive communities are formed when active listening and honest sharing of vulnerability occurs. Healing happens in community.

This book intends to provide awareness on the topic of sex trafficking as a social injustice and a crime against humanity. The book aims to add to the limited existing literature available on the proven benefits of using art therapy with sex trafficked survivors. My intention, as editor of this book, is that fellow art therapists can learn from these empirical case studies to assess and treat this population more effectively. I also hope that the reiterated message throughout the book of self-care provides an extremely important reminder of the recommended practice to the professionals who work with this challenging population and their extensive and horrific problems. This complex work is challenging, and if your well-being is not a priority, the work can be detrimental.

In closing, you are now more aware of the risk factors for human trafficking, the traumatic aftermath of sexual exploitation, and the clear and compelling benefits of art therapy treatment for survivors, and you should possess a better understanding regarding the practices of trafficking in other countries, which may influence or impact survivors everywhere. Sex slavery is not just the curse of underdeveloped or third world countries; this evil exists worldwide despite prosperity. With this information, it is my hope that you are motivated to recognize these disparaged survivors and be inspired to help them prevail and to bring about change in our communities and world. I hope you will become part of the anti-trafficking movement and join me in taking action to provide healing to those who desperately need it most. Everyone deserves the right to live and the right to feel safe.

Every life is worthy.
Every life story deserves respect and is worth sharing.
Every survivor's life is worth saving.

References

Bintliff, A. V., Stark, C., Brown, L. D., & Alonso, A. (2018). Lifelong wellbeing for survivors of sex trafficking: Collaborative perspectives from survivors, researchers, and service providers. *Dignity: A Journal on Sexual Exploitation and Violence*, *3*(3), 1–29. https://doi.org/10.23860/dignity/2018.03.03.03

Centers for Disease Control and Prevention. (2018). *Well-being concepts*. Retrieved from www.cdc.gov/hrqol/wellbeing.htm

Chesnay, M. D. (2013). Psychiatric-mental health nurses and the sex trafficking pandemic. *Issues in Mental Health Nursing*, *34*(12), 901–907. https://doi.org/10.3109/01612840.2013.857200

Childs, K. (2018). The sex-trafficking movement from a survivor's perspective. In L. Smith (Ed.), *Invading the darkness: Inside the historic fight against child sex trafficking in the United States* (pp. 231–246). Vancouver, WA: Shared Hope International.

Clawson, H. J., Salomon, A., & Grace, L. G. (2008, March 15). *Treating the hidden wounds: Trauma treatment and mental health recovery for victims of human trafficking*. Retrieved from https://aspe.hhs.gov/report/treating-hidden-wounds-trauma-treatment-and-mental-health-recovery-victims-human-trafficking

Clawson, H. J., Small, K., Go, E., & Myles, B. (2004). *Needs assessment for service providers and trafficking victims*. Fairfax, VA: Caliber Associates, Inc. Retrieved from www.ncjrs.gov/pdffiles1/nij/grants/202469.pdf

Crawford, M. (2017). International sex trafficking. *Women & Therapy*, *40*(1–2), 101–122. https://doi.org/10.1080/02703149.2016.1206784

Davis, T. (2017). Art therapy exhibitions: Exploitations or advocacy? *AMA Journal of Ethics*, *19*(1), 98–106. https://doi.org/10.1001/journalofethics.2017.19.1.imhl1-1701

Gerassi, L. B., & Nichols, A. J. (2018). *Sex trafficking and commercial sexual exploitation: Prevention, advocacy, and trauma-informed practice*. New York, NY: Springer Publishing Company.

Guarino, K., Soares, P., Konnath, K., Clervil, R., & Bassuk, E. (2009). *Trauma-informed care organizational toolkit*. Rockville, MD: Center for Mental Health, Substance Abuse and Mental Health Services Administration, and the Daniels Fund, the National Traumatic Stress Network, and the W.K. Kellogg Foundation. Retrieved from www.air.org/sites/default/files/downloads/report/Trauma-Informed_Organizational_Toolkit_0.pdf

Hemmings, S., Jakobowitz, S., Abas, M., Bick, D., Howard, L. M., Stanley, N., . . . Oram, S. (2016). Responding to the health needs of survivors of human trafficking: A systematic review. *BMC Health Services Research*, *16*(320). https://doi.org/10.1186/s12913-016-1538-8

Herman, J. L. (1997). *Trauma and recovery: The aftermath of violence—From domestic abuse to political terror* (2nd ed.). New York, NY: Basic Books.

Hook, J. N., Davis, D. E., Owen, J., Worthington, E. L., & Utsey, S. O. (2013). Cultural humility: Measuring openness to culturally diverse clients. *Journal of Counseling Psychology*, *60*(3), 355–363. https://doi.org/10.1037/a0032595

Kara, S. (2009). *Sex trafficking: Inside the business of modern slavery*. New York, NY: Columbia University Press.

Leitch, L., & Snow, M. (2010). *Intervene: Practitioner guide and intake tool*. Vancouver, WA: Shared Hope International.

Levine, J. A. (2017, January 6). Mental health issues in survivors of sex trafficking. *Cogent Medicine*, *4*(1). https://doi.org/10.1080/2331205X.2017.1278841

Litam, S. D. A. (2017). Human sex trafficking in America: What counselors need to know. *The Professional Counselor*, *7*(1), 45–61. https://doi.org/10.15241/sdal.7.1.45

Macy, R. J., & Graham, L. M. (2012). Identifying domestic and international sex-trafficking victims during human service provision. *Trauma, Violence, & Abuse*, *13*(2), 59–76. https://doi.org/10.1177/1524838012440340

Malchiodi, C. A. (2015). Trauma-informed art therapy and group intervention with children from violent homes. In C. A. Malchiodi (Ed.), *Creative interventions with traumatized children* (pp. 258–278). New York, NY: The Guilford Press.

Malchiodi, C. A., & Crenshaw, D. A. (2017). Why children clam up in therapy. In C. A. Malchiodi & D. A. Crenshaw (Eds.), *What to do when children clam up in psychotherapy* (pp. 3–17). New York, NY: The Guilford Press.

Marich, J. (2014). *Trauma made simple: Competencies in assessment, treatment and working with survivors*. Eau Claire, WI: Pesi Publishing and Media.

Mehlman-Orozco, K. (2016, July). What happens after a human trafficking victim is "rescued"? *The Hill*. Retrieved from http://thehill.com/blogs/congress-blog/judicial/289709-what-happens-after-a-human-trafficking-victim-is-rescued

Muraya, D. N., & Fry, D. (2015). Aftercare services for child victims of sex trafficking: A system review of policy and practice. *Trauma, Violence, & Abuse*, *17*(20), 204–220. https://doi.org/10.1177/1524838015584356

National Center for Missing & Exploited Children. (2019). *Child sex trafficking identification*. Retrieved from www.missingkids.com/theissues/cse/1in7

National Human Trafficking Hotline. (n.d.). *Recognizing the signs*. Retrieved from https://humantraffickinghotline.org/human-trafficking/recognizing-signs

Nichols, A. J., & Heil, E. C. (2015). Challenges to identifying and prosecuting sex trafficking cases in the midwest United States. *Feminist Criminology*, *10*(1), 7–35. https://doi.org/10.1177/1557085113519490

Office for Victims of Crime. (n.d.). *About human trafficking*. Retrieved from https://ovc.ncjrs.gov/humantrafficking/about.html

Oram, S., Stockl, H., Busza, J., Howard, L. M., & Zimmerman, C. (2012). Prevalence and risk of violence and physical, mental, and sexual health problems associated with human trafficking: Systematic review. *PLoS Medicine*, *9*(5), 1–13. https://doi.org/10.1371/journal.pmed.1001224

Oselin, S. (2014). *Leaving prostitution: Getting out and staying out of sex work*. New York, NY: New York University Press.

Perry, B. D. (2015). Forward. In C. A. Malchiodi (Ed.), *Creative Interventions with traumatized children* (pp. ix–xi). New York, NY: The Guilford Press.

Polaris. (2014). *In their shoes: Understanding victims' mindsets and common barriers to victim identification*. Retrieved from https://humantraffickinghotline.org/resources/understanding-victim-mindsets

Rafferty, Y. (2017). Mental health services as a vital component of psychosocial recovery for victims of child trafficking or commercial sexual exploitation. *American Journal of Orthopsychiatry*, *88*(3), 249–260. https://doi.org/10.1037.ort0000268

Rothschild, B. (2000). *The body remembers: The psychophysiology of trauma and trauma treatment*. New York, NY: W.W. Norton & Company.

Shared Hope International. (2014). *Domestic minor sex trafficking: Identifying and responding to America's youth*. Vancouver, WA: Shared Hope International.
Smith, L. (2018). Victims charged with the crime that victimized them. In L. Smith (Ed.), *Invading the darkness: Inside the historic fight against child sex trafficking in the United States* (pp. 259–266). Vancouver, WA: Shared Hope International.
Steele, W., & Malchiodi, C. A. (2012). *Trauma-informed practices with children and adolescents*. New York, NY: Routledge Taylor and Francis Group.
United States Department of State. (2014). *Trafficking in persons report: The journey from victim to survivor*. Retrieved from www.state.gov/j/tip/rls/tiprpt/2014/226644.htm
United States Department of State. (2017, June). *Trafficking in persons report*. Retrieved from www.state.gov/documents/organization/271339.pdf
United States Department of State. (2018, June 18). *Implementing a trauma-informed approach*. Retrieved from www.state.gov/documents/organization/283795.pdf
van der Kolk, B. (2014). *The body keeps the score: Brain, mind, and body in the healing of trauma*. New York, NY: Viking.
Vardaman, S. H. (2018). Trafficking dynamics. In L. Smith (Ed.), *Invading the darkness: Inside the historic fight against child sex trafficking in the United States* (pp. 75–84). Vancouver, WA: Shared Hope International.
Williamson, E., Dutch, N. M., & Clawson, H. J. (2010, April 15). *Evidence-based mental health treatment for victims of human trafficking*. Retrieved from https://aspe.hhs.gov/report/evidence-based-mental-health-treatment-victims-human-trafficking
Zimmerman, C., Hossain, M., Yun, K., Gajdadziev, V., Guzun, N., Tchomarova, M., . . . Watts, C. (2008). The health of trafficked women: A survey of women entering posttrafficking services in Europe. *American Journal of Public Health*, *98*(1), 55–59. https://doi.org/10.2105/AJPH.2006.108357

Appendix A

Glossary

Body betrayal: Physical response of pleasure experienced during sexual abuse (Miller, 2012).

Bottom girl: Individual appointed by trafficker to help manage and control other individuals; she may have seniority (Polaris Project, 2017).

Branding: Carving, mark, or tattoo on trafficked person displaying ownership by another (Shared Hope International, 2014).

Breaking/seasoning: The abuse, manipulation, and/or threatening of an individual to ensure obedience and submission (Polaris Project, 2017).

Brothel/cathouse/whorehouse: Location where sexual acts are sold.

Circuit: Established route between cities within a specific region for trafficking purposes (Shared Hope International, 2014).

Coercion: Intimidation or emotional pressure acquired by manipulation, identification confiscation, bondage, and threats to subvert and compel another (United States Department of Health and Human Services, 2019).

Commercial sex act: Any sex act that is exchanged for money or anything of value (National Human Trafficking Hotline, n.d.).

Commercial sexual exploitation of children (CSEC): Sex act with a minor in exchange for anything of value (Miller-Perrin & Wurtele, 2017).

Daddy: Mandated nickname for exploiter (Polaris Project, 2017).

Date/john/trick: Person who pays/trades for sex (Polaris Project, 2017).

Debt bondage: Coercive technique enforcing financial burden on victim (National Human Trafficking Hotline, n.d.).

Domestic minor sex trafficking (DMST): Trafficking of underage American citizens in the United States (Shared Hope International, 2014).

Family/folks/stable: Victimized individuals under control of one trafficker (Polaris Project, 2017; Shared Hope International, 2014).

Force: Use of physical restraint or harm to acquire and sustain control (United States Department of Health and Human Services, 2019).

Fraud: The offer of false promises of love, employment, or a better life that leads to exploitation of vulnerable individuals (United States Department of Health and Human Services, 2019).

Gang rape: Group raping of an individual used as conditioning method (United States Department of Health and Human Services, n.d).

Grooming: The process of developing a dishonest relationship that appears trustworthy but ends in exploitation.

LGBTQ+ (Lesbian, Gay, Bisexual, Transgender, Queer/Questioning Plus): Inclusive acronym used to represent different identities (BBC Newsbeat, 2015).

Lot lizards: Exploited individuals at a truck stop (Shared Hope International, 2014).

Madam: Female trafficker/pimp.

Nongovernment organization (NGO): Established association that seeks to assist issue such as trafficking.

Palermo Protocol, Protocol to Prevent, Suppress, and Punish Trafficking in Persons: The first international agreement is not only to legally define human trafficking but also to initiate eradication (United Nations, 2000).

Pimp: Individual who profits from exploitation of others by receiving payment (in form of money or other benefit) in exchange for sex with an individual.

Prostitution: Selling sex for money; examples of occurrence are in the military, religion, and tribe.

Quota: Total amount of money that is required each night from trafficked individual (Polaris Project, 2017).

Red-light: Sex trade neighborhood.

Ritual abuse (RA): Severe form of abuse involving beliefs or practices (Miller, 2012).

Satanic ritual abuse (SRA): Ritualized abuse usually perpetrated on children to worship Satan (Miller, 2012).

Sex tourism: Organized trip for the sole purpose of sexual exploitation of individual(s).

Sex trafficking: Forced sexual exploitation of an individual.

Sister wife/wifey/wife-in-law: Nicknames for a group of women who are exploited by same individual (Shared Hope International, 2014)

Slavery: Enforced and sustained exploitation of others.

Squaring up: Process of trying to leave the life (Shared Hope International, 2014).

Stroll/track: Street area designated for selling of sex (Polaris Project, 2017).

Survival sex: Exchange of sex for necessary living requirements (shelter, food, etc.).

The life: Period of time while being trafficked.

Trafficker: Individual, small group, like a family, or a large crime organization, such as the mafia; roles include obtaining vulnerable individuals, purchasing and selling people, transporting individuals, and providing a place for selling of sex.

Trafficking: Forced exploitation of an individual.

Trafficking Victims Protection Act (TVPA) of 2000: The first federal law in United States to address human trafficking regarding deterrence, safety, and prosecution (United States Department of State, 2019).

Trauma bond: Typical reaction of acquiring emotional attachment to abuser during a distressing experience (United States Department of Health and Human Services, n.d.).

Trick: Sexual act for sale (Shared Hope International, 2014).

Turn out: New person who is trafficked (Shared Hope International, 2014).

Vicarious trauma: Empathetic distress due to secondary trauma exposure occurring during/after a helping professional works with and counsels trafficking survivors.

References

BBC Newsbeat. (2015, June 25). *We know what LGBT means but here's what LGBTQQIAAP stands for*. Retrieved from www.bbc.co.uk/newsbeat/article/33278165/we-know-what-lgbt-means-but-heres-what-lgbtqqiaap-stands-for

Miller, A. (2012). *Healing the Unimaginable: Treating ritual abuse and mind control*. London, UK: Karnac Books Ltd.

Miller-Perrin, C., & Wurtele, S. K. (2017). Sex trafficking and the commercial sexual exploitation of children. *Women & Therapy*, *40*(1–2), 123–151. https://doi.org/10.1080/02703149.2016.1210963

National Human Trafficking Hotline. (n.d.). *Federal Law*. Retrieved from https://humantraffickinghotline.org/what-human-trafficking/federal-law

Polaris Project. (2017). *Domestic sex trafficking: The criminal operations of the American pimp*. Retrieved from www.dcjs.virginia.gov/sites/dcjs.virginia.gov/files/publications/victims/domestic-sex-trafficking-criminal-operations-american-pimp.pdf

Shared Hope International. (2014). *Domestic minor sex trafficking: Identifying and responding to America's youth*. Vancouver, WA: Shared Hope International.

United Nations. (2000). *Protocol to prevent, suppress and punish trafficking in persons especially women and children*. Retrieved from www.ohchr.org/EN/ProfessionalInterest/Pages/ProtocolTraffickingInPersons.aspx

United States Department of Health and Human Services. (n.d). *Sex trafficking fact sheet*. Retrieved from www.acf.hhs.gov/sites/default/files/orr/fact_sheet_sex_trafficking.pdf

United States Department of Health and Human Services. (2019). *What is human trafficking*? Retrieved from www.acf.hhs.gov/otip/about/what-is-human-trafficking

United States Department of State. (2019). *Victims of trafficking and violence protection act of 2000*. Retrieved from https://www.state.gov/j/tip/laws/61124.htm

Appendix B

Resources

Global Anti-Trafficking Resources and Directories

- End Slavery Now Antislavery Directory
  www.endslaverynow.org/connect
- Global Modern Slavery Directory
  www.globalmodernslavery.org
- International Justice Mission Resources and Advocacy Work
  www.ijm.org/advocacy
- International Labour Organization, Forced Labour, Modern Slavery, and Human Trafficking
  www.ilo.org/global/topics/forced-labour/lang--en/index.htm
- Polaris Global Safety Net
  https://polarisproject.org/initiatives/global-safety-net
- United Nations Office on Drugs and Crime
  www.unodc.org/unodc/human-trafficking/
- United Nations Protocol to Prevent, Suppress and Punish Trafficking in Persons Especially Women and Children
  www.ohchr.org/EN/ProfessionalInterest/Pages/ProtocolTrafficking InPersons.aspx
- Walk Free Foundation
  www.walkfreefoundation.org

United States Anti-Trafficking Resources and Directories

How to Report Trafficking

National Human Trafficking Resource Center 1 (888) 373–7888
Text Help or Info to 233733 (BEFREE)
Hours: 24 hours, 7 days a week
Languages: English, Spanish and 200 more languages
Website: traffickingresourcecenter.org

Human Trafficking Assessments and Screening Tools

- Center for the Human Rights of Children, Rapid Screening Tool for Youth Labor and Sex Trafficking
  https://luc.edu/media/lucedu/chrc/pdfs/ChildRight_RapidScreeningInstrument_CHRC_FNALDRAFT_JULY%20(1).pdf
- National Human Trafficking Hotline Comprehensive Human Labor/Sex Trafficking Assessment
  https://humantraffickinghotline.org/resources/comprehensive-human-trafficking-assessment-tool
- United States Department of Health and Human Services, Administration for Children and Families, Screening Tool
  www.acf.hhs.gov/sites/default/files/orr/screening_questions_to_assess_whether_a_person_is_a_trafficking_victim_0.pdf
- United States Department of Health and Human Services, Office on Trafficking in Persons, Adult Human Trafficking Screening Tool and Guide
  www.acf.hhs.gov/sites/default/files/otip/adult_human_trafficking_screening_tool_and_guide.pdf
- Vera Institute of Justice Long/Short Screening for Human Trafficking: Guidelines for Administering the Trafficking Victim Identification Tool (TVIT)
  www.ncjrs.gov/pdffiles1/nij/grants/246713.pdf

Anti-Trafficking Resources and Services

- Federal Bureau of Investigation, Human Trafficking/Involuntary Servitude
  www.fbi.gov/investigate/civil-rights/human-trafficking
- Federal Bureau of Investigative Programs, Violent Crimes Against Children/Online Predators
  www.fbi.gov/investigate/violent-crime/cac
- National Center for Missing and Exploited Children
  www.missingkids.com/home
- National Human Trafficking Hotline Federal Laws
  https://humantraffickinghotline.org/what-human-trafficking/federal-law
- National Human Trafficking Referral Directory in United States
  https://humantraffickinghotline.org/training-resources/referral-directory
- Office of Justice Programs' Office of Juvenile Justice and Delinquency Prevention Victim Services
  www.ojjdp.gov/programs/human-trafficking-services.html
- Office of Victims of Crime Programs and Task Forces
  https://ovc.ncjrs.gov/humantrafficking/index.html

- United States Department of Health and Human Services, Office on Trafficking in Persons, An Office of the Administration for Children & Families
  www.acf.hhs.gov/otip
- United States Department of Justice Human Trafficking
  www.justice.gov/humantrafficking
- United States Department of State, Office to Monitor and Combat Trafficking in Persons
  www.state.gov/j/tip/

(State and local resources where available)

Anti-Trafficking and Trauma-Informed Educational Information

- Blue Campaign Educational Materials, Trainings, and Videos
  www.dhs.gov/blue-campaign/share-resources
- Learning Center for Child and Adolescent Trauma with National Child Traumatic Stress Network (NCTSN)
  https://learn.nctsn.org
- Office for Victims of Crime, Training and Technical Center
  www.ovcttac.gov/views/TrainingMaterials/dspOnline_VATOnline.cfm
- Polaris Project Initiative, Survivor Support, Children and Youth
  https://polarisproject.org/resources
- Shared Hope International Policy Research, Educational Materials, and Free Printable Community Handouts
  http://sharedhope.org/resources/
- Trauma-Informed Practices and Expressive Arts Therapy Institute and Learning Center Continuing education courses/workshops and distance learning
  www.trauma-informedpractice.com

Appendix C
Reflection Questions

Chapter 1

1. What do you want to learn from this book?
2. Describe the main cause of human trafficking.
3. What is the most surprising discovery about the sex trafficking industry you have learned?
4. Across the globe, how does sex trafficking differ, and how is it similar?
5. What kind of impact can each of us have in our own communities to help combat the sex trafficking industry and help its survivors?

Chapter 2

1. How do trafficking tactics of force, fraud, and coercion influence and compound therapeutic treatment for the survivors?
2. What trauma consequences have the greatest impact on the sex trafficked survivors, and how does complex trauma affect the future of survivors?
3. Given the reported consequences of trafficking, what goals are crucial in art therapy treatment for survivors?

Chapter 3

1. What makes art therapy treatment different from other modalities for trafficked survivors?
2. Explain three creative interventions that could be used to treat a sex trafficked survivor who has experienced dissociation?
3. From the many modalities presented in this chapter, what is one that might be a fit for you and your practice? What other modalities might you be interested in investigating further?

Chapter 4

1. Describe why individuals from these populations—foster care and juvenile detention system, homeless, refugees, LGBTQ+ community, and those with a history of abuse or substance abuse—are most vulnerable to sex trafficking?
2. How can children be better protected against human traffickers?
3. Explain how a better awareness of sex trafficking vulnerabilities may enhance your therapeutic practice in terms of assessment, diagnosis, and treatment?
4. What problem is consistent in therapeutic treatment for the vulnerable populations of sex trafficking?

Chapter 5

1. What factors contribute to Ohio's problem with sex trafficking?
2. Describe the role of survivor safety in trauma-informed treatment.
3. Provide other examples of art therapy interventions that can be used in collaboration with the trauma recovery phases of trauma processing and adjustment to transition and reconnecting to others.
4. Clarify why empowerment is crucial to art therapy for survivors.
5. How can you use creative writing in your therapeutic practice?

Chapter 6

1. Why are males referred to as the overlooked individuals victimized in sex trafficking?
2. How are the consequences of sex trafficking different for males?
3. Explain how theoretical orientation has a role in art therapy treatment with sex trafficked survivors?
4. How does family involvement during the trauma sex trafficking contribute to the complexity of this dilemma?

Chapter 7

1. What challenges contribute to India's sex trafficking issues?
2. Clarify the cultural limitations in India and how they influence sex trafficking.
3. How do the expressive arts therapies (art, music, and dance/movement) assist in trauma recovery for sexually exploited individuals? Explain the similarities and differences between the expressive therapies for this population.
4. The survivor stories are each poignant in unique ways, which one resonated the most with you?

Chapter 8

1. What cultural factors contribute to Nepal's problem with sex trafficking?
2. How does theme-based art therapy address issues such as reproductive health for the survivor? What other themes specific to sex trafficking can be addressed in a similar format?
3. What is the benefit to using songs, poems, and descriptive storytelling in conjunction with art therapy to treat survivors of sex trafficking?
4. What are the advantages/disadvantages to training of trainers (TOT) program?

Chapter 9

1. How might working with survivors of sexual exploitation impact a counselor personally/professionally?
2. What self-care habits are important to you as a professional?
3. What does resilience mean to you?
4. What practice—intentional practice, agency culture, incongruent expectations, and humans, not machine—is most meaningful to you? Why?
5. What is the benefit of art therapy for those individuals exposed to secondary trauma?

Chapter 10

1. How have your thoughts changed regarding the root of human trafficking?
2. Why do you think some individuals want to exploit other humans?
3. What barrier in treatment is the most challenging for you? Why?
4. How can the complex problem of sex trafficking be addressed on communal, national, and international levels?
5. After reading this book, how have your personal/professional goals changed to help combat the abuses of sex trafficking industry?
6. Reflecting back, what artwork from the book is most meaningful to you?

Chapter 10

Index